The

Reference

Shelf

Cuba

Edited by Martha Hostetter

The Reference Shelf
Volume 73 • Number 3

The H.W. Wilson Company
2001

The Reference Shelf

The books in this series contain reprints of articles, excerpts from books, addresses on current issues, and studies of social trends in the United States and other countries. There are six separately bound numbers in each volume, all of which are usually published in the same calendar year. Numbers one through five are each devoted to a single subject, providing background information and discussion from various points of view and concluding with a subject index and comprehensive bibliography that lists books, pamphlets, and abstracts of additional articles on the subject. The final number of each volume is a collection of recent speeches, and it contains a cumulative speaker index. Books in the series may be purchased individually or on subscription.

Library of Congress has cataloged this serial title as follows:

Cuba / edited by Martha Hostetter.
    p.cm.—(The Reference Shelf; v. 73, no. 3)
  Includes bibliographical references and index.
  ISBN 0-8242-0991-5
  1. Cuba—History—1959– 2. Cuba—Social conditions—1959– 3. Cuba—Economic conditions—1990– I. Hostetter, Martha. II. Series.

F1788 .C759 2001
972.9106'4—dc21

2001026162

 Visit H.W. Wilson's Web site: www.hwwilson.com

Printed in the United States of America

Contents

Preface vii

Timeline of the Cuban Revolution 1

I. The State of the Revolution 5

1) Cuba: Evolution in the Revolution. John Putman. *National Geographic* 9
2) Cuba's Suspended Revolution. Kevin Baxter. *The Nation* 23
3) Cuba's Next Revolution: How Christians Are Reshaping Castro's
   Communist Stronghold. John W. Kennedy. *Christianity Today* 30
4) After Castro—What? Roger Fontaine. *World & I* 44

II. Fidelismo: The Cuban Economy 49

1) What Cuba Can Teach Russia. Ana Julia Jatar-Hausmann. *Foreign Policy* 53
2) Castro Gives Tourism a Try. Linda Robinson. *U.S. News & World Report* 66
3) Against All Odds, Cuban Small Business Finds a Way. Philip Peters.
   Wall Street Journal 73
4) Dotcommies Take Over Cuba. Timothy Ashby and Elizabeth Bourget.
   Christian Science Monitor 76
5) Cuban Discoveries Hold Key to World's Progress in Medicine.
   Daniel Whitaker. *The Times* (London) 79
6) Cuba's Organic Revolution. Hugh Warwick. *The Ecologist* 83

III. Opposing Shores: The U.S. and Cuba 89

1) Trading with Communists: Two Dictatorships, Two U.S. Policies.
   Tom Delay and James P. McGovern. *Washington Post* 93
2) How the Embargo Hurts Cubans and Helps Castro. Stuart Taylor, Jr.
   National Journal 99
3) Washington's Costly Cuba Policy. Wayne S. Smith. *The Nation* 103
4) Cuba Countdown. Alexis Simendinger. *National Journal* 109
5) Inside Look at Human Smuggling. Mark Fineman. *Los Angeles Times* 117
6) Art and Politics in Miami. Jordan Levin. *(ai) performance for the planet* 122
7) After Hurricane Elián. Max J. Castro. *Salon* 126

IV. Life in Cuba: An Island Unto Itself? 131

1) American Academics Invade Cuba and Find a Vibrant Intellectual Scene.
   David Aquila Lawrence. *Chronicle of Higher Education* 135
2) Cuba's All-Stars. Tom Miller. *Natural History* 143

3) Cuba Goes Gayer. John Casey. *Spectator*. 152
4) In Cuba a Vintage Harley Can Epitomize Life Itself. Tracey Eaton.
    Times-Picayune 155
5) Cuba Begins to Answer Its Race Question. Eugene Robinson.
    Washington Post 159
6) Making Waves. Rosa Lowinger. *Art News Online* 167
7) Castro's Children. Dierdra Funcheon. *New York Press* 172

Bibliography 183

Web Sites on Cuba 185

Additional Periodical Articles with Abstracts 187

Index 193

Preface

In his latest novel, *The Return of Felix Nogara*, Cuban émigré Pablo Medina imagines a return to Cuba in a post-Castro age. Medina dresses up his homeland as the fictional island of "Barata" and re-christens Fidel Castro as Nicolás Campión, an aging dictator who, in the novel's opening scenes, is dying in bed of natural causes and confessing his sins to a Catholic archbishop. Campión's death creates immediate reversals—Miami exiles converge on their homeland in droves, while his hand-picked successor, Roberto Limón, decides that the Baratans have suffered too much for the sake of ideals and announces that Barata is now open for business. Limón proceeds to sell off tracts of the once-sacred mountains of the revolution to real estate developers and strikes a deal with the United States to store its radioactive waste. While riding in a taxi from the airport, the title character Felix marvels at the speed of changes in Barata, where there are already American-style shopping malls, fast-food restaurants, and a used car lot flying American and Baratan flags. "So soon?" Felix asks his taxi driver. "Not soon enough," the driver replies.

This exchange captures the hopes and fears swirling around the future of Cuba, where tourists can already purchase revolutionary leader "Che" Guevara's face on ashtrays and berets, and where businessmen from all over the world—except the United States—have begun to invest. For the past four decades, Cuba has been a question mark on the map of the Western Hemisphere, cut off not only by years of U.S. sanctions but also through its approaches to its economy and to its people. While today's politicians, exiles, businessmen, and religious and cultural leaders argue over the nation's future, changes on the island have already begun.

The greatest source of change can be traced to 1991 and the collapse of communism in the Soviet Union and Eastern Europe. Virtually overnight, Cuba lost the massive Soviet subsidies and markets that had fueled its economy for decades. Through the first half of Cuba's 100 years of independence, the nation was highly dependent on the United States and, for the second half, on the Soviet Union. Now, for the first time in its history, Cuba is truly on its own.

In order to survive, the still-officially communist government has instituted an economic transformation based on technology, new markets, and a tourism-fueled dollar economy, thereby salvaging socialism with the "poison" of capitalism. So far, the pillars of the revolution—universal education, health care, and housing—remain intact. Although annual per capita income is low (about $1,300), Cuba maintains the highest literacy rate and the lowest infant mortality rate in Latin America. But Cuba now has two societies—a minority of fledgling capitalists, many of whom drive new cars and wear expensive clothes, and an increasingly discontented majority, for whom getting a ride to work or finding three square meals remains a challenge.

This book presents snapshots of Cuba as it exists today: in a state of flux. Section I provides an overview of the current state of the revolution. The authors collected here assess some of the forces of change in contemporary Cuba, including religion, capitalism, and the new dollar economy, and attempt to predict what might happen in a post-Castro, or even a postrevolutionary, Cuba. Section II takes a closer look at the particular development of the Cuban economy through the 1990s and reports on promising new economic sectors, including biotechnology and organic farming. Section III considers the thorny relationship between the United States and Cuba by touching on the U.S. trade embargo, Cuban refugees and U.S. immigration policy, and the Cuban-American population. Finally, Section IV attempts to move beyond a monolithic view of Cuba as defined by its revolution and its leader, presenting views of Cuban intellectual, cultural, and social life.

I would like to thank the authors and publications that granted permission to reprint the material contained in this volume. I would also like to express my gratitude to all those at H.W. Wilson who contributed to this book: Lynn Messina, Sandra Watson, Jacquelene Latif, Tia Brown, Rich Stein, and Christopher Luna.

Martha Hostetter
June 2001

Timeline of the Cuban Revolution

1952: General Fulgencio Batista overthrows President Carlos Pró Socarrás and cancels elections.

July 26, 1953: Fidel Castro leads 160 rebels in an attack on a military barracks in the hope of sparking a popular uprising. Castro is arrested and—after a trial in which he says, "History will absolve me"—is sentenced to 15 years' imprisonment.

1955: Castro is released from prison under a political amnesty and goes to Mexico. There, he organizes Cuban exiles into the "26th of July" movement.

1956: Castro and Ernesto "Che" Guevara return to Cuba with 81 "26th of July" revolutionaries. After a disastrous battle, Castro and a few followers flee to the Sierra Maestra mountains to regroup and build a base for traditional guerilla warfare against the Batista regime.

January 1, 1959: After Castro's forces win a string of victories over the government's troops, Batista flees Cuba and Castro's rebels take power.

May 1959: Land reforms in Cuba generate friction with the United States.

February 1960: Cuba and the Soviet Union sign sugar and oil trade deals.

June 1960: Cuba nationalizes U.S.-owned oil refineries after they refuse to process Soviet oil.

October 1960: Washington bans most exports to Cuba and imposes stringent licensing rules on sales of food and medicine.

January 1961: The U.S. embassy in Havana closes.

April 1961: Castro declares Cuba a socialist state.

April 17, 1961: 1,297 Cuban exiles supported by the C.I.A. invade Cuba at the Bay of Pigs; the attack collapses two days later.

January 1962: Cuba is suspended from the Organization of American States; Castro responds with calls for armed revolt across Latin America.

February 1962: Washington bans all Cuban imports.

March 1962: Food rationing in Cuba begins.

October 1662: After the Soviets install nuclear missiles in Cuba—within striking distance of the U.S.—the U.S. and U.S.S.R. come to the brink of nuclear war. The "Cuban Missile Crisis" is defused when Soviet premier Krushchev agrees to remove the missiles and President Kennedy promises never to invade Cuba.

1964: The U.S. grants political asylum to all Cubans who manage to reach the United States.

March 1968: The Cuban government takes over most private businesses.

November 1974: U.S. and Cuban officials meet in a highly secret and ultimately failed attempt to improve relations.

April 1980: A refugee crisis starts at the port of Mariel when Castro announces that anyone who wants to can leave Cuba; some 125,000 flee by the end of September.

December 1991: The collapse of the Soviet Union brings an end to subsidies and Cuba's major markets. Castro institutes a "Special Period in Times of Peace," a call for austerity and sacrifice.

1992: Cuba drops the commitment to atheism written into its constitution.

1992: The "Cuban Democracy Act" passes, prohibiting foreign subsidiaries of U.S. companies from trading with Cuba. The law allows American companies to sell medicine to Cuba, albeit with licenses and requirements that in effect make such sales extremely limited.

November 1992: The United Nations General Assembly passes a resolution condemning the U.S. trade embargo, by a vote of 88 to 4.

1993: Cuba lifts a ban on use of U.S. dollars, encouraging Cubans to receive funds from abroad and promoting the dollar-fueled tourism industry.

August 1994: After angry demonstrations prompted by food shortages, Castro allows 40,000 people to leave for Florida. For the first time, many of those who leave are black.

Fall 1994: An agreement is reached between the U.S. and Cuba, mandating the immediate return of any Cubans picked up on high seas and allowing 20,000 Cubans to apply for U.S. residency each year.

October 1994: Private farmers' markets are created in Cuba to help solve food shortages. Some forms of self-employment are legalized.

February 1996: Two aircraft belonging to a Miami-based Cuban refugee and exile assistance group, "Brothers to the Rescue," are shot down by Cuban Air Force jets, resulting in the deaths of four volunteer pilots.

March 1996: In the wake of the "Brothers to the Rescue" incident, the Cuban Liberty and Democratic Solidarity Act, known as the "Helms-Burton" Act, is signed into law by President Clinton. The legislation codifies existing sanctions into law, imposes penalties on foreign companies using confiscated U.S. property in Cuba, and dictates conditions for an acceptable "transition" government in Cuba.

1996: The Miami-Dade County Commission passes a "Cuba Resolution" forbidding any county associates from doing business with companies or individuals that have any direct or indirect business with Cuba.

1998: Pope John Paul II visits Cuba. The Communist Party reinstates Christmas as a public holiday.

1999: The White House loosens travel restrictions to Cuba for business, scholarship, and family visits.

November 1999: Elián González, a five-year-old Cuban boy, is discovered by fishermen clinging to an inner-tube in the Florida straits.

March 1999: The Baltimore Orioles play the Cuban national baseball team in Havana.

January 2000: A U.S. Healthcare Exhibition is held in Havana, the first American trade show to take place in Cuba since 1962.

June 2000: The U.S. Supreme Court rules that local governments cannot make rules that interfere with federal foreign policy, effectively ending Miami-Dade's "Cuba Resolution."

June 28, 2000: Elián González returns with his father to Cuba.

October 2000: Congress lifts most restrictions on selling food and medicine to Cuba. However, legislators impose stiff conditions on such sales, including banning the U.S. government and banks from financing sales and shipments of goods to Cuba. Castro protests these conditions and calls for a full lifting of the embargo.

2001: The *Dallas Morning News* and other newspapers open bureaus in Havana, the first permitted since the *New York Times* was expelled 40 years ago.

I. The State of the
Revolution

During a mass in Havana's Plaza de la Revolución *on January 25, 1998, Pope John Paul II called for a Cuban society of "peace, justice, and freedom" but warned of the dangers of capitalism.*

Editor's Introduction

I n 1999 Cubans marked the 40th anniversary of the revolution with music, parades, and proclamations of the militant motto "Socialism or death!" Castro mounted a scathing criticism of free-market capitalism and the global economy, arguing that the economic solutions offered by the world's richest countries have only made less-developed nations poorer and more dependent. And yet, ever since the collapse of the Soviet Union, which provided subsidies and Cuba's major market, Cuba has taken steps away from socialism and toward capitalism by introducing U.S. dollars into the market and cultivating tourism and foreign investment. What, then, defines socialism in Cuba today? And how will the revolution evolve after the inevitable passing of the 74-year-old leader? A major assumption of U.S. foreign policy is that economic change will inevitably lead to political change, but it is not clear if this will occur in Cuba. "No one would be able to change the line of the revolution because that is what the people believe in," Castro recently told a group of American reporters, "in the same way that the pope couldn't turn his followers into Muslims."

Section I evaluates the state of Cuba's 40-year-old revolution and speculates on the island's economic and political future. In the first article, "Evolution in the Revolution," John J. Putman visits the mountain camp where Castro planned his revolution, a starting point for the writer's journey around the island. Putman encounters a series of figures, each offering a glimpse of the often contradictory truths of life in Cuba: A dedicated doctor in a free health clinic proudly describes himself as a "son of the revolution," even though he must supplement his meager $20-a-month salary by selling jewelry to tourists; the president of a watchdog group keeps an eye out for "antisocials"; and the head of a tobacco company reports on the boom in business.

Putman's description of Cuba as a work in progress is challenged by Kevin Baxter's analysis of "Cuba's Suspended Revolution." Baxter reports on Cuban society five years after the U.S. dollar was legalized as a parallel currency to the peso. He argues that, while Cuba's market reforms during the 1990s have helped to jumpstart the economy, such reforms have compromised the hard-earned social equality that was the hallmark achievement of the revolution. Cubans are now divided between the privileged few with access to dollars and the majority, who must scrape by on meager rations and inadequate salaries. Worst of all, according to Baxter, the tourist boom is producing new forms of ad-hoc capitalism, including young prostitutes who line up outside expensive hotels, making the streets of Havana seem like Cuba in prerevolutionary days.

Writing on the eve of Pope John Paul II's visit to Cuba, John W. Kennedy explores how religion has become an agent of social change in Cuban society. During the 1990s, Castro began to loosen restrictions on religious activity and form strategic alliances with church leaders. There are now about one million active Christians in Cuba—more than before the revolution. Even if the pope's visit produces only symbolic changes, many Cubans believe that religion will occupy an important space in post-Castro Cuba.

A subtext in the controversy over the fate of Elián González involved a *santero* oracle for the year 2000, predicting that a child will conquer death and become a figure of salvation; Elián—who survived hours at sea, suffered no salt burns, and was reportedly visited by dolphins—is, to many *santería* believers, such a figure. In a short article, Kennedy discusses *santería*, a blend of Catholicism and traditional African religions that is the most widespread form of spiritual activity in Cuba.

In the final article in this section, Roger Fontaine poses the $64,000 question: How much longer can Castro last, and what will happen after his death? The "maximum leader" has remained in power much longer than many believed possible; the "autumn of the patriarch," in the words of Patrick Symmes in *Harper's* (December 1997) "has proved to be an Indian summer." But Castro's hold on power must end soon, if only through his death. Arguing that Castro's brother, Raúl, lacks Castro's leadership abilities, Fontaine speculates that power will devolve through the Communist Party to members of Cuba's young technocratic class—sons and daughters of the revolution who will attempt to reinvent socialism for the next generation.

Cuba: Evolution in the Revolution[1]

By John Putman
National Geographic, June 1999

The mountain trail was slick, difficult, rocks, rain, mud. It took me up into a cool, misty world far different from the sun-blasted lowlands below. The trail led to La Plata, the mountain camp where in 1958 Fidel Castro planned the last guerrilla attacks against the army of President Fulgencio Batista.

My companion was Rubén Araujo Torres, 60, a short, sturdy man in a peasant's straw hat. He had joined Castro's cause back then, picking up medicine and soap from secret caches, trading these for food from peasants, then bringing the food up to the guerrillas in their aerie. "It was dangerous. The army was everywhere." Why did he go with Castro? "I was a peasant, illiterate, didn't know anything. But friends said, 'Come on, come with us.' I knew the other guys were burning and killing, so I came with them." Rubén ended up on the winning side; from these mountains, the Sierra Maestra, Castro and his fighters broke the spirit of Batista's army.

We passed guard posts and a few outbuildings, then came to Castro's house of thatch and wood, set on a steep slope above a spring-fed stream in a sea of green.

The house had two rooms. The kitchen held a kerosene fridge with a bullet hole in it. The small bedroom had wooden windows on three sides; you propped them open with sticks. "Fidel built the bookcase, those chairs," Rubén said. "He built this chair for himself, that one for Celia." Celia Sánchez was his aide-de-camp. I went outside, sat on a pole bench. "Fidel would sit there sometimes to write," Rubén said. "It's the original wood, hard; it lasts."

I asked about Celia. "She was very nice," Rubén said, "the mother of the troop." She was constantly by Castro's side taking notes, keeping watch, running errands. She stayed by his side until she died in 1980.

"Celia planted these," Rubén said, "hibiscus, *mar pacífico*." I had noticed the bright red petals on the trail coming in. They seemed to me now souvenirs of a time when everyone here was young and all the world was green.

Forty years after the mountain, Fidel Castro, *el comandante en jefe*, the commander in chief, still dominates Cuba, his hand everywhere. Yet Cuba is changing, its future uncertain. The end of economic and military aid from the old Soviet Union has led to a search for new money, new friends, new ways of doing things. And the comandante is aging; people wonder who will replace him and when. I wanted to look into these questions and also into the questions of how life is in Cuba today and what the people think about their lives, their problems, their future.

I knew that to gain answers, I would have to range the island, talk to people at every level, let them shape their stories, be an honest and patient listener. I discovered to my surprise that almost everyone wanted to talk, and at length. It was as if, controls having been eased, there were thousands of pent-up conversations and experiences to be shared. Only an ear was needed.

I decided to start in Havana, that magnificent and crumbling city of 2.2 million souls. It is said Havana is two cities: One represents the old socialist ways, one the new ways.

I drew a circle around one block on a map of Old Havana, the historic heart of the city. I would dig in there, see what life was like. On one side of the block was Calle Obispo, the tourist street that runs from Hemingway's old hangout, El Floridita, down to the 16th-century Plaza de Armas. The block's other streets were not touristic but narrow, filled with people, potholes, carts, voices, music, dogs, laundry fluttering from balconies, a mattress being lowered by rope from an upper floor. I went to Obrapía No. 508 to meet the block's family doctor, a state employee in a system that offers free medical care to all Cubans.

Dr. Henry Luis Brito, 29, was at work in a small, hot, humid room. As patients came in from a dark passage outside, he would listen attentively, take blood pressure. A woman suffered from depression, another from pain in her knees. A child had asthma. A young man, the doctor determined, was afflicted with *blenorragia*, gonorrhea. By 11:30 a.m. Dr. Luis Brito had seen 20 patients, and he took a break.

"In theory I am responsible for 120 families," he said, "but actually almost 130. More than 500 people in three blocks." The doctor's examining room was spare, dimly lit, missing lightbulbs, it held little medicine. I asked about reports that Cuban doctors are well trained but lack equipment and medicines, that because of shortages hospitals some days can perform only emergency operations, and that many Cubans receive needed medicines from relatives in the United States, sent by way of commercial agencies.

"You must understand," Dr. Luis Brito said, "that I am a son of the revolution. I grew up with the revolution, and I believe there is always a solution here." If one medicine was lacking, he prescribed another. "And there is the possibility of alternative medicines, acupuncture, homeopathy."

For his efforts the doctor received a furnished apartment and 400 pesos ($20) a month. It wasn't enough. So the doctor helped his wife, Yumila, "in a kind of private thing" making ceramic earrings and necklaces to sell in the market to tourists.

The block's rationed-food stores stood at the corner of Obrapía and Villegas, one for meat (sausages of uncertain content) and one for vegetables ("No potatoes today," a smiling young woman said. "Maybe tomorrow, maybe the next day"). Everyone had a little ration book, well thumbed, heavily marked, listing how many

---

"I am a son of the revolution. I grew up with the revolution, and I believe there is always a solution here."—Dr. Luis Brito

---

grams of what each person could buy at cheap prices at the government stores. It allowed one roll of bread per person per day; if you had a few centavos extra, a man would bring your allotment to your house in a pushcart. "You get chicken maybe four times a year," a man said, "but certainly twice." You could buy more food in the private markets but at a much higher price.

At Villegas No. 212 was the house of Lourdes González, a positive woman with a big smile and silver bracelets, president of the block Committee for the Defense of the Revolution (CDR). She saw to fulfillment of socialist tasks: recycling, night patrol of the street, health campaigns such as polio vaccinations for all children.

She had a ledger listing everyone on the block. "Nobody can live here, even temporarily, without control." The CDR was on the watch for antisocials—"those who don't work or study, who hustle or rob, who do nothing for anyone, not even themselves."

What if an antisocial is noticed? "We must tell the police. They meet with that person, give warnings. They watch him. He can face sanctions of up to four years."

Rules lie heavy on daily life. You cannot legally buy or sell a house or an apartment; if you want a change, you go down and join the crowd in the median strip of Paseo del Prado to read the swap notices tacked on trees there.

And if you are a young woman, recently married, and want your new husband to move into the house you share with your brother and stepfather, the first step is to obtain a temporary change-of-residence permit. It's good for three months. It takes that long to do all the paperwork for a permanent permit. You must visit the housing authority and a notary and apply to the architecture office for an inspector to come measure your house. He must verify that with an additional occupant the house still meets the rules—ten square meters per person.

"There is more," the young woman told me. Permit in hand, "you must register with the CDR, go to the identity card office, ration book office, driver's license office to get new documents." But she still had no permit; papers had been lost or found wanting, while the days had ticked by. "If we don't get it all done in three months, we could be fined 1,300 pesos." She laughed. "It's crazy" she said.

Jorge, 28, who drives a *triciclo*, or pedicab, and calls himself a *cochero*, or coachman, was trying to pedal his way into the future. The work was hard. "At the end of the day I am very tired, and some mornings I get up with pain in the legs and back." But with foreign tourists he might on a good day earn $15 (U.S.). He was making payments to buy the *triciclo*. He had one worry, that the state, which allowed this small piece of private enterprise, might change its mind, change the rules. It had done so before. Jorge kept on pedaling.

> *The [U.S.] dollar is helping create two societies in Cuba: one with dollars, the other without.*

Jorge's Journeys took him past the new Cuba as well as the old, for the new is everywhere in Havana: shiny new hotels, new Korean-built taxis with radio telephones and drivers in crisp shirts and ties, swarms of foreign tourists and businessmen. The U.S. dollar is everywhere, the currency used by all foreign visitors, and flowing in by the millions to Cubans as remittances from relatives living in the U.S. The dollar is helping create two societies in Cuba: one with dollars, the other without.

A Cuban grumbled. "All the nice new shops are for dollars only, not pesos." The better hotels, with CNN on the TV and plenty of food, were for dollars only, and mainly for foreigners. Most Cubans were stopped at the door unless they worked with, or were guests of, dollar-wielding foreigners. "It's a sort of apartheid," a Cuban said. With the tourist dollars, prostitutes and hustlers had returned to Havana's streets as in the old Batista days, and a government crackdown was to begin.

But tourism contributed more hard currency to the Cuban economy in 1998 than sugar, the old standby. In 1997 Cuba had 1.2 million visitors, in 1998 1.4 million, and 2 million are expected in the year 2000. Fifty-three percent come from Europe; the rest come mostly from Canada and Latin America. The new hotels represent investments by foreign copartners, mainly European and Canadian.

A new terminal in Havana awaits cruise ships that will bring more multitudes of tourists. "We're talking with all the big cruise lines, the American too," said Minister of Tourism Osmany Cienfuegos. Cuba welcomes Americans. The U.S. embargo, which prohibits commerce with Cuba, says that U.S. citizens, unless exempted, may not spend money there. Many thousands visit anyway.

Everyone expects the regulations to be changed, but nobody knows when. So the impending arrival of the Americans, with their numbers, their money, their demands, lies on the horizon like a great storm cloud over the sea. One day the storm will break, wash over the old city, change it for better or worse.

The ministry has begun using the Internet, another official said. "A million hits a month. It's the future." Meanwhile ordinary Cubans are denied its use. Life in Cuba today is rich in contradictions, if nothing else.

When I visited Habanos, S.A., the state company that controls the marketing and sale of Cuba's famous cigars, I found business booming. Exports had jumped from 72 million cigars in 1996 to 126 million in 1998. More production was wanted, said Francisco Linares, the company president. "We're searching for more suitable land"—with just the right amount of sand in the soil and a microclimate that promises moist nights, cool mornings.

And the government is getting out of tobacco growing, turning land over to farm families to work as their own. Already 90 percent of Cuba's tobacco is grown by 30,000 private farmers working small pieces of land. When experience as well as hard work was needed, perhaps it seemed best to let the farmer make the decisions, enjoy the profits.

I was pleased to see that in the push to produce, traditions endured. The factory I visited in Havana was 150 years old, built by a man with a name famous in cigars, Partagás. In a great room suffused with the dark colors of tobacco, rows of men and women bent to their work. Each had a pile of filler tobacco and wrapper leaves; a *chaveta*, or knife; a *tabla de bonche*, the cigar mold to go in the little wooden press; and a *tabla de rolar*, the darkened wooden block on which they cut and rolled. They worked swiftly, their target about a hundred cigars a day each—Cohibas, Montecristos, Bolivars, as well as Partagases.

As they worked, a *lector*, reader, on a platform with a speaker system read newspapers to them, played the radio for them, made announcements, a custom as old as cigarmaking.

Cuba's prestigious Centre for Genetic Engineering and Biotechnology, on the outskirts of Havana, competes in a more high-tech market. Dr. Manuel Limonta, its director general, described breakthroughs achieved or sought by his scientists: vaccines against

AIDS and dengue fever; medicines to dissolve blood clots; genetic modifications of plants, fish, and animals to promote better yields, resistance to pests and disease, and faster growth.

He said the institute's commercial arm was already exporting medicines and clinical supplies to 47 countries: China, India, nations in Latin America and Eastern Europe. "We are now looking to the European community. We would welcome partnerships there.

"Cuba is no longer an island. . . . There are no islands anymore. There is only one world."—Raúl Valdés Vivó, rector of the Cuban Communist Party's Ñico López school

---

Those companies have big marketing networks, much experience. We can offer lower costs in development and production."

Cuba's low pay, it seemed, was a card that could be played on the global market.

I wondered how the state could maintain its communist ideology as it attempted to edge into the capitalist world market. I went to see Raúl Valdés Vivó, rector of the Cuban Communist Party's Ñico López school for advanced studies outside Havana. It stands close to the state's Marina Hemingway, which welcomes foreign yachts, including those of Americans.

Valdés Vivó, 69, was quiet-spoken, wore glasses. He had been a communist before Fidel organized his revolutionary movement. When Fidel declared communism the guiding ideology of Cuba, Valdés Vivó became a leading ideologue.

"The problem today," Valdés Vivó said, "is to maintain socialist principles when we have to use not only socialist but capitalist means." It wasn't easy. It had led to a change in the school's curriculum. Before, he said, students had studied basic texts: the works of Marx, Engels, Lenin, Che Guevara. Students had been expected to give answers in class that coincided with what was written in those books.

"Now we have a more creative education, one that focuses on the problems of today. The student must talk as much as the professor." If there is a basic text at the school today, he said, it is the "ideas of Fidel, even the example of Fidel."

Valdés Vivó mused a moment. "Cuba is no longer an island" he said. "There are no islands anymore. There is only one world"

Maybe, I thought. But I remembered the young woman who told me of her feelings of isolation living on the island of Cuba. "It's like we live on Mars: We are Martians."

I took the *Autopista* westward, into a countryside of banana groves, lime trees, distant hills, tobacco barns, rice spread to dry along the roadside. A fine superhighway, but cars were few, buses fewer. Big trucks carried people packed rump-to-rump, chest-to-chest. I turned right at Pinar del Río, capital of the province of the same name, and climbed little hills to the town of Viñales.

"*¡Lo cubano—está aquí!* The real Cuba—it's here!" a billboard promised.

The pope had reached out ... to urge Cubans to look at the future with hope, to commit to changing things so all might live in harmony.

The area is indeed beautiful. Early morning mist covered the valley of Viñales, and dark limestone masses rose through it like ancient gods. Birds circled, a rooster crowed, the first workers entered the fields of manioc and beans. It reminded me of Eden.

The town, long a regional agricultural center, seemed little touched by the years. Houses with porches, tall pine trees, a gentle atmosphere. But a new emphasis on tourism had brought change. Here too were two Cubas, the old and the new, and sometimes envy.

Each month workers in tourism could buy at low cost from their employers a bag of soap, shampoo, detergents, cooking oil—scarce and costly items all. Other workers didn't have that benefit and sometimes expressed resentment. A party member defended the system. "Some people, because of human nature, think a bar of soap is a big thing, a higher level of life. But they forget that tourist workers share all the other limitations of life in Cuba today."

The Catholic church stands on the main square in Viñales. The priest, Padre Vicente Cabrera Delgado, was 34. He served eleven churches, said Mass in five every Sunday.

"I start about 5 a.m. and end about 10 p.m. I have a car but not a very good one. Often I have to use a bike." He had been born in the province, his father a mason. He wore no clerical collar but a tan shirt, dark trousers. He thought the church was growing, if slowly. One reason was "younger priests, a change of style. A presentation of God not as a rewards and punishment man but as a God that establishes a relationship of friendship with men."

The pope's visit to Cuba had been very important. "Six busloads of people went from here to Havana to see and hear him." The pope had reached out to join believer and nonbeliever in reconciliation, to urge Cubans to look at the future with hope, to commit to changing things so all might live in harmony. "He spoke," another priest had told me, "like a friend who says things you don't want to hear but you should listen to."

"For four decades the church has faced problems with the state" Father Cabrera Delgado said. At the beginning the revolution seized church property, banned public devotions, drove priests from the country. Even Christmas was abolished.

Now problems were more subtle. "There's a disco next door; they do not respect our services?" And sometimes the city blocked off the plaza for an event, barring access to the church, giving no warning. "But there has been an opening, and we cannot ignore that."

Viñales's link to the world in the old days—shipping out agricultural products, receiving manufactured goods—was La Esperanza, Hope, on the north coast. It's a small fisherman's town now, quiet, its houses drawn up along the main street. I turned down a side road, took a path past goats and fiddler crabs to the beach, and found the local branch of the Cuban Federation of Sport Fishing. There was a shack, a rickety wharf, some 30 skiffs dancing on the blue sea.

The club manager pulled chairs from the shack, and we sat in the sun. He said the club had 400 members. Dues were one peso (five cents) a month. "A good deal," he said. And not only for sport. "You can catch and keep for your family 15 kilos [33 pounds] of fish a day. Over that you must give to the state" The boats were privately owned. A pretty one, *La Gaviota—The Seagull*, was for sale. It had an Italian engine. The price was 7,000 pesos.

It was pleasant there. On the horizon cays lay like dark shadows. I could understand why Hemingway so loved the seas around Cuba, the fishing, and why he wrote so much about these things. Close by was the dock of a state fishing cooperative and the tower of a coast guard station. Atop the tower a man bent over a powerful telescope, scanning the horizon, looking perhaps for invaders, spies, or fellow countrymen setting out for Key West 175 miles to the northeast. From small fishing ports like this, I remembered, thousands of Cuban *balseros*, rafters, had set out in 1994 for the Florida shore, risking all against the sea for a better life.

I noticed the Cyclopean eye of the scope swing to focus on me and the fishermen. The manager was called away, returned to say I must leave. "Why?" I asked. He nodded toward the tower. The fishermen expressed regrets. "I don't know why they do this" one said. "The people who come here are nice."

The next day in Viñales, officer Ira of the immigration police, prim, polite, came looking for me. He took me into his tiny office in the police station, closed the door, unlocked his filing cabinet, removed four pages of blank paper, took pen in hand. Had I been down to the fishermen's club by the coast guard station at La Esperanza? Why had I gone to talk with the priest? Who else had I talked to? Well, I mused, even Eden had interrogations.

Back in Havana an official of the ministry of foreign relations said that the actions by the coast guardsman and officer Ira did not conform to new regulations. Perhaps, he said, the new rules had not yet been absorbed by every officer in every town.

East of Havana lies the great bulk of the island: green seas of sugarcane, mountains, *vaqueros* on their little horses, farmers with oxen. I drove east, then south, and ended up in the town of Trinidad. It had once flourished as a sugar port, but time had passed it by. Its center held 1,200 buildings from the 18th and 19th centuries; these were to be restored, a treasure from the past, a lure for tourists. Sometimes I thought the history of Cuba was written in houses.

Leopoldina Fonseca y Valdés-Busto de Iznaga was 90, ill, abed, white hair on a white pillow. There was a rosary above the bed, an old family servant, Benito, by her side. Leopoldina recalled when the revolution had come to Trinidad. She and her husband had been at their country house when the rebels arrived. "They said we had to leave the house in 24 hours. They said they would help, bring trucks. But much was left behind."

> *East of Havana lies the great bulk of the island: green seas of sugarcane, mountains, vaqueros on their little horses, farmers with oxen.*

It had been the end of a dynasty with thousands of acres of cane, fine houses, a great bell tower. Leopoldina and her husband moved to their city palace, and in time, after her husband died, she had to leave that. She lived now in a modest house the government had given her. "Everything was taken from us," she said, "and they give me a pension of only 120 pesos a month, not enough even for medicine."

Buena Vista, the country house from which she had been expelled, sat on a little hill in a valley of cane, a copy of a Roman villa, of stone, square, strong. It was now a shambles, its occupants a retired cane cutter and his family. But he too might soon be asked to leave. Officials were considering adding Buena Vista to the list of houses to be restored for "social uses" such as tourism.

Down the coast to the east lies Santiago de Cuba, the islands second largest city. Images crowd the visitor's mind: a rim of mountains, undulating streets, houses of pink and green, black faces recalling a slave port past, a dwarf on crutches, begging, horse coaches carrying arrivals from the train station, down by the docks, up into the neighborhoods.

It was Carnival, the festival the city has long held to celebrate the feast day of its patron, Santiago—St. James the Apostle. Night after night teams competed for prizes with dancers, musicians, marchers, towering floats. In the dark city, Carnival streets glowed with light and shook with music—a mix of congas, rumbas, salsas. One young dancer, tall, black, elegant, had her eye on the future. She had joined the team of a well-known dancing school, La Placita. "After its training" she said, "I will get a contract at a tourist cabaret. Then I will make money."

African spirits hung in the air. Santiago is a stronghold of *santería*, a faith based on African gods and traditions that incorporates Catholic saints and imagery. I went to see a *santera*, a practitioner, Vicenta Tejeda, from a family of *santeros*. She performed her ceremonies in a small room at the back of her house. She was a friendly woman wearing a yellow-patterned shirt and navy skirt with rings and a gold bracelet. She was surrounded by paraphernalia: African-looking drums of many sizes, iron pots, dolls, dishes, stones, cowries.

"People come because they have problems" she said. "They are sick or have a sick child or have a problem with the law." She performed rituals, would counsel a sick person to give food to the gods or take special baths. If needed, "I will sacrifice a goat."

Vicenta said that in her parlor she practiced spiritism, another religion popular in Santiago. "It's based on the spirits of different protectors. We work with a table, many glasses of water, candles, perfume, petals of flowers."

During that busy Carnival week there was also a political celebration, one marking the anniversary of the revolution. Fidel himself was to speak. The venue was the Moncada barracks, a handsome yellow-and-white art deco building. Castro had attacked it as a young man in 1953; the battle had been fierce, a number of men killed, Castro captured, later released. It was a milestone in the revolution.

I went to the barracks early, saw rows of blue chairs on the parade ground awaiting guests. I decided to spend the evening in the neighborhoods. As I moved through the dark, crowded streets, I noticed loudspeakers had been set to carry the comandante's message to everyone. Block to block, I heard his voice, reciting the achievements of the revolution: "Cuba counts one teacher for every 42 inhabitants . . . 98.8 percent of infants up to age two are immunized against ten diseases . . . 7.3 hospital beds per 1,000 inhabitants . . . total of doctors: 63,384 . . . electricity production capacity multiplied by ten. . . ."

"He always cites statistics," a young man later remarked. "I should know them by heart." Before I went to bed that night, I looked out my hotel room window and saw the floodlights at the Moncada barracks still blazing. The comandante was still speaking. Among his concluding words: "We will never surrender. . . . Socialism or death!"

Fidel seemed everywhere. I wondered what had shaped this man. His boyhood home lay north of Santiago in the village of Birán. I drove there through fields of cane rimmed by mountains. At the gate to the family *finca*, or farm, I was stopped by a guard. To visit, I would have to get special permission from the secretary general of the Communist Party in nearby Holguín. It was given, and the next day I entered.

The *finca* was in truth a hamlet. There was a small wooden hotel, a store, a post office, a one-room school, an arena for cockfights, thatched huts for Haitian workers. On a rise was the family house, handsome, rimmed by a porch and topped with a lookout room. The house stood on posts so that animals and supplies could be sheltered underneath. All the buildings were beautifully restored, empty of people.

Inside, the house was light, airy, had an interior gallery. The parlor held two photographs. One depicted Fidel's father, Ángel, on horseback. He had come from Galicia in Spain as a penniless boy, worked his way up. He sat erect in jodhpurs, leggings, a tightly buttoned jacket, his face as stern as a conquistador's.

The other photograph showed Fidel's mother, Lina, willowy in a white dress, holding flowers. She was from a peasant family, had been a maid in Don Ángel's household.

Another room held Fidel's baby bed, simple but snug, the crib of the revolution, you might say. The lookout room was the parents' bedroom, windows on all sides. Here Ángel could survey his domain in every direction. The room reminded me of another: the one in the little house that Ángel's son built on the mountain when he was the guerrilla chief.

Graciano Gómez, 78, a peasant's son who grew up with Fidel and now lives nearby, recalled the family. Ángel demanded hard work but was fair. Lina was nice, could talk easily with any peasant. As for Fidel, "he was always the leader. We would be playing one game, and he would say, 'Let's do another.'"

The *finca*, in a way, brought to mind Washington's Mount Vernon: a handsome setting preserving a glimpse of life in a bygone time and linked to a historical figure. There was indeed a plan to open the *finca* to tourists, I was told. "But not yet."

Back in Havana, I visited one of the 50 or so dissident organizations that protest the rule of the Castro government or charge violations of human rights. I found the headquarters of the Pro Human Rights Party of Cuba in the basement of a house in southeast Havana. The basement was also home to Odilia Collazo Valdés, president of the party. She was 48.

To argue with Fidel had its risks. The founders of the party, she said, had been jailed in Cuba and were now in the United States.

To argue with Fidel had its risks. The founders of the [opposition] party . . . had been jailed in Cuba and were now in the United States.

"Our program is to defend the 30 points of the United Nations Declaration on Human Rights" Because the government controlled the media in Cuba, she said, the party denounced violations through international organizations such as Human Rights Watch. It was in constant touch with those organizations by phone. It was also in touch with Cuban Americans in Miami and with Radio Martí, the U.S. government-sponsored radio station in Miami. Once the phone rang. Another party member answered, talked, hung up. "Radio Martí," he said.

Odilia said there were between 350 and 400 political prisoners in Cuba. Her father had been a political prisoner, held six years in La Cabaña, a sprawling Spanish fortress overlooking Havana's ship channel. "They let him out when he was very ill; they always do that. He died shortly thereafter."

She said the party had links in every province. Members exchanged visits and information, sometimes demonstrated. "Earlier this month we planned to demonstrate at a religious procession at a church and gathered at a house nearby. But security forces came, and we were not allowed to leave the house."

She had taken along her *ropa de calabozo*, cell clothes—soap, spare underwear—just in case. She had been to jail before, she said, sometimes for hours, sometimes for days. Unlike her father, not for years. Still, rules governing public dissent can change.

A small notice appeared in *Granma*, the newspaper of the Communist Party, early last June." *Información a la población*—Information to the people" the headline said. It announced that the U.S. Interests Section, the de facto U.S. embassy in Havana, was holding another lottery to give Cubans a chance at immigration visas. The lottery would open June 15, close July 15. Entries had to be postmarked within those dates.

The lottery is part of an agreement between the U.S. and Cuba designed to discourage the chaotic flight of boat people to U.S. shores. The U.S. allows 20,000 Cubans to immigrate to the U.S. each year, of which the lottery provides about 15,000. The Cuban government, for its part, tries to control illegal departures.

When I visited the Interests Section, the lottery had just closed. I asked a diplomat how many letters had been received from applicants. The answer was 541,100. That is about 5 percent of Cuba's population.

I wondered what the youth of Cuba thought about the future; it would belong to them. I ascended the great stairway leading to the University of Havana. The university had been one of young Fidel's favorite venues. As a student there he had carried a gun, demonstrated, agitated, speechified.

I would find today's students more circumspect. I walked through the gate into a pleasant quadrangle: trees, paths, benches, law students taking a break. They gave varied answers to my question about the future. "About the same . . . more privatization . . . the government will take the private things back . . . much different . . . the same . . . we have to see who is coming after."

One graduate student, slim, swarthy, had been mulling the question. "We are living in an age of reorganization," he said. "We see it every day in class and in daily life. The Cuban economy is going to be restructured, decentralized, become more spontaneous, and Cuba will be inserted into the global economy. I hope we can survive." Would economic changes lead to political change? "This is not the current tendency" he said.

Who might follow Fidel? People I spoke with mentioned three or four leading government officials. They often cited 61-year-old Ricardo Alarcón, president of the 601-member National Assembly, the "Congress" of Cuba. Considered Cuba's top expert on the U.S., he had spent years as Cuba's ambassador to the United Nations in New York.

Alarcón assured me there was no jockeying to succeed Fidel. "If Fidel is not president or is not working for any reason, his successor is the vice president of the Council of State, Raúl, automatically. Raúl was elected to that post by the National Assembly. If somebody else wants that position, it would be illegal. It's in the constitution"

Raúl, Fidel's brother, is also chief of the army—an army that has gone into business with hotels, car and aircraft rental agencies, the growing and marketing of food. But Raúl is 68, reported to be frail. So the question of who will lead Cuba in the years ahead remains unanswered, as does the question of what direction a new government might take. Future possibilities, a U.S. official said, include a gradual, peaceful transition to democracy, or chaos, or something else. No one knows.

Fidel was the one subject Cubans seemed reluctant to discuss. I asked one man if it was perhaps time for the comandante to step down. He bristled. "To retire would be cowardly." Later he added an old Spanish proverb: *"No hay mal que dure 100 años ni cuerpo que lo resista*—There is no illness that lasts 100 years and no body that could endure it."

On my last night in Havana I walked in the garden of the old Hotel Nacional de Cuba. The garden overlooks the sea. By day peacocks stroll and caged birds sing. By night you watch the beam of the El Morro fortress lighthouse flash from across the ship channel. I thought of my first visit to Cuba, just days after Castro's army seized the capital in 1959. He was then 32, fresh faced. I was a young journalist, curious to see a revolution.

I had stayed at the Nacional, walked the streets, looked at everything. But I remembered little except the *guerrilleros* in their fatigues, weapons hung from belts, shoulders, chests—young, exultant, shouting, smiling, swaggering. You don't see much exultation in faces today, I thought. Rather, you see struggle, uncertainty, maybe hope.

In my room I switched on the television. The face of el comandante filled the screen.

He looked old, tired; he is 72. At times, making a point, he would lift a finger, raise his eyebrows, and an expression of satisfaction would pass over his face. Forty years takes a toll on all of us. I switched off the TV. Tomorrow is another day.

Cuba's Suspended Revolution[2]

By Kevin Baxter
The Nation, August 24, 1998

On many nights, just after dark, the lights and fans in Osmel and Milay Casa's Alamar neighborhood flicker and then go out. In today's Cuba, there's not quite enough electricity to go around. So in a practiced routine, residents slowly file out of the stuffy concrete-block bunkers that serve as apartment buildings in this working-class part of suburban Havana, a neighborhood that, back in the sixties, was showcased to foreign visitors as a model of socialist progress. Then, flashlight in hand, Osmel and Milay join their neighbors in parading up and down the dusty, potholed streets until the humid night cools enough for them to go back inside. Before dawn, they'll be out in the streets again, Osmel pedaling his bicycle toward the city center with Milay balanced precariously over the back tire. It's a long, tiring trip in the tropical heat, but taking the bike instead of a bus to work six mornings a week saves them pennies a day—pennies that add up quickly in a household with a monthly income of less than 400 pesos, or about $20.

But across town in upscale Miramar, where late-model luxury cars ply the wide, well-kept boulevards, passing embassies, seaside hotels and expensive nightspots, Constantino Torres keeps the air-conditioner in his spacious six-room home going all night. A semi-retired college professor, Torres rents out two of his rooms to foreign tourists for a nightly fee nearly twice what the Casas earn for a month of full-time labor. By the way, that rent is payable in U.S. dollars only—that green stuff once called here the "currency of the enemy."

That's just one of the ironies that characterize Cuba today. Forty years after Fidel Castro's radically egalitarian revolution, social classes have re-emerged. Cuba can and should take pride in being the only country in the Americas that has managed to thwart US hegemony. But now, in the post–cold war era, the social fabric of the revolution is unraveling.

Nine years after the collapse of the Eastern bloc wiped out Cuba's major export markets and erased roughly $4 billion in annual subsidies from the Soviet Union, the island still teeters on the brink of insolvency. To stave off a complete meltdown, the government has

---

introduced a number of free-market policies. It has participated in more than 200 "joint ventures" with major foreign capitalists—with the Cuban state's "investment" often no more than its supply of a cheap and disempowered work force. The US dollar has been legalized as a parallel currency and has, to no one's surprise, created a parallel speculative economy.

As a result, the free fall of the Cuban economy has been slowed, but at a devastating social cost. The government still exhorts youth with slogans like "Socialism or Death." But as any Cuban will tell you, any one of the teenage hookers who crowd Miramar's Fifth Avenue, or for that matter any of the parking valets who work tourist restaurants for hard-currency tips, make more in an evening than a "revolutionary" state-employed doctor or researcher does in a month. Cuba's political leadership would argue that while it has had to perform some impressive philosophical gymnastics to avoid directly renouncing four decades of socialist orthodoxy, the market reform strategy appears to be working. After falling by a third between 1989 and 1993, Cuba's GDP grew nearly 8 percent in 1996. Nickel production, with the help of Canadian entrepreneurs, is way up, as is tobacco; agricultural exports, produced with Israeli and Chilean investment, are also on the rise. With hundreds of millions of dollars in Spanish capital invested in classy resorts, the tourist industry is raking in more than a billion dollars a year. Still, based on current projections the standard of living won't return to the 1989 level until 2014.

> *Now, in the post–cold war era, the social fabric of the revolution is unraveling.*

But supporters of the revolution are concerned about more than the standard of living, and many Cubans who sacrificed for decades in the name of revolutionary equality are asking themselves just what sort of society Cuba is evolving into. They ask, Just what is the point of continuing to sacrifice for a regime that in the name of those principles of equality is fostering a society ever more split along class lines? Castro spoke of his own dismay over the rise of the dual economy in a speech to the National Assembly in July, when he said, "We now have elements of capitalism [in our society] . . . we know that only too well. The more contact we have with capitalism and the more we perceive what happens, the more repulsion I feel." But as Angel Tomás González, a lifelong communist says, "The problem is, people just don't see an alternative." Adds Gonzalez, a small, intense man who once edited *Juventud Rebelde*, the newspaper of the Communist Youth, "Well, there are alternatives but none seem better than what we have now."

For González, the most damning economic reform was the 1993 legalization of dollars. That one measure, he and others argue, quickly erased many of the social gains of the revolution by strengthening, then legitimizing, an existing—but until then illegal—parallel economic system and giving an advantage to those Cubans with ready access to foreign currencies, either through their work in the tourist industry or from relatives living abroad. Overnight, chambermaids were making more than heart surgeons; having in the family a Miami-based political defector—traitors the government has long called *gusanos*, or worms—went from being a political liability to a much-coveted asset. Indeed, according to González, last year Cuban exiles abroad sent more than $800,000 to relatives still on the island. But those who remained steadfastly loyal to the revolution got screwed. Which is why González fondly recalls the more egalitarian period before 1993 as "the time when there was socialism." "What we have now is not *socialismo*," he laments, "it's Fidelismo."

> *"What we have now is not socialismo, . . . it's Fidelismo."*—Angel Tomás González, a lifelong communist

That's a common analysis in the streets of Havana these days. Over the past five years the gaps have been widening between rich and poor, black and white, urban and rural dwellers, those with access to dollars and those without, leaving Cubans themselves frustrated as the country's "special economic period"drags on. But as he takes another long draw on a cigarette, González admits there's no going back. If the government originally erred by allowing foreign currencies to circulate freely, it's only compounding that error by trying to manage an increasingly capitalistic economy through the old state-controlled apparatus. "The government wants to control every dollar [but] the state can't control everything from the building of a nuclear power plant to the price of ice cubes," he says. "The big picture is fine. It's the microeconomics that are a mess."

It takes about $100 a month to live comfortably in Havana today, but government salaries in pesos are worth, at most, a fifth of that. Basic necessities, which are rationed, are available at affordable prices, but the ration amounts generally last just two weeks, forcing people to pay exorbitant free-market dollar prices to survive the rest of the month. "Why work hard all week when you can go to a street corner [and] wash a tourist's windshield for $1?" asks González's companion Yolanda, a Spanish journalist. "Then you can spend the rest of the week at home watching TV."

But hustling for dollars isn't confined to street corners. Mispronounce a word in Spanish, forget to speak in the slurred, consonantless Cuban manner or ask directions to a well-known landmark—in short, commit any act that stamps you as a foreigner—and you're immediately surrounded by a sea of anxious salesmen offering everything from cut-rate cigars and rum to preteen prostitutes. It's all part of the growing Latin Americanization—what some even call the Haitianization—of Cuba. Although nearly one in eleven Cubans holds a university degree and the island boasts more doctors and teachers per capita than almost any country in the world, the familiar characteristics of other Latin American cities are now present in Havana: beggars and prostitutes in the streets, delinquents in the most affluent zones and government officials and simple citizens shaking down unwary visitors. Havana seems to be devolving back to its prerevolutionary status.

By my second morning in the downtown Hotel Inglaterra, I had to search out a little-used employees' entrance that opened discreetly onto a side street. The hotel's side doors were closed after dark, however, so there was no way to avoid the nightly parade of prostitutes. At dusk they'd begin to gather in front of the tourist hotels: young women—girls, really—wearing stiletto heels and short, skin-tight dresses. By midnight the seaside parking area shared by the first-class Riviera and Melia Cohiba hotels was filled with as many as 100 girls—known locally as *jineteras,* or jockeys—and dozens more lined Fifth Avenue, the main drag between the hotels and the plush homes and nightclubs of Vedado and Miramar. Where as recently as a few years ago Cuban State Security agents and uniformed cops would quickly extinguish any flickering of prostitution in these tourist areas, today they not only look the other way, they also profit from protection schemes.

Many of the young prostitutes are like Anel and Laura—well-educated and intelligent girls from the Cuban interior who hate what they're doing yet cannot live without the material rewards. Together they march back and forth like sentries guarding the 123-year-old Hotel Inglaterra. When I speak to them, it's a weeknight, so business is slow and the girls take a break on the hotel's patio, which is officially off-limits to them unless they've got a date.

"We're only doing this for the money," says Anel, a 19-year-old who seems embarrassed to be out in public in the black spandex dress she's wearing. A third-year medical student, she came to Havana from far-away Holguin to go to school. Because her studies don't allow her enough working time to support herself legally, most nights she acts as a "Cuban girlfriend" to tourists, a job description that can mean anything from accompanying a lonely businessman

to dinner and a few hours of dancing to something much more intimate. Both women say they've been beaten or abused, an experience they shrug off as an occupational hazard.

"They can't protest the treatment because they don't exist," says
journalist Yolanda, her comments colored by emotion and indigna-
tion. "They're invisible. It's illegal but the government looks the
other way. And the parents are doing the same thing the police are
doing. As long as the girls bring home the cash to buy color TVs,
nice things, they'll look the other way."

Cuba is undergoing a tourism boom not seen since the fifties,
when mob-run hotels lured foreigners with casinos, cheap rum,
cigars and prostitutes. If you leave out the casinos, the current government is using the same bait and achieving even better results.
Indeed state-owned Cuban tourist agencies in places like the
Bahamas now do record business booking cheap, thinly disguised
weekend sex tours to Havana. Last year more than 1 million tourists contributed $1.5 billion to the island's economy, about half a
billion more than Cuba earned from sugar, its leading export crop
and long the cornerstone of its economy. And in the first four
months of 1998, tourist-related revenue was up 15 percent compared with the same period last year.

"The tourists can find better beaches, better hotels and better
service elsewhere in the Caribbean. They can even find better prostitutes. But not as cheap," says Yolanda, who has written exten-
sively on the Cuban flesh trade. "So the government lets them
work to keep the tourists coming."

Out on the hotel patio, Anel has lost her sheepishness and has
launched into a fervent, disorienting defense of the revolution.
"Here we have freedom," she says. "We live in a democracy where
we are free to say and do what we want. If I don't like something, I
can go and complain. I can go to the government. I can go to Fidel
and tell him." But isn't Fidel the problem? she's asked. "Excuse me,
but the problem is the United States," she answers. "Clinton and
the government of the United States can't allow a socialist country
to exist ninety miles from its shores. That's the problem."

Despite Cuba's lingering economic crisis and the new glamour
given all things North American—from dollars to well-paid baseball players—Anel's views are widely held in Havana. While many
Cubans freely and openly criticize the government in even the
most public of venues (though no organized opposition politics are
tolerated), blame for the island's difficulties is more often placed on
policy-makers in Washington and Miami, not Havana. And in
some ways, Cuba has already beaten the US embargo. The economy hit rock bottom long ago, yet ordinary Cubans have managed
to dig, scratch and claw beneath the bedrock.

René Alvarez, who works in a souvenir shop down the street from El Floridita, one of Hemingway's favorite Havana watering holes, is among those who remain staunch defenders of the revolution. Yet he must strain to find a silver lining in Cuba's current gloomy outlook. "Well, right now there isn't any medicine," he offers, "but we do have a lot of doctors." He quickly smiles at the paradox, then shrugs his shoulders.

In fact, the healthcare system, once the jewel of the revolution, is, like everything else in Cuba, in tatters. Many physicians, unable to live on their $20 monthly salaries, are abandoning their hospitals

---

"In what country in the world is it mandatory that each child under seven have a liter of milk every day? . . . But how can we keep that up? We can't. Capitalism has never been in favor of human dignity."—**a Cuban revolutionary**

---

and clinics to take jobs in the tourist industry, where they are paid in pesos but tipped in dollars. The doctors who have stayed behind are forced to work in conditions that rival those in the world's poorest nations. In the operating rooms of the Calixto Garcia Hospital, surgeons reuse disposable plastic gloves until they split open and operations aren't scheduled until the patients provide doctors with the needed medicines and suturing thread. The hallways are dark because there are no lightbulbs and needed equipment goes unused because the hospital lacks the spare parts to keep it running.

Even though Cubans have a life expectancy rate equal to that in the United States, the strains on the health, water and sanitation systems have begun to take a toll. The death rate from diarrheal diseases rose 250 percent in the five years between 1989 and 1994, for example, and nutrition levels have dropped by a third since 1989 in some areas because of shortages and poverty. Havana is crumbling, and many of the city's buildings have grown as tired as their weary inhabitants. Few appear sturdy enough to withstand even a strong breeze—indeed, dozens of Havanans die each year in building collapses.

All over Havana, however, new commercial buildings are quickly sprouting, among them the recently completed Carlos III Mall, four stories of fast-food outlets and boutiques stocked with the latest from Lancôme, Yves Saint Laurent, Konica and Panasonic. Opened seven months ago on a site that once housed a "people's market," the mall, which appears to cater mainly to Cubans with dollars, is no different from many of LA's suburban shopping centers. That it lies in the middle of revolutionary Cuba and not capitalist California is betrayed only by the trendy two-tone Che Guevara watches on sale for $17.50—almost two months' wages for a middle-class Cuban worker. These new temples of consumerism stand in stark contrast to a sewer system that is a dysfunctional mess, public transportation plagued by crime and overcrowding, and a telephone system decades out-of-date.

One night I invited a veteran of the revolution, now a technician at the government-run TV Rebelde, to a baseball game. He brusquely waved off my offer to pay for the tab, paying himself and then thrusting the tickets into my hand in some sort of desperate act of national dignity. For him, the revolution wasn't defeated, it surrendered. "In what country in the world is it mandatory that each child under seven have a liter of milk every day?" he asked as we waited for the game to start. "But how can we keep that up? We can't. Capitalism has never been in favor of human dignity."

Cuba's Next Revolution: How Christians Are Reshaping Castro's Communist Stronghold[3]

BY JOHN W. KENNEDY
CHRISTIANITY TODAY, JANUARY 12, 1998

In 1994, Cuban secret police arrested Eliezar Veguilla after the pastor organized a Baptist conference in Havana that attracted 5,000 youth. Police charged him with being a counterrevolutionary spy working for the CIA.

Cockroaches crawled over Veguilla's body during confinement in darkness up to 16 hours a day. Authorities told Veguilla that if he refused to confess to being a CIA operative he would be placed in a cell with a ferocious bear, visible through a screen.

Then prison guards threw him into a dimly lit dungeonlike room with a bear. A frightened Veguilla prepared to meet his Maker. "I decided at that moment never to confess anything to the government," Veguilla, 39, told *Christianity Today*. But he had been tricked. This was a different bear, declawed and chained.

Two days later, the mind games returned. Moments after hearing gunfire and screams, authorities lined Veguilla up against a wall as a firing squad raised its guns. Ordered to confess, Veguilla, emboldened by the life-changing encounter with the bear, shouted *"Cuba for Christ! Cuba for Christ!"* The rifle triggers clicked, but the firing chambers clinked empty. Veguilla, now a refugee in the Miami area, will never forget the sound of soldiers laughing after his mock execution.

When Will Cuba Open?

Although few Cuban Christians are subjected to such terrifying experiences, church leaders are keenly aware of the state's ruthless exercise of power under Fidel Castro. Soon after seizing power in 1959, Castro implemented hard labor and so-called re-education programs for those he considered the dregs of society: drug addicts, prostitutes, homosexuals—and pastors. Nearly 40 years later, the

3. Article by John W. Kennedy from *Christianity Today* January 12, 1998. Copyright © *Christianity Today*. Reprinted with permission.

re-education camps are gone. But physical beatings and other ill treatment of prisoners remain potent weapons of the communist regime.

"As long as Castro is alive he will be able to maintain control," says 53-year-old church historian Marcos Antonio Ramos, a Baptist pastor who is dean of the South Florida Center for Theological Studies in Miami. "Sooner or later, Cuba will open. *When* is the $64,000 question."

As Castro, 71, this month begins his thirty-ninth year as dictator, Cubans sense that their island's next revolution has already begun.

The Vatican, the Cuban exile community in southern Florida, the

---

> ### *The Vatican, the Cuban exile community in southern Florida, the U.S. government, Castro loyalists, and Cuban minorities ... are all vying for an influential role in Cuba's future.*

U.S. government, Castro loyalists, and Cuban minorities—including evangelical Protestants—are all vying for an influential role in Cuba's future.

Some hope that this month's visit of Pope John Paul II will be the catalyst to bring a swift conclusion to the Castro era. The pope's presence spurred on the collapse of communism in heavily Catholic Poland in the 1980s. "This could be a watershed event that galvanizes change, either peaceful or revolutionary," says Nina Shea, director of Freedom House's Washington, D.C.–based Puebla Program on Religious Freedom.

In the short term, Christians hope the papal visit will open the gates to additional religious liberties. But some are wary, believing it could spark religious persecution of an intensity not seen since the early days of the communist revolution.

The pontiff will celebrate open-air masses in Havana, Santa Clara, Camagüey, and Santiago. The Cuban Council of Churches will distribute 100,000 Bibles as gifts during the papal visit, and Protestants are hoping to be in the crowds to worship outside their church walls for the first time in nearly four decades.

In June, Havana's archbishop, Cardinal Jaime Ortega, 61, conducted the first outdoor service permitted in the country since 1961. Since then, the government has permitted door-to-door visitations in which Catholic volunteers distributed photos of the pope and invited residents to church. Large outdoor banners declaring "John Paul, messenger of truth and hope, welcome" are on display.

After months of wrangling, the Cuban government in November finally authorized the January 25 docking in Havana of a Miami cruise ship of 1,200 Catholic faithful to see Pope John Paul II. With U.S. State Department approval, Miami's Roman Catholic archdiocese is sponsoring the cruise 90 miles off the Florida coast as a likely last opportunity for parishioners to see the 77-year-old pontiff. The move has caused deep division among Cuban exiles in Miami, many of whom denounce it as inappropriate as long as Castro still rules.

In Cuba, some Protestants fear a potential backlash from the papal stay if the Catholic church becomes cozy with the government. "I hope the visit means a greater freedom of religion," says Richard Luna, Miami regional director for Open Doors with Brother Andrew. "But if this turns out to be a meeting between two heads of state, each with a specific constituency that does not include the evangelical church, it could be very harmful for evangelical Christians."

Ortega himself believes euphoria generated by the papal stopover will not last after John Paul II returns home. "There is great openness in anything that has reference to the pope's visit, but not in other areas," Ortega, who had been forced to work in a military camp in 1966, told *CT*. "We have more frequent dialogue with the state now, but many of the problems have not been solved."

"We expect only trouble out of the pope's visit," says Assemblies of God (AG) national superintendent Héctor A. Hunter, who is concerned about a new wave of oppressive restrictions on Protestants. Unlike the block-long compound that serves as Catholic diocese headquarters in Havana, Hunter's unadorned office is in a simple house in a poverty-stricken neighborhood.

Secularist Paradise?

Before Castro came to power, Cuba was the most secularized Latin American country, with only 6 percent of the population regularly attending church. Unlike most other Spanish-speaking Latin American countries, Cuba does not have a history of Catholic dominance, and that could hinder the impact of John Paul II's tour. "The pope is not visiting Poland; the pope is not visiting Mexico; the pope is visiting Cuba," says Ramos, author of *Protestantism and Revolution in Cuba* (University of Miami, 1989). "One single event won't change Cuba. It's a controlled society, a secular society, and the church in Cuba is not that strong."

Early on in Castro's reign, a few religious leaders inserted themselves into social movements, figuring cooperation with the communist government would be the only way to secure vehicles or building materials. But most clergy went on the defensive, and some spent time in prison. There had not been a tradition of ecumenism in Cuba. When Catholic priests and Protestant preachers found themselves in the same prison camps, seeds of cooperation took root. Today, about 40 percent of the population has been baptized Catholic—including Castro, who was raised Catholic and attended Jesuit schools.

After nearly four decades of unrealized communist dreams, Cubans are ripe for change. There is a spiritual hunger in the land, a void that Marxism has been unable to fill. Out of a population of 11 million, the number of active Christians is approaching 1 million, the most ever.

Castro realizes Christians now represent a potent force. He met with 70 representatives from 31 denominations, primarily members of the Cuban Council of Churches, in a nine-hour meeting on November 24. Castro asked the religious leaders to pray for the nation's economic problems, including decreased sugar production, declining foreign investments, and a dearth of international credit.

The dictator is willing to bend in order to preserve his revolution—and his power. In 1990, as the Soviet Union came apart, Castro faced fresh demands for reform and decided to allow religious meetings in homes. Previously, Christians had not been allowed to build new churches or repair existing cramped, crumbling structures because of shortages in everything from cement to nails.

But the response caught the government off guard. Now at least 3,000 Protestant house churches are active, spurring an ongoing revival that has affected virtually all Protestant denominations as well as the Catholic church.

A house group of Camagüey AG evangelist Orson Vila grew to more than 1,500 people, 80 percent of them young professionals disillusioned by economic hardship and ideological emptiness. Two-thirds of the AG's 50,000 adherents meet in house churches. The denomination had only 7,000 followers a decade ago. "It is the Spirit of God moving among the young people," the AG's Hunter told CT. "There is a spiritual hunger for God."

Other denominations report similar growth, both numerically and in enthusiasm. "God has his time to do his work, and now is his time in Cuba," says Roy Ruiz, president of the Council of Methodist Churches in Cuba. Attendance at Methodist churches has tripled to 40,000 since the authorization of house churches.

"This is the most important moment in our evangelical history," says Western Baptist Convention of Cuba president Leoncilo Veguilla, Eliezer's father. "People are coming to church without invitations. Every church is packed in each service."

The revival has a Pentecostal bent, not only among traditional charismatics, but also among many Methodists, Presbyterians, and Baptists. Yet denominations have retained their distinctiveness. "Our service is very lively and experiential," says Hector Mendez of Havana's First Presbyterian Church, which has grown from 60 to 400 since he became pastor in 1991. "But we are within the Reformed tradition."

The Cost of Cooperation

Yet, more unity existed in the 1960s when people of faith faced communism as a common enemy. More freedom has brought more squabbling over how—or whether—to cooperate with government authorities and with one another.

For example, the government has designated the Cuban Council of

---

"There are more elements in socialism that coincide with my faith than elements of capitalism."—Raúl Suárez, pastor of Ebenezer Baptist Church in Havana

---

Churches as the only agency to be allowed to import and distribute Bibles. Since the decade began, the council says, an average of 100,000 Bibles has been imported each year, an annual amount equal to the number of Bibles imported during the previous 20 years.

But the council of churches has only 25 out of 54 denominations as members. Bible distribution is supposed to be pro-rated according to church membership, but some American evangelicals complain the Bibles do not reach their intended destination through the council of churches. Thus, many denominations have resorted to bringing in Bibles and videos through foreign tourists and Americans on government-sanctioned religious visits.

"We have never been a member of the council of churches, and we hope we never will," says AG superintendent Hunter. To be ecumenical in Cuba, Hunter says, is to be too closely identified with the government.

Raúl Suárez, pastor of Ebenezer Baptist Church in Havana and director of the Martin Luther King, Jr., ecumenical center, has not only chosen to cooperate with the government, he is part of it. Six years ago he became one of the first three Christians elected—unopposed, as is the case of all representatives—to the national communist legislature. As such, he has been able to secure food, medicine, medical equipment, and school buses from the United States for different churches.

But Vicente Calvo, a Baptist who is also a human-rights activist, blames Suárez for politicizing the church. Calvo criticizes Suárez for defending the government's human-rights record and denying that the government ever placed restrictions on Bible distribution. Suárez admits to being a proponent of liberation theology and identifying with the social-justice element of Castro's revolution.

"Between Christianity and the revolution there is no contradiction, but neither is there identification," Suárez, says. "There are more elements in socialism that coincide with my faith than elements of capitalism. Marxism is a Latin American concept that emerged from poverty and misery. It's important not to just think about faith, but live among the poor."

While Cuba and the United States are worlds apart on many matters of faith, there has been upheaval over the same doctrinal differences that divide Christians in the United States. For example, Western Baptists in Cuba, who have ties to U.S. Southern Baptists, booted out Suárez over political and theological differences, such as women's ordination.

Church Relief Expands

The granting of limited religious freedom reveals Castro's pragmatism, not a change of heart. He has consented to churches taking the lead in humanitarian aid efforts in part because it saves the government money. After the collapse of Soviet aid beginning in 1991, Castro has, out of desperation, sought foreign investment, permitted limited self-employment, and allowed the U.S. dollar as a parallel currency.

Caritas Cubana in Havana, one of the few independent nongovernmental organizations, is a Roman Catholic agency that dispenses $5 million a year in relief aid. "The government is suspicious that any organization like this offering humanitarian aid is undermining the government," says Rolando Suárez Cobián, director of Caritas Cubana. "There is always a political interpretation for any humanitarian action."

The government allows Caritas Cubana to monitor U.S. supplies that have been approved for sale in government-run hospitals, such as x-ray film, pacemakers, and prescription drugs. Caritas, which has 6,000 volunteers, must certify that the supplies are not being used to help soldiers. "This is the only way the Cuban government can buy low-priced medicine," Cobián says.

Embargo Hinders Ministry

The United States has enforced a full trade embargo against Cuba since 1961, when Castro nationalized all U.S. property. The embargo, defended vigorously by the powerful Cuban expatriate community in southern Florida, limits what ministry can be conducted on the island.

Some Cuban officials see the papal visit as a means to weaken American resolve for the embargo and expose the U.S. embargo to papal criticism.

"The visit will show not only the strength of the revolution but our willingness to improve relations with the church in Cuba," Ministry of Foreign Affairs spokesperson Rafael Céspedes told *CT* in Havana.

"If the pope calls directly for an end to the U.S. embargo, the U.S. Congress would have to listen."—**Rafael Céspedes, Cuban Foreign Affairs Minister**

"If the pope calls directly for an end to the U.S. embargo, the U.S. Congress would have to listen. The pope, of course, is a moral authority."

Other church leaders have tried but failed to weaken the embargo. Pastors for Peace in Brooklyn, New York, has circumvented the embargo but has been ineffective in forcing the government to reevaluate it. "The U.S. is pathologically obsessed with the need to force Cuba under its control," asserts Lucius Walker, a Baptist pastor who heads Pastors for Peace. "The blockade is a violation of international law to use food and medicines as weapons." Walker questions why the U.S. government is providing famine relief for its communist enemy North Korea, but refuses to do the same for nearby Cuba. Walker's group has shipped 1,500 tons of medical equipment, bicycles, medicines, toys, and school supplies to Cuba, all without U.S. government approval.

"The embargo is contrary to the gospel," Walker told *CT*. "We stand under condemnation from our faith if we say that the way to help children is by starving them. As nonsensical as it seems, we cannot deliver a cup of cold water from a U.S. port." Americans may not enter Cuba without going through a third country, such as Mexico, Canada, or the Bahamas.

While the United States has prohibited trade with Cuba since President Kennedy's first year in office, the Helms-Burton Act in 1996 has further tightened the embargo. The measure passed both chambers of Congress less than two weeks after the 1996 Brothers to the Rescue shootdown. Critics contend Helms-Burton will cause more disease and malnutrition as supplies of everything from bandages to syringes dwindle.

"The Cuban people are suffering a lot because of this policy," says government affairs spokesperson Céspedes. He calls Helms-Burton a "brutal policy" that is "trying to destroy Cuba."

Among the staunchest supporters of the embargo is Republican congressional representative Lincoln Díaz-Balart of Miami. He says the embargo has prevented "complicit slave labor" that exists in China, where U.S. corporations are investing heavily in enterprises but workers never see the money. Other foreign firms are deterred from trading with Cuba because U.S. business interests have no access to the Cuban market, says the 44-year-old Díaz-Balart, in Congress since 1993.

Religious Persecution

Although Christians are a minority and unorganized, Castro sees the church as his primary rival.

Subsequently, any religious activity—from the pope's outdoor mass to a small congregation's purchase of pencils—requires extensive bureaucratic approval.

Historically, if certain congregations have experienced too much growth or seem too influential, the Castro regime devises new restrictions. Rules implemented in October prohibit churches from buying electrical goods such as fax machines, computers, and photocopiers. The new rules also prevent religious charities from buying diapers, cribs, cooking utensils, and soap.

"Castro is the law of the country," says 63-year-old Miami pastor José M. Vera, who had been national Open Bible superintendent before fleeing in 1961. "He allows Christians a certain amount of freedom, but they are always like fish on a line."

"The government hasn't changed toward religion and always sees Christians as the main people against the government," says Alexander Pons Palaez, a 26-year-old refugee resettled by World Relief in July in Carol Stream, Illinois. He had been incarcerated for three years beginning at age 15 for erecting "Down with Fidel" posters. "Fidel can't accept that Cuban people love God more than the state."

Government spokesperson Céspedes disagrees. "We have never been antireligious," he asserts. "We had some problems early on with certain religious leaders, but in 1991 we opened our party to religion. Atheism has been dropped as the official creed of the party."

Uncertain Boundaries

Yet, constraints that limit Christian expression are formidable. Religious literature distribution outside church buildings is illegal. Airing Christian television or radio programs is banned. Praying for God to heal the sick is considered an illegal practice of medicine. Denominations cannot operate elementary or secondary schools.

"There are restrictions on how churches can organize, raise money, evangelize, and proselytize," says Freedom House's Shea. "People are uncertain where the boundaries are. Everything is a privilege, not a secure right." The constitution declares that no freedoms are allowed that are "contrary to the decision of the Cuban people to build socialism and communism."

Despite criticisms that he is too sympathetic to the government's policies, Suárez is responsible for the biggest threat to the regime: In 1990 he convinced Castro to permit Christians to meet in homes.

"In one sense he is cooperating with the government," says Sam Williams, a Cooperative Baptist pastor from Richmond who has visited Suárez's church four times. "But he has been instrumental in the government loosening restrictions on Christians practicing their faith and dropping the requirement that one must be a practicing atheist to be in the government."

Nevertheless, many house churches keep meeting underground. "The state has been acting prudently in the face of illegal house churches," Suárez says. "If they close them, there will be an international scandal."

Castro learned a lesson from what happened to Camagüey evangelist Vila in 1995. Government officials presented Vila, a regional AG director, a list of 85 house churches to be closed immediately. He refused, and four months later 30 police officers arrested him. The same day, Vila received a 23-month hard labor prison sentence for allowing "illicit meetings." Vila's wife, Naomi, also a licensed AG pastor, took over supervision of 200 cell groups that continued to thrive. Meanwhile, in prison, Vila's preaching converted hundreds.

Despite theological differences with the AG, the Cuba Council of Churches intervened to free Vila, even though council leaders felt he had disobeyed the government's order. Catholic hierarchy also protested on Vila's behalf. He ended up serving nine months in prison.

The new freedom of religious expression exists in tension with state control. "There is a great opening, but it's happening hand in hand with the greatest oppression since the early 1960s," says Open Doors' Luna, who discovered first-hand in 1995 that repression still occurs. Plainclothes officers told Luna they had files of photographs and signed affidavits to prove he had been a CIA agent "involved in espionage, sabotage, and blowing up bridges and electrical plants." Luna's real mission had been smuggling Bibles. Officials expelled him from the country immediately after interrogation.

Pastor Shortage

Most Cuban denominations are short of pastors and resources for theological education. There are a dozen small seminaries and Bible schools for Cuban Protestants. Enrollment is limited, largely because denominations cannot afford to provide books, food, class space, and scholarships for more than a few dozen students.

Santería Holds Cuba in Thrall

The most widespread form of religion in Cuba today is neither Protestant nor Catholic, but a syncretistic belief system called *santería*—"way of the saints."

Santería is the largest of the Afro-Cuban religions brought by slaves as a way to trick slave owners. While publicly confessing Catholic saints, the slaves privately venerated animistic gods and goddesses of their homeland. Believers worship these African gods, *orishas*, through plant, food, and animal sacrifices offered during chants and dancing initiations.

Santería worship is conducted in homes, and as many as 3 million Cubans may be involved. Some Catholic priests welcome it as a way to attract parishioners to Christian teachings while others see it as demonic. Though evangelicals believe *santería* is evil, the movement has found its way into mainline Protestant denominations.

Pablo Odén Marichal, vicar general for the only Episcopal diocese on the island and head of the Havana-based Cuban Council of Churches, sees no contradiction in mixing the beliefs, goat and chicken sacrifices notwithstanding.

"Why should I view *santería* as a threat?" Marichal asks. "In one of my Episcopal congregations, three *santería* people come with [ceremonial] dresses and preach."

There are more *santería* priests in Havana than Catholic priests in all of Cuba. But with no hierarchy or centralized leadership, the religion has never been a threat to Castro. *Santería* has spread throughout the Caribbean and to the United States, where there are an estimated 800,000 devotees of different nationalities.

In the United States, the Supreme Court in 1993 struck down a city ordinance and ruled that live animal sacrifices in religious rites are constitutionally protected. Residents in the Miami suburb of Hialeah had complained about the stench from animal sacrifices at the Church of Lukumi Babalu Aye.

In the Baptist Convention of Western Cuba, for instance, there are only 63 pastors for 310 preaching sites. There are only 41 students enrolled in ministerial courses at Baptist Theological Seminary of Havana, although 150 are on a waiting list.

Seminary training is especially important now as young professionals flock to the faith, most of them from non-Christian backgrounds. Churches have managed to grow through local lay-leadership training programs.

Some of the best Cuban seminary professors and pastors, including 90 percent of Methodist ministers and two-thirds of Presbyterian clergy, fled when the revolution showed its socialist face, often leaving untrained teenagers to replace them. Virtually all 250 U.S.-based missionaries had fled or been deported by 1961.

"The Cuban church has proven it can survive and develop without the help of missions and foreign missionaries," says Ramos, who immigrated to Miami in 1966. "They lost along the way many of their finest leaders and a good portion of their resources. But new leaders have risen to the cause, and lost resources have been replaced by a new quota of local and personal sacrifice."

U.S. missionaries or pastors can enter Cuba if they are invited by a denomination and they obtain a religious visa that includes a detailed itinerary. In 1994, Cuban authorities ousted several U.S.-based missions organizations, including Campus Crusade for Christ, Open Doors with Brother Andrew, and Youth With a Mission (YWAM). Many U.S. groups bring in not only Bibles, tracts, and Christian videos, but also medicine, clothes, hygiene products, even auto parts. The Bartlesville, Oklahoma-based Voice of the Martyrs (VOM) takes materials—which are sometimes confiscated—to Cuba on a weekly basis through tourists entering via Mexico and Costa Rica.

Tom White, now U.S. director of VOM, is not afraid of being caught. He spent 18 months in a Cuban prison after his plane crashed on the island in 1979. White, 50, had tossed thousands of packets containing the Gospel of John from planes for seven years. White's book, *God's Missiles Over Cuba*, now in its fourth printing, describes his 24-year sentence for counterrevolutionary activities and his confinement with rats and in refrigerated prison cells. Castro released him after international pressure, which included a personal plea from Mother Teresa.

Spiritual Imperialism?

While appreciative of the relief flowing to Cuba from humanitarian Americans, religious leaders in Miami hope there will not be a deluge of overbearing missionary activity when Cuba opens again. "It's important for people to go in to help people, not to manipulate them," says Humberto Cruz, a 60-year-old Baptist pastor in Miami who immigrated in 1967. "The leaders are already there. They don't need Cuban-American imperialism."

But San Antonio evangelist Sammy Tippitt says he goes not out of any colonialist ambitions but because he is invited by Cubans hungry for Bible teaching. He makes an annual trip in conjunction with an Eastern Baptist Convention retreat for pastors. Tippitt's ministry, God's Love in Action, finances the trip because Cubans simply do not have the money. The government offered no explanation when it canceled his scheduled journey in November.

American evangelicals, mindful of how cults invaded post-communist Russia, also want to make sure that materials sent have sound doctrine. "Christian leaders in Cuba have a heart to disciple young people, but they don't have tools available," says YWAM's

---

"There is a huge thirst for knowing God, and this will help in ushering in a democratic transition."—**Cuban refugee Pons Palaez**

Steve Tackett of Nashville. "They can't go to a Christian bookstore and buy discipleship materials. When the government falls, we don't want there to be a vacuum like there was in the Soviet Union."

Barry Owensby, president of World Street Evangelism in Jacksonville, Florida, has made two dozen trips to Cuba following invitations from churches. "We are strategically set because I have established contacts with 100 pastors," he says. "As soon as freedom comes, I will move in a matter of days to set up outdoor crusades with various pastors."

While acknowledging that U.S. missions agencies must be aware of their own paternalistic tendencies, Gregory C. Wallace of Overseas Council of Indianapolis says Cubans must have financial assistance to keep training new Christians. Overseas Council is facilitating the theological education of 45 students at New Pines Seminary in Placetas. The six professors are Cuban, but the financing is American, including money for constructing student apartments and a dining hall.

Although there are no Christian media on the island, residents are able to hear Christian broadcasts from other countries. A 500,000-watt Trans World Radio signal north of Venezuela beams 32 hours of Spanish language programming to the island each week, including U.S.-based shows, such as *Back to the Bible* and *Our Daily Bread*. The various programs receive an average of 200 letters per month from Cubans.

Post-Castro Bloodbath?

As Cuba enters its season of transition, Castro continues to reiterate long-held tenets.

In October, communists convened their first party congress in six years and made it clear that further reforms will not happen any time soon. The dictator also reaffirmed that his 66-year-old brother Raúl, who is head of the armed forces, will be his successor.

Amid turgid praise of the one-party socialist system beneath a banner with portraits of Ernesto "Che" Guevara, Karl Marx, and Vladimir Lenin, the platform declared "the party is in a better position today than ever to perfect its role as society's guide."

The embargo will prove its worth when Castro loses power, Rep. Díaz-Balart believes. He says that with no access to the American market, Castro's successor will be forced to accept U.S. conditions for lifting the embargo: legalizing political activity and providing for free elections. "The embargo is the only reason the provisional government will respect the Cuban people," Díaz-Balart says.

"There is a huge thirst for knowing God, and this will help in ushering in a democratic transition," says Palaez, the recent refugee.

Renovating Cuba physically will very likely be easier than renewing the country spiritually. Vera says Cubans have suffered profound damage inside their souls, and much bitterness and hatred extend toward the Castro regime: 50,000 people have been killed by firing squads for refusing to conform to communism; 500,000 have been religious or political prisoners.

"When Castro falls from the scene there will be a bloodbath," predicts exiled Seventh-day Adventist pastor Noble Alexander. "There are lots of people with pent-up anger. I know thousands who have been killed."

In a real sense, what happens with the military could determine Cuba's future. While secret police and neighborhood communist committees are "deeply involved in daily oppression," Díaz-Balart says the armed forces have remained aloof from the repression.

The Cuban-American Military Council in Washington, D.C., is trying to support any efforts of Cuban armed forces to break ties with Castro. Founded last year by retired general Erneido A. Oliva, the organization of nearly 1,000 military personnel of Cuban origin has intercessory prayer as its first line of defense.

The council's goal is a peaceful transition to democracy, which will include assisting Cuban military leadership in the post-Castro era to become answerable to a government freely elected by Cubans.

"This goal must and will be accomplished free of hate or revenge and in the spirit of understanding, reconciliation, cooperation, and justice," says the 65-year-old Oliva, who graduated from the Cuban Military Academy in 1954 and came to the United States in 1960 to assist in military operations against the Castro government. He participated in the Bay of Pigs as the second-in-command of exile invasion forces.

"Through faith in Jesus Christ, and with his grace and peace, reunification can be achieved in Cuba," Oliva says. "We consider the Cuban armed forces the only element that can accelerate the transition of democracy in Cuba."

Praying for the Day

Many exiles are praying for that day. "I don't want to die before I see Cuba free again," says Miami pastor Vera. "I am ready to go back to Cuba to preach the gospel."

Regardless of whether the transition is peaceful or swift, Cuba's Christians will be in a stronger position than when Castro ushered in the 1959 revolution.

Despite economic distress, international politics, and domestic repression, evangelical Protestants are proving to be faithful.

After his encounters with a bear and a mock firing squad, Eliezer Veguilla is in the United States working with Baptist World Alliance, Trans World Radio, and Open Doors with Brother Andrew. His 67-year-old father, Leoncilo—who spent nearly six years in prison beginning in 1965 as one of 48 Baptist pastors indicted for alleged ties to the CIA—is now president of the Western Baptist Convention of Cuba and Baptist Theological Seminary in Havana. "I'm not afraid anymore of prison," Leoncilo Veguilla told *CT*. "I remain in Cuba because God is with me to the end."

Missionaries who are ready to mobilize when the country opens need to remember that persecution has a way of vitalizing faithful believers. "We don't need to take Christ to Cuba," says Open Doors' Luna. "Christ has been there all along."

After Castro—What?[4]

By Roger Fontaine
World & I, June 1999

There is a scene in Billy Wilder's *The Apartment* where a tipsy lady in a bar asks an equally inebriated Jack Lemmon what he thinks about Castro. The film was made in 1960. And yes, it's been that long.

So exactly what happens to Cuba after the passing of Fidel Castro? That question has been asked from the beginning of Castro's long reign. Many—and not just hard-shell *batistianos*—once thought that the eccentric *jefe de barbudos* would last no longer than six months. The Soviets, for certain, had their doubts and did not really entertain the possibility of a permanent anti-American redoubt so close to the main enemy until at least a year after Castro's triumphal entry into Havana.

Yet, here we are 40 years later and the question is still debated, with responses varying from the absurd to the possible with no certainty yet in sight. What is certain, however, is that Castro has lasted longer than any Latin American ruler in history. No dictator, viceroy, or president for life has endured for so long. Not Batista. Not Duvalier. Not Trujillo. Not Stroessner. Absolutely not Pinochet. Not even Mexico's Porfirio Diaz.

The Maximum Leader has been in office longer than any current head of state anywhere unless one counts Queen Elizabeth II, a notion to which, no doubt, the Windsor family would sorely object. Still, Castro at 72 is visibly slowing down, but despite the daily medical bulletins from the Miami rumor mill, he remains in apparent good health.

After all these years, there is little doubt that Castro can stay in power for as long as he likes or is physically able. He and his regime may face a discontented populace, but it's one that's incapable of insurrection. Meanwhile, the security apparatus remains intact, and, despite a few bad years following the Soviet Union's collapse, its morale is high. Dissidents, as always, are given no slack.

---

4. Article by Roger Fontaine from *World & I* June 1999. Copyright © *World & I.* Reprinted with permission.

To be sure, the actuarial tables are immutable and suggest that Castro is not, after all, immortal, merely long-lived like his father (Ángel Castro died at 81). Unlike papa, the son has access to world-class medical care. That alone could give him at least another decade of life to flog his socialist fantasy.

But even at 82 and with 50 years of governing, he could go on a bit longer (although it would be hard for him to match Ramses II's 66-year reign). Castro himself speaks little of retirement or even passing on, but he has prepared his succession. If Kim Il Sung could pass the torch to his son Kim Jong Il, Fidel Castro long ago decided that his brother Raúl, younger by five years, would assume command after his passing.

Raúl Castro would be in good political shape to carry out his brother's wishes. He has commanded the armed forces from the beginning and, for at least a decade, has populated the other security services with his own men. No one in the Communist Party would be in a position to challenge him. Cuba's immediate future after Fidel, therefore, is likely to be continuity with another Castro in charge. At least for a while.

> *What is certain . . . is that Castro has lasted longer than any Latin American ruler in history.*

But Raúl has problems. If his brother were to die in his 80s, the junior Castro would be in his late 70s, which promises a rather short regency. Moreover, Raúl's health has always been more questionable than his brother's. Among other things, he once had a well-established reputation for being a binge drinker.

Analysts have also doubted whether Raúl could outlast Fidel, leaving the succession in some doubt. Even if Raúl managed to survive his brother, there would be other problems. Raúl Castro may, for example, hold the loyalty of Cuba's military officers, but he conspicuously lacks his brother's charisma and overall intelligence.

The Question

Then there is the Question, namely, is General Castro a closet liberal? Some have suggested he is, but the answer is "not exactly." True, there is evidence that during the economic crisis after the Soviet demise, Raúl did urge a recalcitrant brother to loosen up Cuba's stifling command economy—for one reason only: survival of the regime.

Poorly paid army officers with no mission were becoming restless, and many analysts believe that Raúl makes up for his other deficiencies by staying in touch with the real world far better than Fidel does. But once the immediate danger passed and Cuba's supreme *comandante en jefe* made clear that socialism would never be abandoned, Raúl conspicuously and vociferously agreed with that view—in public at least.

If Raúl were to succeed his brother, then thanks to his lack of popular support, he might liberalize the economy a bit, but political controls, including the Communist Party's monopoly on power, would remain untouched. Indeed, it is quite possible that Raúl would even strengthen the party; in the past, it has suffered neglect from Fidel, who has always been leery of anything that could dilute or check his personal authority.

But what about a Cuba without either of the Castro brothers? First, let's eliminate one possibility. There is no chance whatsoever that Fidel would ever do a Kim Il Sung. Castro's acknowledged son, Fidelito, was unceremoniously fired from the one job he has ever held—head of the country's atomic energy agency—for gross incompetence. But if the Castro family passes into history, what would happen next?

One scenario—and not a very dramatic one—is that the PCC politburo would meet, the old guard would choose a new leader, and that choice would be duly ratified by the National Assembly of Popular Power, Cuba's Potemkin legislature. But the old guard would have difficulty in running the country by itself. The remaining members of Castro's cohort are not only old, they are bereft of any ideas, and most are frankly incompetent.

Real power would likely devolve—and rather quickly—to a younger generation of officials such as Ricardo Alarcón, the brilliant president of the National Assembly, or Carlos Lage, economic whiz kid. While they would remain loyal to Castro's memory, they would also feel free to reinterpret the meaning of *socialismo* for the next millennium.

One can almost anticipate the slogans already. *Un nuevo socialismo para un nuevo siglo* would do for a starter. So, what would that look like? The next generation would certainly preserve what they could of the old cradle-to-grave welfare state. Most of them know, however, that Cuba needs to generate wealth to take care of an aging population. That means efforts at attracting foreign investment will be increased, requiring further liberalization of property laws.

On the domestic front, market reforms may well include tax cuts and less regulation for small businesses. It is not clear how far this new group would go. Almost certainly it would attempt to retain power through the party, although the pressure on dissidents might be relaxed somewhat. But how long the party of any generation could maintain a monopoly on power remains an open question.

How Long in Power?

Another possibility envisions Cuba evolving much more rapidly than often anticipated. Already, there is on the island a widespread feeling, really a deep longing, for change after so many years of stagnation, repression, and boredom. Unfortunately, those powerful sentiments are not channeled in any political direction other than a desire to escape.

Still as we know from experience in Eastern Europe, seemingly insignificant opposition groups can quickly spring to life given even a wisp of political oxygen. How effective they would become depends on leadership that is inherently unpredictable. Here the Roman Catholic Church can play a major role. After the Castros depart the stage, it is likely that the church, the

> *There is on the island a widespread feeling ... for change after so many years of stagnation, repression, and boredom.*

country's only other source of moral authority and legitimacy, could play a major role in encouraging the growth of civic politics without ever endorsing any faction. With that kind of tutelage, free elections could be held beginning with the National Assembly, where a voting procedure is already in place.

All that's needed, as occurred with the Polish *Sejm* [Poland's parliament] in 1989, is that the PCC relinquish its stranglehold on power. As they did in Poland and Bulgaria, younger leaders might even change the party's name and program—in effect, become a Social Democratic party and then subsequently pass on to oblivion (Bulgaria) or become unrecognizable to the remaining supporters of the ancien régime (Poland).

Can the Transition Be Peaceful?

Such a peaceful evolution is possible, but weighed in the balance of Cuba's tragic political history, it remains a long shot. One crucial factor will be the United States. Alas, here may be the real fault line running hidden and underneath any optimistic scenario.

While the Catholic Church's part may be a positive one, the United States can never be the arbiter of Cuba's destiny. Washington tried in the past and failed miserably. The U.S. government can do relatively little to encourage democracy on the island without reverting to its old proconsul role, which did much to cement Castro's grip on power in the first place.

Unfortunately, there is at present little sign that we have learned from our past mistakes. Three years ago, Congress passed and President Clinton signed the Helms-Burton Act. Most attention has been paid to the sections punishing third country investors benefitting from the sale of seized U.S. property confiscated in the early, Jacobin days of the revolution. Although these provisions have tied our relations with Canada and Europe in knots, their impact has not been fully felt because Clinton has chosen not to enforce them.

Far worse, however, is Title II of Helms-Burton, which lays down detailed demands on Cuba's post-Castro governments if they are to enjoy normal relations with the United States. Unfortunately, the consequences of such an undertaking are predictably bad. We have never succeeded in the micromanagement of regime building since the defeat of Germany and Japan in 1945.

But Cuba will not be a conquered nation after the Castros leave. Rather, it will be struggling to survive and overcome the legacy of decades of Marxist misrule. Cuba's political history since independence from Spain has featured a well-meaning but often meddlesome Washington, telling Havana how it should conduct its affairs. The resentment over that unwanted tutelary role helped fuel the animus that led to the Castro upheaval. If we try this approach again, the United States could well poison Cuban politics for another generation, which in turn would produce the gloomiest post-Castro scenario of all.

There is the distinct possibility, after all, that the transition away from Castroism would not be a peaceful affair. Cuba has never managed one in the past. Violence marked the passing of the Machado and Batista eras as well as Spain's control of Cuba. Any upheaval following Castro would only be exacerbated if exile groups joined the fray unimpeded by U.S. authorities. There is no question that the Cuban military would be drawn into any fight that it considers foreign in origin. And once the blood begins to flow, political forces in this country could and likely would push Washington into an unwise intervention, further reducing Cuba's chances for genuine independence and political stability, not to mention democracy.

This suggests that Fidel Castro's passing will not necessarily spell better days for Cuba. That will require a good measure of patience and restraint on both sides of the Florida Straits, qualities seldom evident in the past. Still, there is time to learn from past mistakes, and with the end of the cold war, a largely laissez-faire policy might allow Cubans to work out their problems for themselves.

With any kind of democratic stability, the economy could begin to take off with U.S. and other foreign investment pouring into the island. Cubans have clearly not lost their knack for making money—hundreds of thousands of them are doing that right now under conditions that would stifle most other entrepreneurs. Perhaps that is the best hope. It may well be the only one.

II. Fidelismo: The Cuban Economy

A booming farmers' market in Havana, one sign of Cuba's improving economy.

Editor's Introduction

No one could accuse the Cubans of lacking a sense of humor. One of the more popular jokes of recent vintage is that, to get by in Cuba, you have to have *fe*, which means "faith" in Spanish, but can also mean *familia en el exterior,* or family abroad. Another joke depicts a drunk who, after being stopped by police for rowdiness, shouts that he is a baggage-handler at Havana's swanky Hotel Nacional. When the police phone his wife she exclaims, "Oh, delusions of grandeur! He's the chief surgeon at the hospital." These jokes point to some of the ironies of life in contemporary Cuba. Cuban exiles—whom Castro has long referred to as *gusanos*, or worms—send remittances back to Cuba that represent the major source of income for many families; and Cubans who work in prestigious government or medical jobs now live at poverty wages, while those who work for dollars in the tourist economy have become relatively prosperous.

Section II looks at what one Cuban has called "Fidelismo"—the strange brew of socialism and capitalism that defines the Cuban economy today. In the first article, "What Cuba Can Teach Russia," Ana Julia Jatar-Hausmann contrasts the course of the Cuban economy of the 1990s with that of Russia, Cuba's cold war sponsor. While Russia has enacted far-reaching free-market reforms, causing its economy to flounder, Cuba has taken small steps toward creating a fledgling capitalist sector, a gradualist approach that, Jatar-Hausmann argues, is beginning to pay off. Cuba has instituted a tax system, reduced state subsidies, and diversified its traditionally sugar-based economy; while not exactly a free market, Cuba today has an improved version of state capitalism.

In the next article, Linda Robinson reports on Cuba's newly resuscitated tourist industry. Europeans, Canadians, Latin Americans, and—increasingly—Americans are flocking to Cuba, drawn by the history and romance of Old Havana and the gleaming new beach resorts along Varadero peninsula. This industry has created new jobs and opportunities for Cubans, but, for Robinson, the question remains: Can Cuba encourage tourism without returning to the freewheeling days before the revolution, when gambling, prostitution, and political corruption were pervasive?

Philip Peters is an economist who recently conducted a survey of independent Cuban businesses. In his *Wall Street Journal* article, Peters refutes the U.S. State Department's contention that Cuba has "resisted any credible effort to adopt market-based policies" since the Soviet bloc vanished. An economic transition is underway, Peters writes, with the legalization of small businesses, the introduction of incentive pay in state enterprises, and joint ventures between government and foreign companies.

The U.S. trade embargo prevents many goods from reaching Cuba, but technology has a way of slipping through borders, as Timothy Ashby and Elizabeth Bourget reveal in their report on Cuba's information-technology industries, "Dotcommies Take Over Cuba." With a mandate to bring the revolution into the Internet age, the Cuban government has created profitable computer and telecommunications businesses, and has invested heavily in training and research. Foreign companies are now looking to Cuba, with its educated population and developing communications infrastructure, to become a digital hub for the Caribbean region.

The final articles in this section were published in British publications—*The Times* of London and *The Ecologist* of Sturminster Newton, England. In addition to the content of their reports, both articles offer useful perspectives on Cuba outside of the American context, where opinions of Cuba tend to be sharply divided. Daniel Whitaker reports on the biotechnology industry in Cuba, where scientists have made impressive discoveries. These innovations include a meningitis vaccine that was recently licensed by the American pharmaceutical company SmithKline Beecham, which successfully lobbied for an exception in the trade embargo. Medical research is big business in Cuba, and many foreigners travel there each year to take advantage of their facilities and expertise. However, as Whitaker relates, the average Cuban does not benefit from this system. Although all Cubans receive free health care—at levels unknown in most poor countries—clinics lack basic supplies, a consequence of the U.S. embargo and the ailing economy.

Hugh Warwick reports on the overhaul of Cuban agriculture in the 1990s. No longer able to rely on food imports or expensive fertilizers, the Cuban government has encouraged sustainable food production, including urban gardens, organic farms, and farmers' markets. In a related article, Edward Metcalf describes Cuba's attempts to produce its own energy sources and its success in converting sugarcane residue into electricity.

What Cuba Can Teach Russia[1]

BY ANA JULIA JATAR-HAUSMANN
FOREIGN POLICY, WINTER 1998

"The pace of economic and social demise was accelerating. Popular discontent was spreading and the economy was deteriorating at growing speed. Only fear of the unknown prevented a popular rebellion. . . . Whatever time Castro had left in power, his failure to change with the times seemed almost sure to condemn his once-acclaimed revolution to a lonely death."

Thus wrote Pulitzer Prize–winning author Andres Oppenheimer in 1992 in *Castro's Final Hour*, a book marketed as a "historical account of the disintegration of Castro's Cuba." Oppenheimer was not alone in his assessment. To most observers and analysts, the collapse of the Soviet Union meant the imminent fall of Cuba. Few thought that the only remaining communist stronghold in the Western Hemisphere could survive without subsidies, aid, and preferential trade treatment from the Soviet bloc. This conviction deepened with Cuba's failure to follow Russia down the path of market democracy. Intent on maintaining its socialist regime, Cuba not only had to overcome the loss of its cold war economic partners without any outside help but also to contend with a tightening U.S. embargo and its extraterritorial enforcement through new legislation.

Nevertheless, to the surprise of all, disappointment of many, and joy of a few, Russia today is the world's leading economic charity case, while Cuba has become the lone soldier of state socialism, marching on long after it was supposed to have surrendered to superior capitalist forces. Even as Russia's gross domestic product (GDP) shrank by a staggering 42.5 percent between 1989 and 1997, Cuba's economic output—after plunging initially by 35 percent between 1989 and 1993—has managed to recover and grow every year since then. True, in contrast to Russia, Cuba remains a police state whose people are denied fundamental freedoms. Although Cuba has seen respectable rates of economic growth, daily life remains a harsh struggle for the vast majority of a population that cannot openly complain. Yet in spite of Cuba's slow and timid reforms, not only is it prospering relative to its former cold war patron, but U.S. efforts to topple President Fidel Castro have

1. Article by Ana Julia Jatar-Hausmann from *Foreign Policy* Winter 1998–99. Copyright © Carnegie Endowment for International Peace. Reprinted with permission.

actually propped up his regime. What happened? Why has Cuba "succeeded" where Russia has "failed?" Why were outsiders' expectations so wrong? And what lessons, if any, can be derived from the Cuban experience for Russia and other countries facing wrenching transitions?

A Bleak New World

Russia's decision to forsake communism for market democracy won it badly needed political and economic support from the United States and its partners in the Group of Seven. In 1991, Russia faced a fiscal deficit equivalent to 30 percent of its GDP and an economy that had contracted by 13 percent from the previous year. Backed by the International Monetary Fund, the Russian government launched a drastic program of economic reforms in 1992 that unified its exchange rates, privatized state industries, and freed prices. Multilateral agencies rewarded Moscow with financing and assistance. Doors to new export markets swung open. Russian exports to countries that did not belong to the former Soviet Union grew by 20 percent from 1993 to 1994.

Russia today is the world's leading economic charity case, while Cuba has become the lone soldier of state socialism.

In contrast, Cuba confronted a post-Soviet world that was more bleak than brave. Its trading relationships with other members of the Council for Mutual Economic Assistance or COMECON—the Soviet economic bloc, which accounted for 87 percent of Cuba's trade—rapidly disintegrated. Its annual subsidy from the USSR—which averaged $2.1 billion per year for three decades and accounted for 10 percent of its total economy in 1989—disappeared. And instead of multilateral assistance, Cuba has faced ever tighter unilateral sanctions from the United States. For most Cubans, the end of the cold war was not the fall of the Berlin Wall on CNN. It was the collapse of their lives before their very own eyes, an all-too-real nightmare of constant blackouts, closed schools and hospitals, no spare parts, no consumer goods, no fertilizers, and little food. On the roads, 200,000 Chinese bicycles substituted for cars; in the fields, 300,000 oxen took the place of useless Russian tractors. A four-hour wait for a bus to work became normal; once the jobs were gone, it became irrelevant. People stayed home earning 60 percent of their salaries in unemployment payments, which they had a hard time spending since there were no goods to buy.

Soviet aid to Cuba had always represented far more than just an inflow of dollars; it was the source of discretionary spending in the hands of the state. The Cuban government had used it to finance

An Exceptionally Blunt Instrument

Among the most controversial features of the U.S. embargo against Cuba is the Cuban Liberty and Democratic Solidarity (LIBERTAD) Act, better known as the Helms-Burton law (1996). Its sponsors, Senator Jesse Helms and Representative Dan Burton, had hoped it would deal the final blow to a Cuban economy badly weakened by the collapse of the Soviet system.

The law has four sections: Title I imposes additional sanctions intended to deepen the isolation of Cuba's economy; Title II instructs the U.S. president to develop an assistance plan for a post-Castro transition government; Title III calls for the return of properties expropriated by the Cuban government and allows U.S. citizens to sue anyone who currently invests in these properties; and Title IV directs the U.S. State Department to deny visas to executives of foreign companies who are deemed to benefit from these holdings.

International criticism of Helms-Burton has centered on Title III, which has caused a serious diplomatic rift and near-trade war between the United States and some of its closest allies. As Sir Leon Brittan, the European Unions Trade Commissioner, remarked in July 1996 when President Bill Clinton imposed Helms-Burton sanctions (but temporarily suspended the implementation of Title III), "The best way to get change in Cuba is not to clobber your allies, and that's what they have done."

For their part, Cubans worry that Title III will bankrupt the country. As Ricardo Alarcón, president of Cuba's National Assembly, has said, "We can't pay the estimated $100 billion we supposedly owe to those who left," he said. "It represents for us 50 years of exports."

Even more offensive to many Cubans, however, is Title II, which specifies that an "acceptable" transition government must legalize all political activity, release all political prisoners, establish an independent judiciary, and commit publicly to holding free, multiparty elections within 18 months. Most importantly, the new government must not include President Fidel Castro or his brother Raúl. Such sweeping conditions help explain why Helms-Burton has actually strengthened Castro's domestic support. The government has translated the law and made it widely available, deepening its citizens' distrust of the United States.

More importantly, perhaps, Helms-Burton has fallen far short of its goals. Although Cuban officials have admitted that the law has slowed credits to Cuba and deterred prospective investors, foreign direct investment has continued to flow, and Cuba's economy has continued to expand.

—*FP*

not just annual import levels of about $8 billion (almost $800 per inhabitant), but generous *libretas* (rationing cards) that included everything from rice, beans, and rum to cigarettes, clothing, and toothpaste. To replace these subsidies, Cuba's hardliners (*los duros*) argued for the development of a tourist sector isolated from the rest of the socioeconomic structure. In their view, this capitalist enclave would provide enough dollars to sustain the economy and Cuba's socialist system.

Yet Cubans quickly learned that capitalist investments in tourism were a poor substitute for communist subsidies. Dollars that came into the country as foreign direct investment (FDI) would simply have to go back out to pay for the machinery and equipment used in new tourist projects. And 60 percent of the dollars that tourists brought in ended up leaving in order to pay for the imported goods they consumed—such as the caviar allowed back into the country after 30 years.

From 1990 to 1993, Cuba's crisis continued to deepen. With the economy increasingly afflicted by the shortage of hard currency, imports and local production went into a free fall. Even as salaries and social programs—the core of the socialist promise—remained unchanged, the fiscal deficit ballooned to more than 30 percent of GDP. The government responded by printing more money. Faced with a dwindling supply of official goods and an increasingly worthless currency, Cubans tried to buy what they needed on the black market, pushing prices and the unofficial exchange rate for dollars through the roof. Officially pegged at 1 peso to the U.S. dollar, the exchange rate on the streets shot up to 130 pesos per dollar in 1994. Although it was illegal to hold dollars and many Cubans went to jail for doing so, no one seemed to care. After all, in 1994 the average monthly salary was 160 pesos—not enough to buy a pound of pork. The black market for dollars and goods grew beyond the state's control—fueled in part by state workers who used their positions to smuggle goods. Cubans quickly learned to live in illegality, and the government to turn a blind eye to it.

In August 1994, rioters, exasperated by power cuts, food shortages, and the summer heat, took to the streets, and the government finally realized that tourism alone would not save socialism. Instead of adopting cosmetic changes at the periphery of its economic system, Cuba would have to redefine its socialist order. The basic problem was that too many pesos were chasing too few official goods at controlled prices. The solution was either to increase the supply of goods (by local production or imports) or decrease demand. Increasing the supply of goods would take time. By contrast, decreasing demand would be easier and faster: Following Russia's example, Cuba could massively devalue the peso to its black-market level. This option would immediately increase prices, reduce the purchasing power of consumers, and trim "excess demand" to conform to the availability of goods in the market. But Cuba's government had little stomach for the consequences of devaluation and resulting depreciation of real salaries. In Russia, the massive devaluation and unification of exchange rates in 1992 had sparked an average inflation rate of 1,527 percent, with year end inflation reaching 2,500 percent. The specter of something similar terrified Cuban leaders.

There was another, more politically attractive alternative: to replace Russian funding by tapping not just an increased flow of tourist dollars (and, in the long run, other types of FDI) but also the growing stream of remittances sent by Cuban exiles to their families. Cubans were anxious to spend the dollars they were receiving from tourists and relatives in Miami on products and services inside Cuba. The government needed to establish a mechanism that would channel those dollars into the formal economy rather than the black market. The idea was not only to enable Cubans to buy more products and services but for the government to gain control over this precious hard currency and use it to pay for imports and increase the supply of goods.

This approach required profound changes in Cuba's economic structure. Most significantly, given Cubans' unequal access to remittances and tourist dollars, it would alter the carefully crafted egalitarian distribution of income. In the words of Cuban reformist Pedro Monreal: "All this had a very negative impact on a worker's society. . . . wage—the economic and social reason to work—ceased to be the fundamental route for obtaining individual and family well being." That was a chance that Cuba's more reformist leaders were willing to take. In contrast to the hardliners, reformers such as Roberto Robaina, now minister of foreign affairs; Carlos Lage, vice president; José Luis Rodriguez, minister of economics; and Ricardo Alarcón, president of the National Assembly, were mostly younger, with stronger academic backgrounds, and more in touch with the international community and reformist thinkers elsewhere. But they did not see themselves in transition to anything but a more effective version of socialism—with the existing political system intact and the same elites in control. As Lage, the principal architect of the economic reforms, said in 1993: "In our Revolution, the ideas are always being renewed and enriched; but the base, the root, the political assumptions, the socialist option chosen by the Cuban people and undertaken by the vast majority, never changes. On the contrary, it consolidates with each renewal."

Despite such seemingly doctrinaire sentiments, the economic free fall opened the door to economic reform in 1993. With GDP falling by 15 percent and the dollar trading in the black market at a rate equivalent to the average monthly wage, ideology had to give way to practical answers. Consequently, reform went from being unthinkable to becoming a topic of fervent debate in Cuba's National Assembly. Finally, Castro himself had to intervene, saying in July 1993 that "life, reality . . . forces us to do what we would have never done otherwise. . . . we must make concessions."

The economic initiatives launched in mid-1993—and implemented in fits and starts during the last five years—have focused on three goals: first, increasing the flow of foreign exchange; second, reducing government expenditures; and third, increasing the supply of goods and services. Moreover, these goals have had to be achieved without jeopardizing the political continuity of the regime. The existing ideas, doctrines, and leaders have had to remain intact.

Dialing for Dollars

Two important reforms were designed to wrest dollars from private hands: first, the legalization of dollar holdings, which enabled Cubans to spend them freely for the first time and thereby spur the flow of remittances; and second, the creation of state-owned dollar retail stores so Cubans could easily buy goods in hard currency. As economics minister Rodriguez explained in 1994: "The objective is to sell products to those who have dollars at very high prices; then the government will be able to redistribute the profits among those who need it more." With good reason, some Cubans have referred to these stores, where consumers can buy everything from Italian marmalade to roller blades, as "the government's dollar cash register."

Cuba in the Black
Percent Increase in GDP: 1990–97

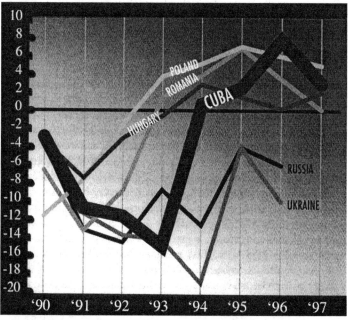

Sources: *World Tables*, International Bank for Reconstruction and Development (Baltimore: Johns Hopkins University Press, 1995). *Poland: The Path to a Market Economy* (Washington: IMF, October 1994). *Banco Nacional de Cuba Monthly Bulletin of Statistics* (New York: United Nations, 1998).

By 1997, dollar sales in these stores represented 17 percent of Cuba's total dollar income; that same year, dollar remittances accounted for 20 percent of the island's total dollar income.

The Cuban government has also worked hard to persuade as many countries as possible to bring their dollars to Cuba, encouraging investment in specific sectors of its economy (such as mining), permitting 100 percent foreign ownership, and creating free-trade zones. As the minister of basic industries Marcos Portal declared in 1995, "We went to bed one night and when we woke up, the Soviet Union was gone, so we had to begin all over again. The

---

"We went to bed one night and when we woke up, the Soviet Union was gone, so we had to begin all over again."—**Marcos Portal, minister of basic industries**

---

same thing had occurred years before with the United States. This is not going to happen again to us." Cuba's new commercial strategy involved flirting with as many countries as possible. In October 1998, the government announced that $6 billion of foreign direct investment would be entering the country, with $1.7 billion committed or delivered by 25 countries including Australia, Canada, France, Germany, Great Britain, Israel, Italy, Mexico, and Spain. Meanwhile, in Russia, FDI has fallen from $6.1 billion to approximately $3 billion in the past year. Foreign direct investment has continued to flow into Cuba despite the U.S. embargo: $620 million in 1998 and an expected $700 million in 1999. Moreover, foreign firms have also promoted more fundamental changes by training thousands of Cuban employees in managerial, financial, and marketing techniques.

Ending the Free Lunch

In May and June of 1994, the Cuban government adopted a series of measures to reduce the fiscal deficit. It cut subsidies to state enterprises (80 percent of which were operating at a loss); jacked up prices on cigarettes, gasoline, alcohol, electricity, and other goods and services; and—for the first time since the revolution—established a tax system. Partly as a result, Cuba's fiscal deficit fell from 30.5 percent of GDP in 1993 to 2 percent of GDP in 1997. In contrast, by 1997 Russia's fiscal deficit was still 7 percent of GDP.

Cuba's efforts to cut its losses at state-owned enterprises are particularly noteworthy in two respects: First, the government's willingness to convert many of them into joint ventures has brought much-needed cash and expertise. The end result has not been privatization but improved state capitalism. All foreign investment has been made through joint ventures with the state. In 1997, the government shared over $200 million in profits with its Italian partner in the Cuban telephone company. Second, the active involvement of the Cuban military in restructuring sectors such as the food industry has both made it a strong supporter of reform and helped redefine the armed forces' institutional role in the post–cold war era.

Like the boat people who still leave Cuba's shores, these would-be capitalists are the "land rafters" of the socialist economy, embarking on a perilous and uncertain journey.

Stocking the Shelves

To increase the supply of food, the government implemented agricultural reforms that created new incentives for workers. Big state-owned farms were converted into cooperatives whose members set their own goals and shared in profits. As a result, the proportion of land in the hands of the nonstate agricultural sector grew from 24.8 percent in 1992 to almost 70 percent in 1994. The farmers' markets that Castro had closed in 1986 as part of a campaign against "neo-capitalists" were reopened, allowing farmers to sell part of their production to the public and set their prices in dollars.

To meet the demand for more services, the government legalized self-employment in more than 170 different occupations, from hairdressing, plumbing, and automechanics to the well-known *paladares*, small family-owned restaurants. Professions requiring university degrees were excluded, condemning much of the Cuban intelligentsia to an embarrassingly lower standard of living unless they stooped to moonlighting for dollars. Self-employment has provided a safety valve for the jobless. About 600,000 Cubans, or roughly 15 percent of the work force, were estimated to be working directly or indirectly within the self-employed sector in 1996. The government gets its share of the money spent on these private services through a combination of monthly fees and income taxes.

These liberalizing trends may mislead the casual observer into believing that capitalism is quickly spreading through Cuba's economy and society. This is not the case. In Cuba, capitalism is a long way from winning ideological acceptance. Despised by the traditional elite, the self-employed have been legalized but not legitimized. Like the boat people who still leave Cuba's shores, these would-be capitalists are the "land rafters" of the socialist economy, embarking on a perilous and uncertain journey.

Transition to What?

Since the implementation of reforms, Cuba's economy has been growing and is likely to continue to do so (GDP has expanded by 15 percent since 1994, with 4 percent growth expected for 1999). Also, in spite of the distortions generated by keeping the official exchange rate at 1 peso per dollar, the unofficial exchange rate has stabilized at 19 pesos per dollar, and the fiscal deficit has been kept at 2 percent of GDP.

More importantly, perhaps, these reforms have given Cubans and the Cuban government room to breathe. A family with $100 in hand is no longer forced to chase scarce, expensive goods on the black market. It can now legally spend $40 in the farmers' market, $10 in the *paladares*, $20 in the state-run retail stores (where it can also buy goods produced by joint ventures), and $30 on services provided by the self-employed. The economy has become less socialist, and the government is back in control of it. As unpopular as some of these reforms have been—especially the new tax system—the government did keep one promise: The Cuban peso was not officially devalued.

Yet the price of success has been the creation of two Cubas that are drifting apart. The self-employed owners of *paladares*, farmers, artisans, joint-venture employees, and prostitutes are enjoying their taste of capitalism and want more. But the doctors, educators, scientists, and government employees who have sacrificed years climbing up the traditional socialist ladder rightly feel left behind. For them, still trapped in the peso economy, it is the end of the revolution, despite Fidel's message to the contrary. Growing inequalities are generating increasing criticism and discontent not only among the traditional professional elite but also among Communist Party leadership.

Cuba's ability to defuse these tensions and continue its progress will depend on the resolution of two central paradoxes. First, in spite of the success generated by these new policies, the Cuban government has slowed down the reform process, delaying long-awaited changes in property rights, such as the legalization of small and medium enterprises. Second, notwithstanding the positive impact of foreign investment on private-sector development in Cuba, the United States has passed a series of laws that has tight-

Cuba's Long-Distance Civil War

President Fidel Castro's triumph in the Cuban Revolution ended a hot local conflict, but it also began a colder long-distance confrontation between Cubans who lost their assets and social positions and those who took them over.

The losers joined forces with the United States, attempting military action before settling on the trade embargo as their weapon of choice. In the early years, the Cuban exile community was too weak to sway the U.S. political process, and U.S. corporate interests and geopolitical concerns took precedence over civil confrontation. But over time, as the exiles became U.S. citizens and learned how to use their new country's political system, their influence has expanded dramatically. The Cuban American National Foundation (CANF), founded in 1981 by the charismatic Jorge Mas Canosa, has built a strong lobby that has worked to tighten the embargo on Cuba. Together with groups such as the Institute for Democracy in Cuba and former major property holders in Cuba such as the National Association of Sugar Mill Owners of Cuba and the Bacardi rum company, CANF played a major role in drafting punitive legislation such as the 1996 Helms-Burton law.

Those individuals who took over farmland, real estate, and productive assets in Cuba needed a political system that would prevent the losers, who were supported by an awesome geopolitical player, from regaining power. In addition to the backing of the Soviet Union, the winners' weapon of choice was an "internal" embargo that has kept Castro in place but constrained political and economic freedom. Today, the Cuban government still sees private ownership, freedom of the press, the multiparty system, and even the growing number of self-employed Cubans as vehicles that will allow wealthy enemies in Florida to regain economic power and buy electoral support.

As with many wars, chief among the casualties have been ordinary civilians. Sanctions have retarded Cuba's development and hurt families. Harsh efforts by Cuban authorities to keep their external enemies at bay have ruined lives and deterred Cuba from putting its resources to better use. On the eve of the revolution, Cuba enjoyed one of the highest standards of living in Latin America, ranking first in the per capita availability of telephones, newspapers, and private automobiles; second in per capita income (after Venezuela); and third in average food intake (after Argentina and Uruguay). It now lags behind most of the region in all these areas.

The long-distance civil war is not over, but its intensity seems to be diminishing. Disillusioned by the failure of the U.S. embargo to remove Castro from power, the American foreign-policy and business establishments increasingly advocate a more open U.S. policy toward Cuba—witness the proposal made in October 1998 by a group of Republican and Democratic senators, with the endorsement of three former secretaries of state, to initiate the first comprehensive review of U.S. policy on Cuba since 1959. Demographic changes within the Cuban exile community are tipping the balance of power away from those who seek to regain their properties toward more recent arrivals who have closer ties to their families in Cuba. Finally, in Cuba itself, a taste of capitalism and freedom has created a constituency for further liberalization.

—FP

ened the embargo, thereby undermining the same forces that it has championed so vocally in its policies toward China and Vietnam.

Efforts to resolve these two paradoxes tend to focus on one of two alternatives: either to get rid of Fidel or end the embargo. Unfortunately, this analysis is incomplete. Cuba's harassment of its budding entrepreneurs and the tightened U.S. embargo are merely the latest manifestations of a long-distance civil war that has been raging since the overthrow of Fulgencio Batista's dictatorship and triumph of the Castro revolution in 1959. This continuing conflict pits those who won against those who lost out. For all their totemic significance, neither Castro nor Senator Jesse Helms holds the key to bridging the bitter psychological divide that separates the two camps. Unlike the experiences of its former "revolutionary" brethren in Eastern Europe, Cuba's revolution was a homegrown affair that institutionalized communism well after the fact. As such, the end of the cold war has not changed the constellation of factors— property rights, power struggle, racial discrimination, and 100 years of frustrated nationalism—that caused the revolution in the first place.

In spite of the post–cold war resurgence of the civil war taking place on both sides of the Florida strait, Cuba has chosen a relatively successful transition process that allows for steady, moderate economic growth. Of course, as the Cuban and Russian experiences each show from different vantage points, the transformation of a centrally planned economy into a market-driven one requires more than the willingness of governments and assistance of the international community. Searching for the invisible hand is inherently difficult. Taking into account the distinct characteristics that make Cuba's reform process more of a parable than a blueprint, what lessons can be drawn from its experience?

In Troubled Waters, Don't Throw Away the Anchor

Fiscal austerity should come before exchange rate liberalization. Before balancing its budget, Russia freed exchange rates and induced hyperinflation. The ruble went from 1.7 per dollar in 1990 to more than 4,640 per dollar in 1995; in October 1998, the rate reached the equivalent of approximately 16,000 old rubles. Cuba, however, initiated in 1993 an aggressive and unpopular fiscal adjustment and has not yet unified the exchange rate. In the unofficial market, the dollar has stabilized, remaining at 19 pesos per dollar since 1996. Having a free exchange rate cannot be the first priority when you have a fiscal mess.

Create the New before Destroying the Old

Abandoning socialism is a bit like jumping off a cliff. As the experiences of various transitional countries show, it inevitably involves a precipitous economic decline, at least temporarily. Since the leap is unavoidable, the question is how to make it as safe as possible. In this context, Cuba has something to teach its former cold war patron. As opposed to the Russians, Cubans have chosen to create opportunities for investment and growth in tourism, mining, and the service sector before dismantling the existing system. They have also developed strategies for attracting remittances from exiles while creating markets where these dollars can be easily spent. These strategies to attract hard currency have been successfully fueling growth since 1994. In the meantime, as in Russia, inefficient state-owned enterprises have been restructured with varying degrees of success, with some kept running just to avoid unemployment. In other words, Cubans seem to have successfully put into practice what has been called the monkey theorem: When moving from tree to tree, monkeys never let go of one branch until they have a good grasp of the next.

> *Abandoning socialism is a bit like jumping off a cliff.*

The State Is Better Than the Mafia

Privatizing inefficient public enterprises is an important step for liberalizing economies. Nevertheless, privatization alone does not guarantee success and efficiency. There are hundreds of bankrupt privatized companies in Russia and other former socialist countries. The Cuban experience suggests that, in some cases, changing the incentive structure is more sensible than changing the ownership structure. Especially in the absence of state market-regulating mechanisms (i.e., commercial codes, antitrust laws, a reliable tax system), the managers of newly privatized firms have huge incentives to search for short-term benefits. Joint ventures between foreign investors and the state have worked well for Cubans by making private and public incentives compatible. On the one hand, joint ventures help assure the private sector that the government will not mess up conditions for success, since it stands to benefit. On the other hand, joint ventures reduce the odds of managers exploiting their companies for personal gain. When faced with increased market freedom and absence of control by a withering state, managers in Russia ruined enterprises under their control, selling and expropriating assets and wasting and diverting resources. Dominance over important sectors of the economy by Mafia-like groups in Russia was possible because the state dramatically reduced its enforcement capacity. In Cuba, the alliance between government and foreign investment has created market-oriented incentives while keeping out organized crime. Even capitalism needs a state.

Keep the Military Busy

Cuba has so far succeeded in harnessing its military as a potent force for reform, whether through its political support or the economic success of military-run ventures such as La Gaviota, the country's biggest tourist company. During the transition, the military can provide an efficient alternative coordinating mechanism for business organization in the absence of market institutions. But as the recent experience of China has shown, weaning the military off its reliance on commercial ventures can be a delicate political task.

There is one central lesson, however, that Russia has for Cuba, even if it is expressed in the negative: Avoid total-victory scenarios. The idea that the end of communism would come in the form of a glorious final victory (à la Russian president Boris Yeltsin on top of a tank in 1991) created the paradigm that U.S. politicians have envisioned for Cuba. However, after seven years of gridlock in Russia, with a reformist president and conservative Duma, the finality of that triumph seems much less obvious. Working toward the resolution of the continuing civil war between Cuba's exiles and its inhabitants is bound to prove more successful than attempting to achieve "total victory." If an armistice took place that eliminated the potential for outright victory by either side, the reform process in Cuba could naturally continue building a country that is more prosperous and more democratic.

Castro Gives Tourism a Try[2]

By Linda Robinson
U.S. News & World Report, January 12, 1998

For years, Bert Traeger and his dad booked front-row seats for Havana's exuberant Carnival. From their balconies at the Hotel Pasaje, the Miami men watched conga dancers and lavish floats cha-cha by. Then came free daiquiris in the Havana Club tasting room, burlesque at Chinatown's Shanghai Theater, cockfights at Río Cristal, and all-night gambling at glittering casinos. Josephine Baker might be strutting in her plastic-banana skirt and faux-fruit necklaces, Tony Bennett singing at the Sans Souci, or Beny Moré playing the Alibar. "Everybody," Bert Traeger recalls, "was dying to go to Havana."

And go they did. In the 1940s and 1950s, the "Paris of the West" was flooded with carefree Americans. From Florida, the Pan Am Clipper flew six times a day to Havana, Cubana Air four, and a rail-ship link whisked New Yorkers down in 48 hours. Miami residents seemed to go all the time. Bert Traeger celebrated his high school graduation in Havana, taking his buddies over on the Key West ferry. As a naval reservist, he led fellow sailors on a merry jaunt through the seaport. His father, who did business with Cuba, knew the island tip to tip.

The nonstop party ended with Fidel Castro's 1959 revolution. Tourists and rich Cubans decamped, and their pleasure palaces were seized by a militant regime bent on creating a socialist paradise. Now, after 39 years of communism, the Caribbean's moribund playground is coming back to life. Tourist buses ply the old Gray Line route to cigar factories, massive Spanish fortresses, and the restored section of La Habana Vieja, the hemisphere's largest collection of colonial buildings. Venerable hotels on the treelined Prado boulevard have been rescued from years of penury and neglect. Since 1990, when Castro began to revive tourism to replace the billions of dollars lost in Soviet aid, arrivals have grown by 20 percent a year. In 1997, a record 1.2 million foreigners came to Cuba, and 1.4 million are expected in 1998, including Pope John Paul II, who this month will visit the officially atheistic island for the first time.

Heritage

Cuba's tourist appeal, while faded, remains strong. Many attractions that made the island the "Pearl of the Antilles" survive, and more are being resurrected. True, visitors are often shocked by the poverty and decay of a country now in deep economic crisis, but the decades of socialism have not erased a rich cultural history. Founded by Spain in 1519, Havana became a gracious city of parks and wide avenues, of opera, ballet, and theater. Sugar barons built fine homes and elegant clubs that, though run down, still stand. Cuba's 300 beaches draw almost half of the island's visitors. Package tours are competitively priced—a more important factor to most vacationers than the fact that Cuba is still communist.

> *The surge in tourism is occurring despite Castro's ongoing ambivalence over the contamination of his socialist island with the virus of foreign capital and free-wheeling outsiders.*

The surge in tourism is occurring despite Castro's ongoing ambivalence over the contamination of his socialist island with the virus of foreign capital and freewheeling outsiders. In addition, an embargo imposed during John Kennedy's presidency still bans American tourists from their once favorite island. Last summer, a spate of bombs shook several Havana hotels and killed an Italian tourist. Cuban officials accused exiles in Miami of plotting the attacks, which stopped after a Salvadoran was charged with planting the bombs. Whoever wanted to scare off tourists has yet to succeed.

Among the landmarks still intact is the fabled Tropicana, where Nat King Cole played February gigs and learned to sing in Spanish. It looks the way it did in 1957 when a *Holiday* magazine correspondent wrote, "Nowhere in the world have I seen a club like this, in beauty and sweep of setting; the main attraction is a colossal open-air cabaret [in which] stand the tallest royal palms, the starry sky its ceiling." On a recent night, long-legged dancers in red-and-white organza and sequined headdresses swished through the aisles and sashayed on platforms high in the trees. When a singer asked the tables of *mojito* drinkers where they were from, the names of a dozen European and South American countries were shouted back.

Tarzan and the Duke

The grand dame of Havana hotels, the Nacional—designed in the 1930s by the same architects who created the Breakers in Palm Beach—has been faithfully restored down to its Spanish tiling and breezy patio overlooking the seaside Malecón promenade. Guests are greeted by a mural depicting past visitors, the likes of Johnny Weissmuller, Ava Gardner, and Winston Churchill. Sepia-tinted on the wall of the hotel's Gulf View Bar are pictures of former regulars Frank Sinatra, Errol Flynn, and John Wayne. In the Nacional's Salón de Aguiar, a boisterous group of Mexicans eats lobster and snapper at the same long table where American mobsters, stogies puffing, decided in 1946 to off Bugsy Siegel.

Although foreigners had visited for decades, it was America's Mafia that turned the Cuban capital into a 24-hour, no-bet-limit paradise for gamblers. Gangsters took over the posh Casino Nacional and the Sans Souci and opened casino hotels like the Capri, where movie tough guy George Raft played host, and the turquoise Riviera, built by Meyer Lansky, the Miami mob boss.

Forty years later, Reinaldo Naves, still a Riviera bellman, remembers the inaugural bash that Ginger Rogers headlined in the hotel's Copa Room: "The ladies were so elegant in their long white gloves. The men were betting ten, twenty thousand at roulette and blackjack." He points toward Lansky's 20th-floor quarters, now redone as executive suites. "The boss was even shorter than me," the 5-foot-tall bellman recalls, "but he had two big blond bodyguards with him all the time." As Naves hustles off to meet an Italian group, a long line forms outside the Copa Room, now the Palacio de la Salsa, where the dance floor will churn till dawn.

Four decades ago, as clubs rocked in revelry, Castro's guerrillas were attacking President Fulgencio Batista's government. When Batista dined at the Countess of Camargo's mansion—now the Museum of Decorative Arts—guests laid joking wagers on whether bombs would go off before dessert. When rebels finally took control of Havana, Lansky's Riviera was still full of high rollers.

"Get your family and come with me to Las Vegas," the Mafia don told his longtime chef, Gilberto Smith.

"I'm staying," the *cordon bleu* cooking champion replied. "I'm a Communist."

Lansky wished him well. "You never told me," he said. "But I knew."

Within months, tourism dried up. Castro made the new Hilton his headquarters, shut the casinos, and razed the Shanghai. The brothels closed, and the deserted hotels grew dank and dreary. Havana's festive whirl was over.

Over $600 million invested in hotels is reviving the dormant economy. Net revenues from tourism, estimated at $567 million in 1997, have become the country's No. 2 source of cash (No. 1: money sent home by exiles). The change since 1990 is palpable: More food is in the stores, more cars travel once deserted streets, and ordinary Cubans have a chance to earn dollars by driving private taxis, running in-home cafes, and renting out rooms. Although the regime is wary of even such tiny entrepreneurial ventures, the gloom is beginning to lift. Havana is not living "to a Cole Porter rhythm"—a '50s travelogue boast—but it is rousing from its coma.

Former wealth, current poverty, and future hopes are juxtaposed in the seaside Miramar district. A grizzled man in an undershirt leans from the balcony of a decaying mansion that was divided into a multifamily dwelling after the revolution. On either side of him are refurbished homes used by an embassy and a foreign business. Down the street, work crews toil until 3 a.m. to finish a 409-room luxury hotel, a joint venture between Cuba and the Spanish Meliá Group.

At Miramar's western end the grand old Biltmore Yacht and Country Club is rising again. Architect Teofilo Addine is using old photos to re-create the decorative masonry. "We've got a budget of $10 million, and all the marble we need is already imported," he says, showing where a second pool, a spa, a golf course, tennis courts, and restaurants will go. The club was part of the tourist empire built by Biltmore hotelier Jack Bowman, who helped make Cuba a rival of the French Riviera in the Roaring Twenties. Rich Americans like the Vanderbilts and Annenbergs flocked to his Sevilla Hotel, designed by the Waldorf-Astoria's architects, watched horses run at the Oriental Park track from the dining terrace of his Jockey Club next door, and gambled at his ritzy Casino Nacional.

Guests from Tampa

Not far from the Biltmore, at the Marina Hemingway, a piece of Cuba's nautical past has returned. José Díaz Escrich, president of Club Náutico, recounts his success in restarting the once popular U.S.-Cuba regattas. "Last May, 127 boats raced from Tampa to Havana," he says. "It ran every year from 1930 until the revolution, and last year we finally did it again." In November, 40 U.S. boats sailed from Key West to Varadero, a regatta that had been revived twice in the Jimmy Carter years. To comply with the embargo's curbs against spending money on the island, American sailors paid their home clubs instead of Cuba. "U.S. officials briefed us before we left Key West," says Pat Smith, aboard her namesake. "They said it was a privilege to travel to Cuba, but I consider it my right." Others tied up at the marina ignore rules entirely. A retired Brooklyn ironworker named Buzz is on his fourth visit. "I go drinking every night with my Cuban friends," he says, "and I don't answer to anyone."

One aspect of old Cuba that's still absent is gambling—a source of huge corruption and Mafia penetration under Batista (who got half the take from Lansky's slot machines). "There are no casinos in Cuba," says Cuba's vice minister for tourism, Miguel Brugeras, "and there will be no casinos in Cuba."

Brugeras cannot say the same for prostitution, which is escalating as a result of the influx of tourists and the poverty caused by the end of Soviet aid. "We're working for family tourism and against sex tourism," says Brugeras as he cites new laws aimed at pimps and traffic in minors. But powerful market forces are working against the government initiative: Cubans need dollars desperately, and many tourists come for sex. Except for hotel workers who get dollar tips, most Cubans are paid in pesos, yet essentials like cooking oil can be found only in dollar stores. *Jineteras*, as prostitutes are called in Havana, work the discos and streets outside hotels.

One of them is Judy, 21, in an iridescent halter dress and upswept hairdo, who slips into the Habana Club disco to look for a man willing to pay $100 for her services. She is matter of fact about her main goal: "I want to marry a foreigner and leave the country—preferably for Spain, since I speak the language." The club she scouts each night is part of the Comodoro Hotel, where Santo Trafficante Jr. ran gambling and prostitution and, he once boasted, watched then Sen. John Kennedy frolic with three of his whores. The resurgence of the oldest profession has caused an alarming spurt in Cuba's HIV infection rate, which had been kept low by aggressive testing, condom distribution, and a much criticized policy, now relaxed somewhat, of quarantining AIDS victims in sanitariums.

Cuba's brisk sex trade includes the emergence of huge underground gay discos and Miss Transvestite contests. But the racy side of Havana remains a far cry from the 1950s, when the harbor and other neighborhoods were lined with brothels and porno shows (like the Superman "exhibitions" immortalized by Graham Greene and *Godfather II*). And what occurs today could be curbed if other jobs were created; many hookers say they would do something else if it paid. The sad truth, reports one hotel executive, is that "the two jobs worth having in Cuba right now are *jinetera* or waiter."

Some visitors are plainly bothered by the sights of poverty. Alicia Sosa, a Uruguayan doctor, spent a week in Havana and left depressed. A man from Spain who had backed the Cuban Revolution changed his mind once he saw Havana. "I can't support this government any longer," he says. "I bought dinner for a girl last night after she told me she hadn't eaten all day." Such reactions are part of the risk Castro incurs by opening doors to tourists, but Brugeras, the tourism chief, insists that Cuba wants visitors to see "the realities, our daily struggle, our gains, and our difficulties, that this is neither heaven nor hell."

While many Caribbean islands are poor, it is Cuba's plunge from a higher standard of living that creates a sense of loss. Havana as museum is an eerie place. The physical remains of great wealth and a glamorous heyday are all around, but the upper and middle classes who once inhabited that world have gone. "It was a great

---

Brugeras, the tourism chief, insists that Cuba wants visitors to see "the realities, our daily struggle, our gains, and our difficulties, that this is neither heaven nor hell."

---

city, and it's still endlessly revealing to walk through its ruins," says Micky Wolfson of Miami, 58, heir to the Wometco movie chain fortune, who often visited Havana as a teenager and, with State Department permission, returned recently for a tour. Throughout the visit, he couldn't shake "the tragedy and horror of a society completely destroyed."

A few society ladies remain, like Zaida Carrera, 94, but her life is profoundly changed from the days of tea at the Country Club and the gala balls at the Havana Yacht Club. Chandeliers and porcelain plates bearing the seals of titled Cubans adorn her stately home, but she cannot get cement to repair the cracks that keep occurring. She doesn't suffer as much as her neighbors, she says, but "little by little, we've had to sell our things to eat."

Beach Boom

An entirely new chapter of Cuba's tourism story is being written in the beach resorts that have mushroomed across the island. Two hours' drive from Havana, Varadero's sandy peninsula—which had only a few hundred hotel rooms before the revolution—is now lined with two dozen hotels. In October, Club Med opened a 500-room canary-yellow resort complex decorated with fountains and modern art; ground already has been broken for expansion. Even before the winter's high season began, French tourists windsurfed and paddled around the calm waters while a multilingual volleyball game took over the beach in front of a new Spanish Meliá hotel. Though developed for tourists only recently, Varadero has long been a haven for the rich. A mansion built atop a bluff for Irenee du Pont is now a restaurant. So is the "Casa de Al," a former hangout for Al Capone.

The government has embarked on a massive plan to develop its many virgin keys and islets for tourism. Caribbean competitors are watching nervously; some, hoping to get a share of Cuba-bound traffic, have offered joint-destination packages. On Cuba's north shore, Canadians are mobbing Cayo Coco. In the south, on Cayo Largo, a half-dozen hotels now line the inland shore, and thatched huts dot the beach. Scuba diving centers have popped up all around the island; Cuba's northern coral reef is the world's second largest after Australia's Great Barrier Reef. Sport fishing is expanding from the

---

Some hotel executives in the United States are distressed that American companies are excluded from Cuba's tourist boom.

---

famous marlin-fishing tourneys (swept by American anglers last year) to bonefishing off the southern coast and trout fishing in teeming lakes.

Some hotel executives in the United States are distressed that American companies are excluded from Cuba's tourist boom. "The most important time to enter a new market, as in the case of Cuba, is at the beginning of its commercial, economic, and political transformation," says Peter Blyth, the president of Radisson Development Worldwide. Non-U.S. competitors, he complains, have already nailed down the specific locations that his company deemed ideal. And Cuba, he notes sardonically, "is unlikely to increase in size."

If future projections are borne out, Blyth may grow more peeved. By the year 2007, even without any change in its policies or in the U.S. embargo, Cuba can expect 4 million tourists a year, according to a study by Nicolás Crespo, an independent travel consultant. His estimate jumps to 5 million visitors if Cuba adopts a free-enterprise system that allows Americans to invest in Cuban tourism.

The leap in a decade from 1.2 million visitors to 4 million or more hinges above all on whether Cuba can build rooms fast enough. Cuba's master plan called for construction of 5,000 hotel rooms in 1997; in fact, only 2,800 were added, for a total of 29,678. Some foreign investors fault the myriad restrictions that Cuba imposes in its attempt to keep control of tourism's golden goose; only one third of the rooms are managed by foreigners or joint ventures. But with occupancy running 90 percent at some hotels and 60 percent overall, Vice Minister Brugeras is convinced that Cuba has "a lot left to develop." The operative theory is build and visitors will come. Tourism, the revisionists conclude, just might be Cuba's manifest destiny after all.

Against All Odds, Cuban Small Business Finds a Way[3]

BY PHILIP PETERS
WALL STREET JOURNAL, NOVEMBER 20, 1998

This is the only country in Latin America where the state employs three in four workers; the only one where government agencies plot the nationwide distribution of food; the only one without a convertible currency.

It's a place where, "to resolve the problem of shoes," the president of the "Blas Roca" farm cooperative had to perform a small economic planning feat just to set up a cobbler's shop to service his 300 workers. One is tempted to believe the U.S. State Department's view that Cuba has "resisted any credible effort to adopt market-based policies" since the Soviet bloc vanished.

But it's not that simple. A series of limited economic reforms since 1993 have injected doses of capitalism throughout the Cuban economy. The results are modest when measured in national accounts, but for many thousands of Cubans and their families, the reforms have brought higher incomes and a measure of security. The greatest significance may be ideological: even though socialism still reigns, Cuba is slowly deviating from old principles.

Microenterprise is now legal. Today over 150,000 Cubans work in an incipient entrepreneurial sector—mainly small restaurants, lunch stands, and service businesses. A March 1998 survey that I conducted with Joseph Scarpaci of Virginia Tech found that these businesses made an average monthly after-tax profit of 743 pesos, over three times the average Cuban salary. The entrepreneurs have brought commerce back to Cuban streets, and they have some tangible economic freedom, along with some handicaps that have made the pace of change erratic.

Many entrepreneurs quit state jobs to work for themselves. "There is no job in the state that I could have that would be better than this. Here, I'm in charge," says a Havana glass cutter I first met in 1996 when he was nervous about start-up risks. Today his business is steady, and he is slowly renovating his house. Granted, restrictions are many: most entrepreneurs are barred from hiring employees, wholesale supply sources are lacking, and tax collec-

---

3. Article by Philip Peters from *Wall Street Journal* November 20, 1998. Copyright © *Wall Street Journal*. Reprinted with permission.

tions and regulatory enforcement have reduced the sector by about one-fourth since it peaked in size in 1996. But new businesses continue to open, suggesting that the longer term trend may be upward.

In the government sector as well, the link between pay and output is being rebuilt as the government now uses incentive payments as a tool to spur production. Not every workplace can afford to pay them, but their use is spreading. The official press trumpets the productivity of cigar workers who receive incentive payments in both pesos and U.S. dollars. Near the resort center of Varadero, state construction laborers explained to me how they boost their income by exceeding production targets and avoiding absenteeism. Farm cooperatives pay monthly productivity bonuses.

Once taboo, foreign capital is fueling joint ventures with the Cuban government, and foreign practices are changing the workplace. Tourism, Cuba's new top foreign-exchange earner, benefits from foreign investment as does mining, energy, telecommunications, and some other sectors. Critics complain that foreign investors pay "slave wages" because joint venture workers receive modest peso salaries from state employment agencies, but in fact the workers receive very substantial supplemental payments on the side. One Cuban I met earns $300 monthly, twenty times his former state salary, selling industrial equipment for a European company. Another, a 33-year-old administrator for a Canadian firm, effectively earns nine times the average Cuban wage by virtue of the fact that 90% of his salary is paid in Canadian dollars. He no longer worries about feeding his family.

These workers also learn capitalism. "On the day I started working for the Canadians, I realized I didn't know how to work," he says. Like his counterparts in other joint ventures, "discipline" and "transparency" lace his description of his new job. At the phone company ETECSA, employees say an infusion of Italian capital has brought better customer service, a stronger work ethic, a profit sharing plan, and the printing of the first phone directory in a decade.

Soviet-style state planning is dying. The Economy and Planning Ministry has seen its workforce reduced by two thirds since 1990. "Everything is changed, except for the building," Vice Minister Alfonso Casanova says in an interview. Where his predecessors once decided the precise amount of each raw material to be allocated to each state enterprise, Mr. Casanova spends his time slashing subsidies. He is interested in financial results, which he monitors online in his office.

One of the most important changes is that the state no longer monopolizes food production. The Blas Roca cooperative, one of 1,500 that resulted from the breakup of larger state farms in 1993, is part of a new system of quasi-private food supply. In exchange for fuel and supplies, the cooperative delivers a quota back to the state—but it also produces a surplus which it is free to sell in the private market. Agriculture ministry officials readily admit that not all cooperatives are profitable, and further reforms are necessary. For guidance they are looking to "credit and service" cooperatives—small groups of private farms that were never collectivized and have the highest productivity.

Since 1994, bustling farmers' markets have returned to Cuban cities, creating an alternative to the state's unreliable food distribution system. Prices move freely according to supply and demand, but they are out of reach for Cubans who earn only a typical state salary. At October market prices, a pound each of pork, rice, beans, and tomatoes, plus some onions, limes, and garlic would consume one third of the average monthly wage. The state supplies only a fifth of the produce in these markets; the rest comes from surplus production of cooperatives.

Will further reforms follow? Officials hint at possibilities, such as a new property law and reduced restrictions on entrepreneurship, but no action seems imminent. Still, it's a mistake to dismiss the significance of reforms achieved so far. They will not produce dramatic growth, but they have pulled Cuba out of its post-Soviet crisis. Add hundreds of millions of dollars in cash from family remittances from abroad, and the theory of current American policy—economic collapse leading to popular revolt—becomes fantasy. As policy makers theorize about "transition scenarios," an economic transition is already underway, one enterprising Cuban at a time.

Dotcommies Take Over Cuba[4]

By Timothy Ashby and Elizabeth Bourget
Christian Science Monitor, December 20, 2000

Another revolution is sweeping through Cuba.

Today, Fidel Castro seems as determined to create a world-class information-technology sector as he was to overthrow the Batista dictatorship in the 1950s. Anticipating an end to the United States trade embargo, Cuba is preparing to become the Caribbean's digital hub.

Largest of the Caribbean island states, with a land area of 43,000 square miles and 11 million people, Cuba has been economically and politically isolated from its giant neighbor 90 miles to the north for more than 40 years.

Despite what one may think about Fidel Castro, none of the profound economic changes taking place in Cuba today would be possible without his direct guidance. Mr. Castro and his still officially communist government have undertaken Cuba's economic transformation by following a policy based on technology, markets, and new capital.

The aging revolutionaries who followed Moscow's model have been replaced by a new generation of well-educated, pragmatic officials. Among members of the Cuban National Assembly, the average age is 40; the foreign minister is 35, and the minister of foreign investment is a 49-year-old woman. They read *The Wall Street Journal* and George Gilder's *Telecosm*, a US bestseller on the revolution in broadband, and shake their heads when foreign leftists spout Marxist dialectic at them.

In January 2000, the Cuban government established a Ministry of Information Technology (MINIT) with a mandate to make Cuba an "information society" and quickly develop an information-technology industry and e-business. MINIT has various subsidiaries operating as profitmaking businesses focusing on telecommunications, software, hardware, wireless, e-commerce, and training.

Eight Cuban universities offer degrees in information technology, and the Institute for Science operates 40 branches around the island providing adult education in computer science. Several Internet service providers are available, owned by government ministries but functioning like competing dotcoms.

---

4. Article by Timothy Ashby and Elizabeth Bourget from *The Christian Science Monitor* December 20, 2000. Copyright © Sonrisa Foundation. Reprinted with permission.

Cuba has an established electronics manufacturing industry. Semiconductors, radios, televisions, and Cuban-designed computers are assembled with foreign parts. There are 30 software-development companies; none existed three years ago. Total software exports for 2000 may seem paltry at $14 million, but they have grown 650 percent since 1999.

Computer youth clubs are springing up everywhere. A club in Havana has work stations with modern Pentium computers on the ground floor, used by young Web designers looking like dotcommies from a Silicon Valley start-up. The walls are emblazoned with slogans and posters—but not quite the ones expected in a club owned and operated by the Cuban Communist Party. The predominant slogan is *"Creemos en el Futuro"* ("We Believe in the Future"). Posters advertise courses in software programming, multimedia, computer repair, and e-commerce. Classes upstairs are packed with serious teenagers learning HTML and Microsoft Office.

Global information-technology companies plan to make Cuba a premier location for Internet data centers.

Students swap copies of *Giga*, a slick Cuban computer magazine. Recent topics include Internet security and a review of new hotel-reservations software developed by the Cuban firm Softur. Despite the embargo, *Giga* carries ads for US brands such as Microsoft, IBM, Macintosh, and Oracle.

Cuba is ideally positioned to be a digital hub. The telephone system is being upgraded after a $1 billion investment by Mexican investors. Full digitalization of the telecommunications network is expected in 2004, and more than 2,000 post offices offer Internet access to the local population. Cuba has a cellular telephone system, satellite earth stations are being built, and a new fiber-optic cable connects the island to Florida.

Global information-technology companies plan to make Cuba a premier location for Internet data centers, providing Web-hosting services for businesses throughout the Western Hemisphere. As a likely future member of the North American Free Trade Area, Cuba will offer tax advantages to US firms investing in electronics manufacturing for export. The island has more college graduates per capita than any other Latin American country, and skilled workers earn the equivalent of $30 a month.

Cuba's government has extended an invitation to foreign businesses interested in helping to develop the information-technology industry. Although Cuba would prefer to obtain US expertise and products directly, other nations are currently providing American technology.

"Trading with the US is an American problem, not a Cuban one," says Daniel Fernandez Lopez, vice president of Grupo de la Electronica, a division of MINIT responsible for telecommunications. "We welcome American business, but we can't wait."

Americans who are frustrated by the embargo can begin rebuilding business bridges now by providing charitable IT training, used computer equipment, and exchanges between US and Cuban IT executives, a legal practice under the current embargo. By doing so, we can generate cultural goodwill while laying foundations for future business.

Cuban Discoveries Hold Key to World's Progress in Medicine[5]

By Daniel Whitaker
The Times (London), March 15, 2000

Walking in from the heat of the Havana afternoon to the cool of the cavernous Farmacia Sarra, you can plainly see Cuba's economic hardship. Only a few brown-bottled medicines are forlornly displayed on the mahogany shelves rising up behind the marble counter of this ornate 19th-century chemists. These are supplemented by herbal remedies.

A doctor from a nearby district hospital implores: "When you come back, please try to bring some omeprazole (currently the world's biggest selling drug, for stomach ulcers). My patients really need it and we have none."

Yet just 30 minutes' drive west from the Sarra lies the Polo Cientifico biotechnology park, where 38 research and production facilities drive one of the biotech world's most remarkable success stories. Between them, these centres have developed products that are drawing the attention—and money—of some of the capitalist world's largest pharmaceutical players.

Examples include the discovery of vaccines for dengue fever, hepatitis B and the only effective vaccination against meningitis B (which accounts for more than half of all meningitis cases), policosanol, a medication from sugar cane that lowers cholesterol and can treat lipid disorders, and advanced monoclonal antibodies for the treatment of cancer.

Last year, after nearly two years of negotiation, SmithKline Beecham (SB) convinced the American Government to allow an exception to its draconian embargo legislation, letting SB sign a deal with the Cubans worth up to $20 million (Pounds 12.5 million) for a five-year exclusive right to market the meningitis vaccine. York Medical, a Canadian company, has gone further, signing a joint-venture agreement to market or out-licence four anticancer products, now undergoing clinical trials. Having spent $18m on testing so far, York hopes to bring these to market by 2002. A number of

---

5. Article by Daniel Whitaker from *The Times* (London) March 15, 2000. Copyright © *The Times*. Reprinted with permission.

other big manufacturers have been sending steady streams of senior staff to Cuba for talks, though fear of possible US sanctions makes them loath to comment.

The success is remarkable given the lack of resources on the poverty-stricken island. Many of the breakthroughs occurred during the 1990s, when the collapse of trade with the former Soviet Union and a tightening US embargo all but paralysed the Cuban economy. Multinational drug companies can easily spend close to $1bn developing a single new product, and it has long been assumed that nothing of interest would emerge from outside the developed countries where these companies carry out their research.

The dynamism of Cuban biotech development contrasts with most of the rest of the island's economy. In the countryside, oxen-drawn ploughs still till the land, the sugar industry is stagnating and home-produced manufactures are famous for their low quality.

Cuba's achievements in medicine discovery are due to a number of elements coming together. Within a year of seizing power, Fidel Castro proclaimed "the future of our nation is necessarily the future of men of science." He then put in place policies to back up this sentiment—enormous resources were diverted into education and health care (at the expense of those other parts of the economy now struggling).

A National Centre for Scientific Investigation was set up in 1961, spawning the many research facilities of the Polo Cientifico. Reliable figures are hard to come by from an obsessively secretive government, but total investment is estimated at several hundred million dollars.

Little might have come of it without the dedication of the scientists involved. Even leading Cuban scientists are paid about $15 per month, compared to upwards of $5,000–$10,000 a month for American pharma researchers, excluding share options. Defection is rare, though it would not be difficult, given the many foreign conferences which the Cubans attend. But in talking to off-duty researchers, what comes through is their devotion to duty. This is partly a rare instance of genuine socialist idealism, since many of the products are designed to combat the main diseases that afflict the island's population. But it also draws on a long tradition of medical endeavour in Cuba. Back in Havana, there is a proud museum and several monuments to Dr Carlos Finlay, the Cuban who, as any schoolchild on the island will recount, was in 1881 the first person to identify the mosquitoes that carried yellow fever.

Castro's investment in biotech at so difficult a time has been an enormous gamble, but the research areas that the Cubans embarked into have come up trumps. As David Allan, chief executive of York Medical explains: "When they began looking at antibody therapy as a way to fight cancer, the rest of the world dismissed the idea. Now it is accepted that this will be a major part of future oncology therapies, and Cuba is up there with the scientific leaders."

Current focuses, such as on DNA recombination at the Centre for Genetic Engineering and Biotechnology (CIGB), also look promising. Dr Manuel Limonta, the CIGB's exuberant founder and now head of the island's blood supply, likes to quote a line of his favourite author Gabriel García Márquez, "much sooner than later, reality ends up by recognising the imagination was right."

> *Biotech [is] the third biggest foreign exchange earner after tourism and sugar.*

The research centres themselves are in modern (often late-1980s) premises with equipment that is close to state of the art. Dr Limonta's successor, Dr Luis Herrera, arranges tours of his air-conditioned laboratories at the CIGB, where 700 scientists work flanked by mass spectrometers, infrared and ultraviolet microscopes, confident that visitors will leave impressed. Ironically, the standards applied in the production process are those officially set by the US. Some visiting foreign companies are taken with the staff as much as with the buildings. Dr Agustin Lage, head of the Centre for Molecular Immunology, for example, has been made a board member at York—an unusual move for a Cuban official. "We wanted Lage because he epitomises Cuban science—dedicated but practical," Allan explains.

Export income figures are not published. But one local industry-watcher guesses up to $200 million per year, making biotech the third biggest foreign exchange earner after tourism and sugar. The bulk of this goes to Asia and elsewhere in Latin America. While these sums are substantial, if the research programme is to keep up with the capitalist world, they must rise, through entry into the large European or North American markets.

To do this, the Cubans need help. On an isolated communist island, there is little opportunity to learn about commercial marketing, about intellectual property law or how to get medicines approved by demanding foreign regulators. Multinational drug companies know this well. Hence, the deals with SB and York.

Even though some such deals are likely to materialise, there are other clouds on the horizon. Mass tourism, the now legal circulation of dollars and slowly warming relations with the US, all mean that Cuban society is changing, becoming more competitive and unequal. So it will be harder for the island's biotech industry to hold on to staff and their idealism, especially as the product range shifts from local life-savers to what will sell best abroad.

The secretive official culture may also have to change to something more encouraging of local initiative and foreign investment. In 1996, the fugitive US financier and Cuban resident, Robert Vesco, was sentenced to 13 years in prison for misleading potential investors in Cuban biotech. Many see Vesco as the "fall guy" in a mysterious case involving high-level corruption.

The US Helms-Burton Act is also a drag on progress, though in the opinion of Allan this is more because of the confusion it sows than actual provisions. The Act prohibits use of property nationalised by Castro but, as Allan points out, the Polo Cientifico was empty wasteland when the revolutionaries seized power.

Despite these obstacles, the positive currently seems to outweigh the negative and biotech, together with tourism, is an important potential trump card for the Castro regime in its attempt to hold the economy together. This latter-day industrial miracle shows that even so widely accepted a rule as the economic superiority of capitalism must sometimes admit exceptions.

Yet for the regime to survive, some of the fruits of the biotech industry's success will have to be spread to the pockets of ordinary Cubans and on to the bare shelves of the Farmacia Sarra.

Cuba's Organic Revolution[6]

By Hugh Warwick
The Ecologist, December 1999

The Cuban revolution of 1959, which brought Fidel Castro to power, is considered to be the seminal moment in the modern history of the island. But the revolution begun in 1989, with the collapse of the Soviet bloc, is an equally significant, if much quieter, event.

During the early 1960s, as the US tried unsuccessfully to crush the new, revolutionary spirit of Cuba with the most far-reaching trade embargo in history, Castro's Cuba had to forge powerful links with the Soviet bloc in order to survive. And for some 30 years, the support Cuba received from the USSR helped to create the most well-"developed" island in the Caribbean. By 1989, Cuba ranked eleventh in the world in the Overseas Development Council's Physical Quality of Life Index (which includes infant mortality, literacy and life expectancy), while the USA ranked fifteenth.

The help Cuba received came in many forms—the Soviets bought Cuban sugar, for example, at over five times the market rate, and discounted oil was bought and then re-exported. For 30 years, from 1959 to 1989, 85 per cent of Cuba's trade was with the Soviet bloc.

The Soviet Collapse

But in 1989, the Soviet system began to unravel. Imports dropped overall by 75 per cent and oil imports by 53 per cent. Known officially by the Castro regime as the "Special Period in Time of Peace," this moment in Cuba's history saw it slide close to the edge of collapse, as all aspects of life were affected by the crumbling of its international market.

The most significant impact was on food. Some 57 per cent of Cuba's calorific intake was imported, and it was estimated that the population relied on other countries for over 80 per cent of all their protein and fats. The Soviet collapse also led directly to an 80 per cent reduction in fertilizer and pesticide imports. Prior to 1989, most of Cuba's intensive agriculture was dependent on these imports—their disappearance was thus a disaster for its agricultural system.

6. Article by Hugh Warwick, Edward Metcalf from *The Ecologist* December 1999. Copyright © *The Ecologist. www.theecologist.org.*

America's Grip Tightens

This was exacerbated by the implementation in 1992 of the USA's punitive "Cuba Democracy Act," which tightened its existing trade embargo, and further in 1996 with the signing of the satirically titled "Cuba Liberty and Democratic Solidarity Act"(the Helms-Burton Act). On top of an embargo that prevents the sale by any American or American-friendly industries of food or medicine to Cuba, upon pain of sanctions or legal action, the Helms-Burton Act is a deliberate attempt to stifle the re-growth of the Cuban economy by deterring foreign investment. US Senator Jesse Helms, one of the creators of the Act, is remarkably honest about its overall aim—the replacement of Castro's government by one more favoured by the US. "Let this be the year Cubans say farewell to Fidel," he said as the Act was passed in the Senate. "I don't care whether Fidel leaves vertically or horizontally, but he's leaving."

For a less resourceful and determined nation than Cuba, such action by the world's only superpower could have spelled disaster. But rather than roll over and die, Cuba began to foment a new revolution. The nation responded to the crisis with a restructuring of agriculture. It began a transformation from conventional, high-input, mono-crop intensive agriculture, to smaller organic and semi-organic farms.

Urban Agriculture

As oil imports crashed, Cubans looked for ways to reduce their dependency on it. In agriculture, this meant reducing transportation, refrigeration and storage costs by relocating agricultural production closer to the cities. Havana has some 20 per cent of Cuba's population, and at 2.5 million people is the largest city in the Caribbean. Feeding its population was obviously a priority. Urban agriculture was one of the solutions.

Urban agriculture played an important role in feeding urban populations around the world up until the industrial revolution of the eighteenth century, when nearly all food began to be imported from the countryside. Fertile areas inside and surrounding cities were lost to development. But since the 1970s, there has been evidence of a global reversal of this trend. It is estimated that some 14 per cent of the world's food is now produced in urban areas.

Prior to 1989, though, urban agriculture was virtually unheard of in Havana. Thanks to State provision, there was adequate food for all and little need to grow any privately. The post-Soviet crisis incited a massive popular response, initially in the form of gardening in and around the home by Havana's people. This was soon given a boost by the Cuban Ministry of Agriculture, which created an Urban Agriculture Department, with the aim of putting all of the city's open land into production.

By 1998, as a direct result of this policy, there were over 8,000 officially recognised "gardens" in Havana, cultivated by over 30,000 people and covering some 30 per cent of the available land. These farms and gardens have been organised into five main categories—though they are not comprehensive or exclusive, they do give an indication of the style of work.

Huertos Populares (popular gardens): Cultivated privately by urban residents in small areas throughout Havana.

Huertos Intensivos (intensive gardens): Cultivation in

> *Oxen are being bred to replace tractors; integrated pest-management is being developed to replace pesticides no longer available*

raised beds with a high ratio of compost to soil. Run either through a State institution or by private individuals.

Autoconsumos: These belong to and produce for workers, usually supplying cafeterias of particular workplaces.

Campesinos Particulares: Individual small farmers, largely working in the greenbelt around the city.

Empresas Estatales: Many of these State enterprises are run with increasing decentralisation, autonomy and degrees of profit-sharing with workers.

The most common of these are the popular gardens, which range in size from a few square metres to three hectares. The larger plots of land are often subdivided into smaller individual gardens. Usually the gardens are sited in vacant or abandoned plots in the same neighbourhood as, if not next-door to, the gardeners' household. The local government allocates land, which is handed over at no cost as long as it is used for cultivation.

Cuba Goes Organic

The crash in agricultural imports has also led to a general diversification within farming on the island. Oxen are being bred to replace tractors; integrated pest-management is being developed to replace pesticides no longer available; the promotion of better co-operation among farmers both within and between communities is promoted; and the rural exodus of previous decades is being reversed by encouraging people to remain in rural areas.

But the most significant aspect of the post-Soviet agricultural revolution has been the response to the removal of the chemical crutch, as imports of pesticides, herbicides, etc., collapsed. Fortunately for Cuba, it was well-placed to respond to this. While Cuba has only two per cent of the Caribbean region's population, for example, it has some 11 per cent of its scientists. And many of them, influenced by the ecology movement, had already developed a critique of Cuba's intensive agriculture system (to the displeasure of some in the establishment). They had also begun to develop alternatives to chemical dependency, which have since come into their own.

Almost uniquely, Cuba has begun to develop a biological pest-control programme based largely on parasitoids. While this in itself is innovative, the effort has been reinforced by the establishment of "Centres for the Reproduction of Entomophages and Entomopathogens" (CREEs). Over 200 of these have been set up to provide decentralised, small-scale, co-operative production of biocontrol agents, which farmers can use instead of pesticides to protect their crops.

As a result of such necessary innovations, the Cuban landscape, once dominated by chemical inputs, has been changing rapidly. And many of the new control methods are proving more efficient than pesticides. For example, the use of cut banana stems baited with honey to attract ants, which are then placed in sweet-potato fields, has led to the complete control of the sweet-potato borer—a major pest—by the predatory ants. There are 173 established "vermicompost" centres across Cuba, which produce 93,000 tons of natural compost a year. Crop rotations, green manuring, intercropping and soil conservation are all common today. Planners have also sought to encourage urbanites to move to the countryside, as labour needs for alternative agriculture are now a constraint on its growth (organic farming is generally more labour-intensive than chemical farming). Programmes are now aiming to create more attractive housing in the countryside, supplemented with services, and to encourage urban people to work on farms for periods of two weeks to two years.

Cuba Goes Renewable

By Edward Metcalf

While Americans have deprived themselves the luxury of legally imported Havana cigars, for Cubans, the U.S. embargo meant total trade reliance upon the Soviet bloc, and when that collapsed, a bold—albeit forced—move into some form of self-sufficiency.

Nowhere is the struggle to replace previously imported goods with domestic products more evident than in the area of energy consumption. From 1989 to 1992, when the Soviet Union was breaking up, oil imports from the USSR to Cuba plunged from 13 to 6 million tons per year. To cope with petroleum shortages the Cuban government turned to local renewable energy sources, not solely as an emergency measure, but as a permanent alteration in the country's energy dependency.

Over 200 small hydroelectric plants have been built, mostly in isolated mountainous regions, of which 180 are now functioning. Wind energy is also being utilised through the construction of approximately 5,700 windmills. Abundant sunshine makes Cuba a prime candidate for the development of a solar industry, and the government has established a Solar Institute in Santiago de Cuba that is looking at ways of bringing solar energy to the island. To date, there are around 350 solar heating systems operating. The priority at the moment is to install solar panels on the roofs of family doctor clinics and community centres in remote rural areas not already on the electricity grid.

In its search for alternative energy sources, Cuba has been highly successful in converting sugar cane bagasse (the pulpy residue left after extraction of juice from the cane) into electricity. Of Cuba's 160 sugar mills, 104 are powered entirely by their own bagasse. It is estimated that the utilisation of bagasse saves Cuba 700,000 tons of oil per year, while other biogas (methane from manure and waste material) operations represent the equivalent of 370,000 tons of oil per year. Together, almost 30 per cent of Cuba's energy supply now originates from biomass.

Shortage of oil not only requires energy innovation, but conservation too. Cuba's predicament has made her a world exemplar of environmentally sound transport policy: everyone in Cuba rides a bicycle—because they have to! It is not unusual for a Cuban to make a 50 km journey on a bike. The dominant make is a one-speed Chinese model affectionately known as the "Flying Pigeon." In recent years the government has imported 1 million such models from China and it is estimated there are 800,000 of them in Havana alone. Cuba will soon produce bicycles domestically—they are expected to be the principal form of local transportation well into the future. That reliance upon the bicycle is more coerced than voluntary makes the Cuban experience no less of an example to the congested cities of the world.

The embargo makes no special exception for medicine or medical equipment, imports of which (from countries outside the embargo) have dwindled since Cuba's economic crisis of the early 1990s. The response of the Cuban Ministry of Public Health has been to oversee the development of what it calls "natural and traditional" medicine. All medical students are now required to study alternative treatments relevant to their specialty (such as acupuncture and homeopathy); while practicing doctors and nurses are given intensive courses to update their knowledge. The result is that alternative medicine is now available in all medical facilities, as well as at special Centres for Holistic Medicine, lessening Cuba's reliance upon expensive foreign drugs.

Cuba in the 1990s provides a rare example of a poorer country seeking to provide for the basic needs of its people by embracing environmentally sustainable technologies.

III. Opposing Shores:
The U.S. and Cuba

As part of "people to people" relations, a soccer team from Lincoln, Nebraska, plays a Cuban team in Havana on August 16, 1999.

Editor's Introduction

The United States has been entangled in Cuban history for over a century, from its financing of the Cuban sugar harvest, to the intervention of Teddy Roosevelt's "Rough Riders" in the Cuban war of independence from Spain, to the recent conflicts over Elián González. When Castro overthrew General Batista in 1959, the U.S. State Department lent its support to the new government and—thanks to a *New York Times* reporter who trekked to the Sierra Maestra mountains—Castro became an international celebrity. By 1962, however, after Castro had expropriated American property, forged alliances with the Soviet Union, and pledged to spread revolution throughout Latin America, relations with the U.S. had soured. At that time, President Kennedy responded with a full trade embargo on Cuba that has been in place ever since. When the cold war ended, many imagined that there would be a rapprochement between these former enemies, but during the 1990s the U.S. Congress passed two laws that strengthened the trade embargo, and official relations again took a turn for the worse.

The first article in Section III presents opposing viewpoints about trading with communists, written by two U.S. Congressmen after the House of Representatives voted to grant China—like Cuba a communist country with a history of human rights abuses—"permanent normal trade relations" (PNTR). Tom DeLay, a Texas Republican, voted in favor of PNTR with China but supports the full trade embargo against Cuba. While China has attempted to foster democratic principles, DeLay argues, Castro has steadfastly refused to enact political or economic reforms. Therefore, lifting the trade embargo will only help to strengthen Castro's dictatorial regime. James P. McGovern, a Massachusetts Democrat, voted against PNTR for China but has lobbied for the end to the trade embargo on Cuba. McGovern argues that the embargo has failed, and that its continuance only solidifies Castro's position. McGovern suggests that cautious engagement is the best avenue to democratic change, whether it be in Cuba or in China.

In the next article, Stuart Taylor, Jr. posits that Castro is "a ruthless communist dictator who keeps Cubans poor to avoid giving them a taste of freedom," and then argues that, in spite of this fact, allowing Americans to travel and invest in Cuba is the best way to counter Castro's propaganda and produce a ground swell of change. Writing from different ideological quarters in *The Nation*, Wayne S. Smith echoes Taylor in arguing that U.S. policies regarding Cuba are wrongheaded. Smith focuses on Section 109 of the Helms-Burton Act, which provides funding for Cuban-American organizations that are working to bring an end to Castro's government. Smith reports that some of this funding is being illegally channeled to groups within Cuba, thereby giving Castro an excuse to crack down on the political opposition. He contends that inflammatory anti-Castro rhetoric and U.S.-sponsored attempts to subvert Castro do nothing to strengthen civil society in Cuba while making more difficult the work of legitimate opposition groups.

Alexis Simendinger's article in the *National Journal* was written as the 2000 U.S. presidential election approached. Simendinger reports that, while the leading candidates expressed tough views on the embargo out of a need to court the Cuban-American vote in Florida (which, in fact, proved to be a pivotal state in last year's election), the prevailing political winds are beginning to blow in Cuba's direction. An unlikely coalition of interest groups, business leaders, and Midwestern farmers has begun to lobby for changes in the U.S.-Cuban policy, forming the most potent challenge to the status quo in years. (After three years of lobbying, in July of 2000 Congress lifted restrictions on selling food and medicine to Cuba, making the first substantial change to the embargo since 1962. Nevertheless, legislators imposed stiff—many say impossible—conditions, including insisting on non-U.S. financing of any sales.)

Mark Fineman reports on another point of conflict between the U.S. and Cuba: immigration policy. The United States allows any Cuban who reaches American shores to apply for residency status, although Cubans picked up at sea are sent home. The Cuban government regards this "wet foot/dry foot" policy as contradictory and unworkable: Although meant to discourage Cubans from taking the risky trip by sea, it has in fact led to drastic increases in the numbers of Cubans illegally smuggled to the U.S.

The final articles in this section discuss Miami's Cuban-American population. Jordan Levin retells the history of the "Miami resolution," a now-defunct policy adopted by the Miami-Dade County Commission in 1996 that made it illegal for any county office to conduct business with companies or individuals who themselves do business with Cuba. Max J. Castro describes Miami in the wake of the Elián González controversy as a city divided along racial, generational, and class lines; while once the Cuban-American community spoke in one voice, dissenting opinions are beginning to emerge.

Trading with Communists: Two Dictatorships, Two U.S. Policies[1]

BY TOM DELAY AND JAMES P. MCGOVERN
WASHINGTON POST, JUNE 18, 2000

Reward Progress, Punish Dictators

BY TOM DELAY

The struggle against communist oppression did not conclude with the fall of the Berlin Wall. In fact, this struggle to liberate men and women from the evil of totalitarianism continues with great urgency.

In China, 1.2 billion souls live without the most basic of human rights. In Cuba, 11 million men, women and children suffer under Fidel Castro's brand of Marxism. The challenge posed by these dreadful circumstances mirrors the responsibility America shouldered during our cold war with the Soviet Union: We must implement a comprehensive policy that enhances our security by defending and exporting our values.

We must smash the last few remnants of the Iron Curtain by recognizing the particular circumstances present in the remaining repressive states and applying a specific approach to each.

China and Cuba offer the perfect example of how, if we are to transform communist states, we must use different tactics for different countries. America should work to encourage states such as China that are already undertaking changes that promise to foster democratic principles; and we should quarantine regimes that steadfastly refuse to take even incremental steps toward political and economic reform, such as Cuba.

We have good reason to expect that increased trade with China through the permanent normal trade relations (PNTR) recently approved by the House will accelerate the growth of democratic impulses in that country. China's command economy has greatly evolved since the 1970s. At that time, the state and the state alone

---

1. Article by Tom DeLay and James P. McGovern from the *Washington Post* June 18, 2000. Copyright © *Washington Post*. Reprinted with permission.

set prices, planned economic goals, and allocated resources. China had no real private enterprise or foreign ventures. It imported only those goods that could not be made in China.

Today, China is changing rapidly. Free-market forces increasingly drive economic decisions. Beijing has eased restrictions on business enterprises, and loosened the rules governing where and how international firms can operate. As a result, the private sector is growing. Entrepreneurs, once condemned as "counterrevolutionaries," are now the instruments of reform. It is easier for private firms to secure import and export rights, obtain funding, and form joint ventures.

> *By "engaging" Cuba, America would only provide Castro with more funds for his policies of repression.*

Without a doubt, China remains a serious threat to peace and stability. It is still ruled by despots, and trade in the absence of a determined U.S. effort to undermine the communists in Beijing will make little difference.

But all the dramatic shifts now taking place do suggest that a middle class is emerging in China, and I believe that this middle class will eventually demand broad acceptance of democratic values.

Unfortunately, the prospects for even a slow transition to a market democracy through trade are much dimmer in Cuba. Castro has made it clear that he has no free-market or democratic impulses. Cuba strictly limits foreign investment. Cuban contracts have no integrity. Foreign firms operating there must hire employees from the government bureaucracy.

In short, Castro's dogmatic enforcement of pure communist ideology would make trade with Cuba a source of economic support for a despicable system, not a tool for growing a freedom-loving middle class. By "engaging" Cuba, America would only provide Castro with more funds for his policies of repression.

In addition to these fundamental contrasts in their domestic economic structures, China and Cuba maintain other dramatic differences, not the least of which are size and location. The embargo against Cuba—a small island nation in our hemisphere with a population that equals about 4 percent of our own—has, in fact, largely contained an aggressive Marxist who is openly committed to sparking revolution throughout Central and South America.

Applying the same approach to China—a country on the other side of the globe, occupying an enormous portion of an entire continent, and with a population well over 400 percent larger than that of the United States—makes little sense. Withholding PNTR from China, for example, would only limit our ability to reach out to the Chinese entrepreneurs who are so critical to the advancement of free markets and human rights.

Defending and exporting democratic virtues is the proper goal of U.S. foreign policy. Trade represents a means of pursuing this objective, and it is a means that must only be employed when greater commerce will serve to undermine tyranny and promote democratic ideals.

We can never forget that the cause of freedom must be the cause that guides our nation's actions in the world, and we need only cast a brief gaze into the past to find countless lessons about freedom's enormous value and precious nature.

I had such a lesson as a young boy. It is not, to be sure, the kind of lesson that in any way compares to the searing experiences endured by the thousands and thousands of immigrants who seek refuge in America each year. Nonetheless, it is enough of a lesson to merit mention during a discussion about how we can best promote democracy in China, Cuba and around the world.

My dad drilled oil wells in Venezuela. Our family lived there for several years and witnessed three revolutions. Occasionally, we traveled back and forth to Texas, and in those days, Cuba was the refueling stop. I will never forget one short stay on Castro's island. Escorted between rows of soldiers with barking guard dogs, my mother, brother, sister and I were held in a small detention room for hours without cause or explanation. Although she did her best to conceal her fear, I sensed that my mother was not at all certain that we would ever get back on the plane.

We were released later that same day and able to depart without further incident, but by then I had learned an absolutely unforgettable lesson about freedom. I learned that freedom is not an unalterable condition. I learned that freedom, though the greatest gift after life, could be taken away in an instant.

When companies operate in China, they are working in a way that I believe will ultimately deliver freedom to the Chinese people. When such companies operate in Cuba, they strengthen a communist dictatorship dedicated to the destruction of that same freedom. The difference is decisive, and an effective and principled U.S. foreign policy must recognize and incorporate this distinction as we labor to bring these two states into the family of democratic nations.

Be Consistent, or We Lose Leverage

By James P. McGovern

I recently voted against granting permanent normal trade relations (PNTR) to China. At the same time, I have asked President Clinton to travel to Cuba and to lift the current U.S. economic embargo against the island.

Is there a contradiction in my positions? No.

I believe that we should have normal trade relations with both China and Cuba. However, the debates over PNTR for China and whether to lift sanctions against Cuba differ greatly. Granting PNTR to China is about relinquishing some of our leverage, while establishing normal trade with Cuba is about gaining leverage where we currently have none.

It's the "P" in PNTR that bothers me. PNTR is not about the wisdom of engaging China; we've been doing that for decades and should keep doing so. It's about expanding the normal trade relations that China has had with the United States since 1980. Normal trade will continue even if PNTR is not approved, because we each want access to the other's markets.

Conversely, U.S. policy with Cuba has long been about isolating the island by maintaining and even strengthening the economic sanctions. This policy has been in place for more than four decades—and it has been an embarrassing failure.

Until now, Congress has voted annually on normal trade with China. I have consistently supported it. But I ultimately voted against PNTR because I am concerned about jobs in America and human rights in China. I wanted to continue to be able to put these issues squarely on the table each year.

I believe that while the U.S.-China deal will be very good for this country's new, high-tech industries, it will hurt—if not destroy—some of the more traditional industries that remain an important part of our economy. I represent a district that has a mixture of both kinds of industry. I am not a protectionist, but I do believe we have an obligation to answer the question one of my constituents, a 54-year-old textile worker in Fall River, put to me: "Do they really expect me to be a computer programmer if my shop closes?"

I want our relationship with China to continue to grow. But I'm also committed to working for a domestic and global economy that promotes the spread of wealth and opportunity to all working families. I believe in engagement with a heart.

Presidents and members of Congress often talk about "human rights" and "global responsibility." But rarely does that talk translate into concrete action—especially where trade agreements are concerned.

Archibald MacLeish said, "We are deluged with facts but we have lost or are losing our ability to feel them." Maybe in this age of instant news we are so overwhelmed with reports of human rights violations that we have lost our outrage. I feel that my government, which acknowledges that human rights in China have deteriorated dramatically in the past two years, could have negotiated a better agreement—one that would have made clear that fundamental rights are a priority and a necessary part of responsible commerce.

Those rights are equally important for Cuba, which is why our presence there is so needed.

I have visited Cuba several times—first as a college student in 1979, and most recently this April.

The Cuban tourist industry is burgeoning. European and Canadian businessmen and women are everywhere. Small, family-owned restaurants are popping up. A stronger Catholic Church is creating space not just for religious freedom but for nongovernmental community organizing and development as well. The U.S. dollar is a recognized currency on the island. In private, many

---

Fidel Castro has been able to use our embargo as an excuse to crack down on human rights and explain away every failure of his regime. By lifting the embargo, we lift the excuse.

Cubans—including some representatives of the government—talk of ways to move toward a more open society while, at the same time, protecting the positive gains of the Cuban revolution in health care, education and early childhood development.

But there are very serious human rights violations in Cuba as well. People are imprisoned for dissent; according to human rights activists, there are about 400 political prisoners. Some dissidents with whom I have met during my visits to Havana have been arrested and jailed shortly after my departure. They are among the strongest advocates for a change in U.S. policy. They know that it is much harder for their government to stifle their voices when the world is watching. I know this, too, because of one of the most remarkable events I have ever witnessed—Pope John Paul II's visit to Cuba in 1998. I stood in the Plaza de la Revolucion in Havana with hundreds of thousands of Cubans as the Holy Father delivered his message uncensored. A young Cuban professor standing next to me marveled at "the political space being created." He added, "There will be no turning back."

I will continue to publicly condemn human rights abuses in Cuba, as I have condemned them in China, and to call for freedom of speech, freedom of assembly and freedom of the press in both countries. But we should remember that Fidel Castro has been able to use our embargo as an excuse to crack down on human rights and explain away every failure of his regime. By lifting the embargo, we lift the excuse.

It makes no sense to keep our policy in a perpetual holding pattern, waiting for the Cuban leader to die. We need to end our immoral sanctions on food and medicine, and we should lift the trade embargo entirely. We should put fax machines and laptops into the hands of Cubans and give them access to the outside world. Let's flood Cuba with ideas, products and people.

Lifting the embargo would also benefit the United States. Normalizing relations would open a new market for American agriculture, pharmaceuticals, tourism and other industries. And unlike China, Cuba's most important industries—tourism, cigars and mining—pose no significant threat to American jobs.

During the recent House debate on PNTR, supporters spoke about the significant impact an expanded U.S. presence would have in China, a communist country of a billion people half a world away with a traditional antipathy toward the West and a dominant role in the Asian marketplace. Arguably, our presence in Cuba—a communist nation of 11 million, 90 miles off the Florida coast, with a long history of contact with the United States—should make an even greater difference.

Comparing our current policies on China and Cuba goes beyond comparing apples and oranges. It's more like apples and Oldsmobiles. The troubling contradiction is on the part of those who support economic ties with China and continued isolation of Cuba. In the end, I believe we must remain engaged with both countries, through normal trade relations and an unambiguous policy that supports basic human freedoms.

How the Embargo Hurts Cubans and Helps Castro[1]

By Stuart Taylor, Jr.
National Journal, May 13, 2000

In the early 1960s, the CIA plotted to poison Fidel Castro's cigars, to send Mafia hit men after him, and to make his beard fall out by dusting his shoes with a depilatory. These were not good ideas. Now the centerpiece of U.S. policy is the rigid, unilateral economic embargo and travel ban codified by the 1996 Helms-Burton Act. This is not a good idea, either. Nor are the Helms-Burton penalties on foreign companies that invest in properties expropriated by Castro 40 years ago.

At least the CIA targeted the murderous dictator himself. The embargo targets the island's entire population of 11 million, in an effort to strangle the Castro regime. This made sense when the United States first imposed the embargo in the early 1960s, as Castro was becoming a Soviet ally bent on exporting revolution during the most dangerous phase of the cold war. But the embargo has proven so counterproductive since the collapse of the Soviet Union in 1991 as to be almost irrational.

By aggravating the dire poverty in which most Cubans live, the embargo enables the 73-year-old Castro to maintain a siege mentality and blame Yankee imperialists for the disastrous state into which his communist regime has plunged the Cuban economy. No other nation now supports the embargo, which once had the backing of the Organization of American States and others. Virtually every other nation condemns Helms-Burton. These policies bar U.S. businesses from competing for toeholds in a Cuban market that will someday become lucrative. They have manifestly failed to drive Castro from power, to ease his repressive rule, or to lay any groundwork for a peaceful transition to freedom and democracy.

To the contrary, the embargo and Helms-Burton have strengthened Castro in both Cuban and world opinion. Although Castro clamors for an end to it, "I think he loves the embargo," says one high-level former National Security Council official. "It keeps him in power."

Now, thanks to the spotlight on Elián González, more Americans are starting to notice the stupidity of our Cuba policies. To be sure, the embargo seems unassailable in this election year, sustained as it is by the passionate support of the potent Cuban-American lobby, which no President, or would-be President, wants to cross. But that lobby's strength has ebbed. Most Americans disapprove of the tactics of many of the Cuban exiles who have fought to block Elián's father from taking him back to Cuba. This development may broaden opposition to the embargo. Opposition had already been growing among export-seeking farmers; business groups, including

The embargo and Helms-Burton have strengthened Castro in both Cuban and world opinion.

the U.S. Chamber of Commerce; religious leaders, including Pope John Paul II; human rights groups; foreign policy experts across the political spectrum; and some conservative Republicans, as well as liberal Democrats.

Claims that the policy needs more time to "force [Castro] to face the consequences of his misrule [and] reflect on Cuba's desperate need for change," which is how the Cuban-American National Foundation puts it, are getting old. It has been four decades since the embargo's inception, nine years since the end of the billions of dollars in Soviet subsidies that had previously blunted its impact, and five years since Senate Foreign Relations Committee Chairman Jesse Helms, R-N.C., said that the then-pending Helms-Burton bill would give Castro "a final push." A growing minority of Cuban-Americans says it's time to try a different approach, although many won't say so publicly for fear (one told me) of ostracism, or worse.

This is not to say that the next President will, or even should, try to end the embargo in one fell swoop. That would require getting Congress to repeal Helms-Burton. As a political matter, furious opposition from the Cuban-American lobby and its allies, notably Helms, would probably doom any such effort. As a policy matter, a case can be made for relaxing the embargo by increments, and imposing conditions on private U.S. trade or investment, to maximize pressure on the Cuban regime to ease its stifling economic controls and sometimes brutal repression of dissidents.

And any President who wants to lead the nation toward constructive engagement with Cuba will run into a buzz saw if he ignores political realities, suggests Richard A. Nuccio, who was once special adviser to President Clinton on Cuba. One such reality is Castro's

habit of spitting in the face of the United States at politically sensi-
tive moments, as in early 1996, when he sent Helms-Burton sail-
ing through Congress by cracking down on dissidents and having
Cuban fighters shoot down two small civilian planes, killing four
Cuban-Americans who had planned to fly over Havana. President
Clinton signed the bill into law because it was politically expedi-
ent, says then-adviser Nuccio, even though Helms-Burton would
abort the Administration's nascent moves to engage Castro's
regime and Nuccio himself had lobbied against it.

---

*If Castro allows tourism, trade, and invest-
ment to bring in a lot of money, the
inevitable infusion of people, products, and
ideas will ... perhaps crack the thinning
ice under his regime.*

Politics aside, the case for relaxing the embargo does not depend
upon whether one sees Castro as a flawed, but well-meaning,
champion of the common people, or (as I do) a ruthless communist
dictator who keeps Cubans poor to avoid giving them a taste of
freedom.

Let's stipulate that Castro's totalitarian regime is every bit as
bad as Helms and the most anti-Castro Cuban exiles believe; that
it is only sustained by fear and a network of security forces and
informants reminiscent of George Orwell's novel *1984*; that most
Cubans would secretly love to be rid of Castro; that he seeks foreign trade, investment, and tourists not to meet the needs of the
Cuban people or to foster reforms but, as Helms has said, to get
"hard currency to keep his faltering Marxist-Leninist economy
afloat" and to "pay for the ruthless and cruel apparatus that keeps
him in power"; that the regime keeps for itself 95 percent of the
payments it demands from foreign companies in lieu of wages for
Cuban workers; that, unlike China, communist Cuba is determined to minimize any movement toward a free-market economy;
that Castro will always find ways to blame the United States for
Cuba's problems; and that any retreat from the embargo would
prompt the tyrant to crow that he had forced the United States to
recognize the legitimacy and permanence of his regime.

Let him crow. He would be losing his only excuse for Cuba's
grinding poverty and political repression. If most Cubans are
already as disaffected as Helms suggests, then surely they won't be
fooled by more Castro propaganda. Meanwhile, if Castro allows
tourism, trade, and investment to bring in a lot of money, the inev-

itable infusion of people, products, and ideas will feed popular pressure for change and perhaps crack the thinning ice under his regime. Conversely, if Castro is determined to crush any private entrepreneurial activity, then he won't take in much foreign exchange.

There can be no guarantee that relaxing the embargo will succeed in changing Cuba for the better. But if done with care, such a move can hardly make things worse. (Nuccio does caution that sudden U.S. abolition of the embargo can make things worse in the short run by so gravely threatening the communist regime's grip on power as to provoke a new wave of repression, and perhaps a new wave of refugees.)

The harder question is how much to ease the embargo and under what conditions. Even Helms has indicated he would ease up if Cuba's government would institute such revolutionary changes as allowing free and fair elections. But that's not going to happen while Castro is in charge. And the constructive steps taken by the Clinton Administration since Helms-Burton, such as slightly easing restrictions on travel to Cuba and allowing Cuban-Americans and others to send more dollars to relatives and friends there, have been tiny.

The best opportunity for a larger step toward engaging Cuba may be presented by a combination of farm-lobby clout and the humanitarian appeal of sending impoverished Cubans food and medicine. Last August, the Senate voted by a surprising 70-28 majority to add to an appropriations bill language sponsored by Sen. John Ashcroft, R-Mo., to end unilateral U.S. embargoes on exports of farm products and pharmaceuticals to Cuba and some other nations. Although the three Cuban-American House members are likely to block any similar Senate-passed measure this year, the next President will have some potent allies if he chooses to exercise the kind of leadership that Clinton has eschewed.

If Richard Nixon could go to China, perhaps George W. Bush or Al Gore can find a way to sell food and medicine to Cuba. That would be a good start.

Washington's Costly Cuba Policy[2]

By Wayne S. Smith
The Nation, July 3, 2000

The case of little Elián González brought vividly into focus just how contradictory and counterproductive US policy toward Cuba really is. On the one hand, the United States does not want any more floods of undocumented Cubans arriving by small boat—as during the rafter crisis of 1994. So much does it not want them that under a US/Cuban agreement signed in 1995, the Coast Guard picks up on the high seas all those it can apprehend and sends them right back to Cuba. Had Elián, his mother and the others in their boat been picked up by the Coast Guard, they would have been returned to the island immediately. But how then can our embargo and other economic sanctions make any sense? Are they not designed to increase economic distress on the island, thus exacerbating the very conditions that cause Cubans to take to the boats and head for Florida? And is that not exactly what we do not want?

Even before the Elián case, US policy toward Cuba verged on incoherence, with a near total disconnect between what that policy is and what the Clinton Administration says it is. On the one hand, the President has consistently supported legislation to tighten the embargo drastically, but on the other, he would have us believe that his policy has been aimed at improving relations. Asked at a press conference in Hong Kong two years ago why we trade with China but not with Cuba, Clinton responded that he had tried everything possible "to engage Cuba in a way that would develop the kind of reciprocal movement that we see [in the case of] China." He even described the Cuban Democracy Act of 1992 (CDA) as having been a "clear road map" for improving relations and developing that kind of reciprocal relationship. But, he suggested, the Cubans just wouldn't cooperate.

Really? Strange, then, that when Clinton announced his support for the CDA back on April 23, 1992 (as he came out of a dinner with right-wing Cuban exiles with a check for $250,000 in his hand), he said it would give us the opportunity to "put the hammer down on Fidel Castro and Cuba." Then-Congressman (now US Senator) Robert Torricelli, a New Jersey Democrat who was the

CDA's principal sponsor, was even more direct. In a debate with me on CNN's *Crossfire* in December 1992, he said the CDA would bring about the end of the Castro regime "within months." And shortly thereafter, in a panel discussion at Georgetown University, he said the CDA was designed "to wreak havoc in Cuba" and that "Castro must be brought to his knees."

And then, of course, came the Helms-Burton Act in 1996, the most draconian piece of legislation ever implemented against Cuba, which effectively blocks any kind of normalization with the island. In fact, the act prohibits engagement with any Cuban government until Castro is gone and until a whole series of other conditions have been met, such as the return of all nationalized property. Helms-Burton is now the legal basis for US policy toward Cuba, and Senator Jesse Helms was not reluctant back in 1996 to say that its purpose was to get rid of the Castro regime. "Whether Castro leaves Cuba in a vertical or horizontal position is up to him and the Cuban people, but he must and will leave Cuba," Senator Helms vowed.

The Cubans, not surprisingly, took (and take) Helms-Burton as a statement of hostile intentions.

The Administration frequently says that it wishes to see a "peaceful transitional process" in Cuba. And yet, if the objective is to get rid of Castro, then one cannot expect the process to be peaceful, for the hard fact is that Castro will not simply resign or fade away because the United States wants him to; rather, if need be, he would fight, and many Cubans would fight with him. Thus, if one aims to remove the Castro government, then one must be ready for a bloody civil war—a war that would result in tens of thousands, perhaps hundreds of thousands, of Cuban refugees on our shores. Is that what the Administration wants? Is that even what Senator Helms wants?

The Cubans, not surprisingly, took (and take) Helms-Burton as a statement of hostile intentions. President Clinton's continued insistence (as, for example, in a statement on November 5, 1999) that he is still "bending over backwards to try to reach out" to the Cubans, but being rebuffed at every turn, is thus truly puzzling. Can he possibly believe that? True, over the past two years the President has been pursuing what he calls his "people to people" program. To expand contacts with the Cuban people, he has relaxed travel controls, improved communications and expanded cultural and sports exchanges. These innovations are in fact helpful. But "people to people" is not and cannot be taken as an effort to improve relations with Cuba as long as the Administration, seeming to echo Senator Helms, emphasizes that its purpose is to undermine the Castro government or, as the President put it on January 5, 1999, to help the Cuban people "in their struggle against [the existing] system."

USAID Grantees Under Section 109 (As of September 1999)	
The Institute for Democracy in Cuba	$1,000,000
Center for a Free Cuba	900,000
International Republican Institute	725,000
US-Cuba Business Council	567,000
Cuba On-Line	300,000
Florida International University	292,000
Cuba Free Press	280,000
Freedom House	275,000
Cuban Dissidence Task Force	250,000
Pan-American Development Foundation	237,000
National Policy Association	225,000
American Center for International Labor Solidarity	195,000
Partners of the Americas	172,000
International Fund for Election Systems	136,000
University of Florida Measuring Public Opinion	110,000
Rutgers University Planning for Change	99,000
Cuba Net	98,000
Sabre Foundation	85,000
TOTAL	$5,946,000

Note: The list of organizations receiving funding during the present fiscal year was not available of this writing.

Nor is it simply a matter of the rhetoric or of how the objective is stated. On the contrary, one of the Administration's key policy initiatives has to do with funding and channeling support to independent groups in Cuba (see chart). As this support is provided under Section 109 of the Helms-Burton Act, it is taken by the Cuban government as an open US declaration of intent to fund subversion. The Cubans have reacted by cracking down on dissidents and promulgating new measures against those who "cooperate with the enemy." This may be an overreaction on their part, for overthrowing the Castro government is probably not the Administration's real intention. The Cubans can hardly be blamed for believing that it is, however, given the President's own unfortunate words, and given rhetoric such as that used at a press conference on April 20, 1998, by Marc Thiessen, Senator Helms's assistant. In discussing assistance for groups inside Cuba, he stated flatly that "the debate on Cuba has to be about ways to subvert the Cuban government."

As of the end of the last fiscal year, in September 1999, the US Agency for International Development, which administers the funding provision of the Helms-Burton Act, had provided some $6 million in grants to some eighteen organizations. An additional $3 million-plus was appropriated for the current fiscal year. USAID insists that as a matter of policy all grantees are forbidden from using US government funding to provide cash assistance to groups

---

One can imagine the outraged reaction of the US government were some organization in Cuba publicly congratulating itself on the amounts of material assistance it had been able to channel to antigovernment groups in the United States!

---

or individuals within Cuba. Nonetheless, in some cases cash assistance reportedly is being provided. Those organizations providing it, however, can always argue that it does not come from funds provided by the government, and no one could prove otherwise, since they usually do get funds from other groups and money is fungible.

Most of the largesse has gone to the usual gaggle of exile groups— groups that for years have been advocating the ouster of the Castro government. The largest recipient so far is the Institute for Democracy in Cuba, a Miami-based organization comprising nine separate exile groups, including the Support Group for Dissidence, the Association of Former Prisoners and Cuban Political Combatants, the Cuban Alliance and the International Republican Institute. As of September 1999, the Institute for Democracy had received $1 million from USAID and, according to its own brochure, had "been extremely successful in channeling substantial material assistance to activists in Cuba." One can imagine the outraged reaction of the US government were some organization in Cuba publicly congratulating itself on the amounts of material assistance it had been able to channel to antigovernment groups in the United States!

The next largest recipient is the Center for a Free Cuba, run by exile activist Frank Calzon, who is outspokenly opposed to any rapprochement with the Castro government and who has bitterly attacked the Clinton Administration for its position that Elián González should return to Cuba to live with his father if that is his father's wish. As of September 1999, USAID had given Calzon $900,000, and it presumably will provide additional funds during this fiscal year.

While the underlying purpose of the grants may be undermining the Cuban government, most of them could better be described as boondoggles in quest of pie-in-the-sky: everything from drawing up elections plans that will never be used to blueprints for a new Cuban economy. For example, according to USAID one grant of nearly $100,000 is to "support planning for future assistance to a Cuban transition government and, eventually, to a democratically elected government in Cuba." Few serious analysts believe there will be a transition government until Castro dies or otherwise passes from the scene. And even then, the new government will almost certainly come from within the present leadership and not be likely to welcome advice from any US organization funded under Section 109. Thus, the chances that any "planning" under this grant will ever be put to use are slim to nonexistent.

Still, throwing the taxpayers' money away on unworkable projects is nothing new when it comes to Cuba. Take the case of TV Martí. The US government has spent some $100 million so far to keep it transmitting to Cuba, even though it is never seen or heard. Castro has easily jammed it since its first broadcast in 1990, as communications experts predicted he would.

Some recipients argue that the grants can help strengthen civil society in Cuba. In fact, however, they make more difficult the work of Cuban religious groups, legitimate human rights activists and other independent organizations—the very groups that will form the core of a nascent civil society. As the Rev. Odén Marichal, the president of the Cuban Council of Churches, put it to me during a conversation last November: "We want to see expanded freedom of religion and various other adjustments in our society. But we will work with the government and within our own laws to bring that about. Your government's references to supporting independent organizations in Cuba in efforts against the existing system here almost seem designed to suggest that those independent organizations represent a potential fifth column. As such, they are misleading, unhelpful and irresponsible. None of us, I can assure you, would ever accept any of these Section 109 funds."

Elizardo Sanchez, Cuba's leading human rights activist and the head of the Commission for Human Rights and National Reconciliation, put it in even stronger terms. In a conversation with me in early 1999, Sanchez said: "Your government's rhetoric is thoughtless and harmful. It can be used to misrepresent any independent organization in Cuba as being in league with the CIA. Because we value our nationalist credentials and are determined to work strictly within the law in our efforts to bring about reforms, our organization would not even consider accepting support under Section 109. That Section, and in fact the whole Helms-Burton Act, is harmful to the cause of a more open society in Cuba."

Right! The Administration could accomplish far more by moving to rescind Helms-Burton and reorienting its policy generally toward cautious engagement even with Castro still in power. Indeed, if it wishes to encourage a peaceful transitional process, that is its only option. One thing is certain: It could not accomplish less than with what has been its approach to date.

Perhaps . . . just perhaps . . . wiser heads are beginning to prevail. As of this writing, the State Department is reviewing the "effectiveness" of the Section 109 grants. If it's a serious review and not a whitewash, this could prove to be step in the right direction.

Cuba Countdown[3]

By Alexis Simendinger
National Journal, September 18, 1999

Charles M. Custin, the president of Tech Products Inc., a Miami building products company, wrote a $1,000 check last June to attend a George W. Bush fund-raiser in Fort Lauderdale because he thought it couldn't hurt. "My hope is that Bush is going to be a very pro-business President," he said. Asked to elaborate, the 48-year-old, Cuban-born businessman explained that he's looking to back politicians who urge an end to the U.S. trade embargo with Cuba. "Any President who is truly pro-business and behind our capitalistic system has got to look at that and say, 'Hey, I'm keeping American businessmen from a huge market,'" Custin said. "There are millions of dollars of trade that will be done in my products."

Custin, who fled Cuba at the age of 9 in 1960 and who once favored U.S. sanctions against the Cuban government, began to reverse course following a 1992 trip to the island with a group of architects. "After a week there, I came back an avid supporter of lifting the embargo and bringing American capitalism to Cuba. I think that's what would bring down the political walls there, just like it did in Europe."

Custin has been active with a group, the Cuban Committee for Democracy, that urges an easing of U.S. policy, and he traveled to Washington this summer to try—unsuccessfully—to persuade Rep. Ileana Ros-Lehtinen, R-Fla., who is passionately anti-Castro, to consider the value of trade to Cuba as a means of encouraging the end of Fidel Castro and communism.

"It's a very frustrating issue, because for the U.S. government it's not a big enough place. It's no different than China, but China's such a huge market that American business has been able to influence policy," Custin said. "But on Cuba, there's such a strong lobby to the far right to keep the rigid sanctions."

There was a time when Custin believed that President Clinton might be the first chief executive to take a dramatically different tack when it came to Castro and Cuba. But after seven years of watching the President vacillate between signing and ducking embargo-tightening legislation, the Miami businessman is gloomy.

---

3. Copyright © 2000 by National Journal Group Inc. All rights reserved. Reprinted with permission.

"My optimism right now is very low," Custin said. "The only hope is that the [next] President comes in and says, 'Listen, the laws of the U.S. government are to help the overall country, not a small group that has a different agenda.'"

Judging from the campaign speechifying of Bush, Vice President Al Gore, and former New Jersey Democratic Sen. Bill Bradley, Custin's hopes may be premature. All of the leading candidates have been maneuvering carefully on foreign policy issues as they cast their eyes toward the early primaries and the coveted electoral votes of Florida and New Jersey, where the Cuban-American population is heavily concentrated. For 2000, the Hispanic vote everywhere is highly prized.

Presidential candidates have long respected the voting strength and deep pockets of the anti-Castro exile community.

"The cold war is a decade behind us, but politicians still want to look tough and realistic, and they don't want to look like they're making concessions to or being naive vis-à-vis Fidel Castro," said Richard E. Feinberg, professor of international relations at the University of California (San Diego) and a former national security adviser on Latin America in the Clinton White House.

Presidential candidates have long respected the voting strength and deep pockets of the anti-Castro exile community, represented most prominently by the well-organized and lushly funded Cuban American National Foundation, which was created by the late Jorge Mas Canosa. Between 1979 and 1996, individuals and organizations with Cuba-related interests gave more than $4.4 million to U.S. political candidates and party committees. The foundation, its officers, directors, and trustees, as well as its political action committee, the Free Cuba PAC, contributed 73 percent of the total, according to data from the Federal Election Commission and the Center for Responsive Politics, an advocacy group that promotes campaign finance reform.

While Bush, Gore, and Bradley step gingerly, an unlikely alliance of powerful and persuasive interest groups, think tanks, former government officials from both parties, and newspaper editorial writers are all calling for an end to the nearly 40 years of trade sanctions imposed on Cuba, even as the mercurial, 73-year-old Castro remains in power.

"The climate is changing," said Wayne S. Smith, a senior fellow at the Center for International Policy and the former chief of the U.S. Interests Section in Havana from 1979–82. "What has been the situation until quite recently is that you had one small but extremely strident and well-heeled interest group in Miami determined that there would be no opening to Cuba, certainly not until their interests were taken into account, principally their property. . . . You now have the U.S. Chamber of Commerce and American businesses increasingly interested in seeing a change, not so much because of Cuba, but because of business relations with other [countries]," he continued. "Even more importantly, American farmers have become involved."

The most dramatic shift emerged in the Senate in August when 70 lawmakers (36 Republicans and 34 Democrats) voted to add language to the agricultural appropriations bill. Sponsored by Sen. John Ashcroft, R-Mo., the amendment would give farm and pharmaceutical exporters an opening to the Cuban market. The language does not mention Cuba, but it would eliminate most restrictions on exports of agricultural products and medicines.

Midwestern lawmakers, including House Speaker J. Dennis Hastert, R-Ill., are feeling the heat from pro-trade advocates.

If approved by Congress and signed by the President, the language would seriously weaken the 1996 Helms-Burton law, which bundled existing executive sanctions against the Cuban government into law and imposed some much-criticized punishments on foreign companies that do business with Cuba. Senate-watchers expressed surprise at the overwhelming vote for the amendment, which bucked the GOP leadership. "There's a sense that somehow the sand shifted," said Craig L. Fuller, the former chief of staff to Vice President George Bush and co-chairman of the U.S. chamber-sanctioned Americans for Humanitarian Trade with Cuba. Opponents of the Ashcroft language hope to gut or remove it in conference. And if they don't, some in the agriculture community believe Clinton will resist signing it into law, because it limits some of his remaining executive power and hands it to Congress.

So far, the Administration has remained on the sidelines. Audrae Erickson, a director of governmental relations for the American Farm Bureau Federation, thinks Clinton is keeping any misgivings to himself because of the importance of January's Iowa caucuses and Gore's relations with farmers. "I suspect it's real hard for [the Administration] to come out and publicly oppose the Ashcroft amendment, given the 70-28 vote. That had to have been a huge wake-up call for them," Erickson said.

Indeed. What's giving rise to the new climate on Capitol Hill has less to do with a coherent strategy for democracy in Cuba than with the domestic woes of the struggling U.S. farm community. Midwestern lawmakers, including House Speaker J. Dennis Hastert, R-Ill., are feeling the heat from pro-trade advocates. U.S. pharmaceutical, agricultural, hotel, and travel corporations have long complained that the Canadians, the Mexicans, and Europeans have early footholds in a potentially lucrative Cuban market. Now these business interests are part of the emerging counterweight to the clout of the anti-Castro exile community. They argue that changes already seen in Cuba will foster positive governmental and societal changes. Examples they cite include estimates that 7 million tourists will visit Cuba within a decade; increased communications through the Internet; and 400 joint ventures between the Cuban government and companies from 70 countries.

In short, and suddenly, the anti-sanctions interests are better organized and more broadly representative than ever before. They have become impossible to ignore. A collection of about 30 representatives from business, agricultural, pharmaceutical, religious, Cuban-American, and labor groups descended on the State Department last week to meet with the new head of Cuban affairs, Charles S. Shapiro. Also attending from the Administration were officials from the Treasury Department's Office of Foreign Assets Control and from the National Security Council, and an aide to Secretary of State Madeleine K. Albright.

The interest groups sought the Administration's views on the Ashcroft amendment, and they encouraged the President to exercise his existing powers under Helms-Burton more broadly to help forge connections between Cuba and the United States, said attendee Delvis Fernandez Levy, the president of the Cuban American Alliance Education Fund, a group that would like to remove the sanctions. "There is a current there that will inevitably lead to better relations with Cuba," Levy said. "I don't think I'm naive in this area."

But if a growing number of lawmakers and Governors are willing to say increased trade is good for the United States and for relations with Cuba, what should voters expect from the next President?

"It's hard to tell," said Richard A. Nuccio, who was a special adviser on Cuba to Clinton and is now an adjunct professor of government at Georgetown University. "What people say in election mode is almost certainly different than what they do after the election."

Gore is trying to appeal to both sides by advocating people-to-people contacts and increased travel to Cuba—the so-called Track II policies rekindled by the Clinton Administration this year—while keeping the economic barricade around the Cuban government.

Anecdotes and rumors about Gore's harder-line Cuba views, in comparison with Clinton's, are widely circulated among those debating the issues. Nuccio said that when he was in the White House, the Vice President generally argued that any change in U.S. policy would only benefit Castro.

Asked to explain Gore's Cuba platform, the Gore campaign punted the question to the Vice President's foreign policy spokesmen, Tom Rosshirt, who outlined Gore's record, but said he didn't speak for the campaign.

"The Vice President certainly supports Administration policy, which is to keep up pressure on the Castro regime, and at the same time seek to reach out and support the citizens of Cuba in ways that do not strengthen the regime," Rosshirt said. "We are certainly interested in preparing the Cuban people for a life after this regime, for a life of freedom and free elections and free speech. But the embargo is part of our effort to make sure the pressure stays on the Cuban government and that we do not in any way strengthen the regime."

Bradley, Gore's sole Democratic rival, voted for the Helms-Burton law in 1996. He is unlikely to wander far from the other leading candidates in the presidential pack.

Bush has counted on brother Jeb, Florida's Governor, to help him craft his Cuba rhetoric. In New Hampshire in June, Bush said that Cuba is an exception to his free-trade philosophy, as long as Castro is in power. "It's important for America to keep the pressure on Fidel Castro," he said.

Condoleezza Rice, who heads the Bush campaign's foreign affairs team and a senior fellow at the Hoover Institution on War, Revolution, and Peace in California, said that the Governor "sees no reason to change the sanctions against Cuba, because the important thing is regime change."

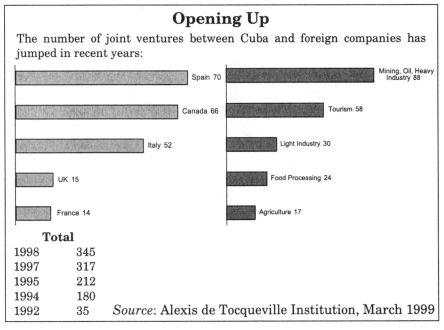

Opening Up

The number of joint ventures between Cuba and foreign companies has jumped in recent years:

Spain 70	Mining, Oil, Heavy Industry 88
Canada 66	Tourism 58
Italy 52	Light Industry 30
UK 15	Food Processing 24
France 14	Agriculture 17

Total

1998	345
1997	317
1995	212
1994	180
1992	35

Source: Alexis de Tocqueville Institution, March 1999

Rep. Lincoln Díaz-Balart, R-Fla., who is a nephew of Castro's and a strident opponent of lifting sanctions until a democratic transition is in place in Cuba, also is advising Bush. The Texas Governor is a good student, said Díaz-Balart, confirming that Bush had embraced as his Cuba policy the core of a memo the Representative sent the Governor last December. In it, Díaz-Balart repeated key elements of the Helms-Burton law that he helped write—that sanctions would remain until Cuba's political prisoners are liberated, political parties are in place, and free elections are scheduled. "Not only has [Bush] taken a firm public position along those lines, his position is very firm and consistent in private," Díaz-Balart added.

> *"There are people who think all we have to do is open up a McDonald's in Cuba, and there goes the regime."*—Dario Moreno, Florida International University

The Havana-born Díaz-Balart, who was first elected to the House in 1992, also said he is confident that Bush would roll back Clinton's more liberal interpretations of people-to-people exchanges. "Bush would not grant visas to Castro lobbyists to pressure the Hill, to go to American interest groups and get them on board," he predicted.

Jose R. Cardenas, the Washington director of the Cuban American Foundation, assailed what he called Clinton's "people-to-party" version of contacts between the United States and Cuba. "It's a stealth accommodation with the Castro regime right now," he said, "and it's being led by Clinton's National Security Council."

U.S. chamber President Thomas J. Donohue—who, with the blessing of the White House, traveled to Cuba this summer and met with dissidents and dined with Castro—is devoting considerable energy to the anti-sanctions endeavor. Donahue is hoping that trading food and medicine, à la the Ashcroft amendment, may be the beginning of a real end for the embargo. "I expect you'll see a liberalization," he said. "The question is, when and how fast?"

Not very fast, answered Dario Moreno, an associate professor of political science at Florida International University in Miami. "There are people who think all we have to do is open up a McDonald's in Cuba, and there goes the regime. I think you have to be very realistic about what's going on, and what's going on is a transition in slow motion."

The next President might not be in office long enough to see a complete transition in Cuba, Nuccio suggested. "Over time, lifting the embargo will have positive benefits for freedom and democracy. But in the short term, the next three, four, five years, it would reinforce Castro's hold on the island."

If Bush is elected, he might "look for ways to open up our activities," Donohue said, ignoring the candidate's rhetoric. "Openness leads to open opportunities for people and then government. . . . For me, it's the whole issue of unilateral sanctions. They don't work. Everyone laughs up their sleeves on that."

A Gallup Poll found that public support for re-establishment of U.S. diplomatic relations with Cuba was the highest it's been in the past 25 years.

As recently as a few years ago, it would have been unthinkable for a presidential candidate, or President, to embrace Donohue's view. But, increasingly, this view seems in tune with public opinion. In May, a Gallup Poll found that public support for re-establishment of U.S. diplomatic relations with Cuba was the highest it's been in the past 25 years, which suggests to politicians that the country may be ready for a change, even if many among the nation's more than 1 million people of Cuban origin are not.

The Gallup survey found that 71 percent of Americans favored restoring diplomatic ties with Cuba, and 25 percent were opposed. Fifty-one percent said they would support ending the U.S. trade embargo, compared with 42 percent who still favored it.

Moreno offers a caveat, though: The public would quickly turn on a candidate who advocated ending sanctions while Castro is alive but didn't get much from the dictator in return. "I think that's why it's so tough for the business sector to try to get the lifting of the embargo, because Castro is not being very cooperative in giving anything of significance to a presidential candidate to hide under," he said. "There's not much they can point to, and there seems to be a political price to pay."

Once in office, a President who seeks to ease or lift sanctions would require a Congress willing to tangle with the Helms-Burton law, which ties any chief executive's hands. Some experts suggest that conditions will improve for additional, albeit incremental, easing of relations with Cuba if a Republican wins the White House, the Democrats take back the majority in the House—and the Senate remains in Republican control.

"You might be in a bizarre world in which you have a coalition between conservative Republican Senators and very liberal Democrats in the House calling for a change in Cuba policy, and the opposition might be moderate Democrats and the White House," Moreno said.

"I think what you're probably going to see in Cuba policy is the continued fraying around the edges. I don't think anything's going to happen in an election year."

Inside Look at Human Smuggling[4]

By Mark Fineman
Los Angeles Times, January 5, 2001

Convicted smuggler Joel Dorta García sat inside the forbidding compound of Cuba's Department of State Security and showed little remorse while describing the journey that killed a man.

Dorta was trying to outrun the Cuban Border Guard and reach U.S. waters in 1999 in an overloaded 32-foot Scorpion speedboat when the cap blew off a 200-gallon gas tank on deck.

The 14 paying passengers screamed as gasoline soaked their legs. The seas were rough. There was no moon. And the Border Guard officers speeding alongside the boat were shouting for Dorta to stop, to save the men, women and children on board from almost certain disaster and to turn himself in.

"I said, 'I'm not stopping,'" the Cuban-American said coolly in an interview room here last month, reliving that night. "I didn't force these people to get on the boat. And I thought, 'If I stop, we'll capsize and I'll never get home.'"

Now, Dorta most likely never will. The Scorpion did flip over, killing 47-year-old Sergio Maurilio Martinez. The Border Guard captured the 29-year-old smuggler and saved the rest of his human cargo, who, according to prosecutors and survivors, had paid $8,000 each for the crossing.

Dorta is among nearly a dozen Cuban-Americans who have been convicted under Cuba's tough new anti-smuggling laws and one of two sentenced to life in prison in this nation's effort to deter the multimillion-dollar trade in illegal migrants.

But the smuggling continues to grow exponentially, driven by the yearning of about 1 million divided families, the Border Guard's limited resources and, critics say, a U.S. policy that permits any Cuban who illegally reaches American soil to remain. Virtually nonexistent before the implementation of that policy in 1996, the smuggling of Cubans for profit has roughly doubled in each of the past four years, Cuban statistics show, while scores of people have died in failed attempts to illegally cross the treacherous seas between here and the U.S. shoreline.

---

4. Article by Mark Fineman from the *Los Angeles Times* January 5, 2001. Copyright © *Los Angeles Times*. Reprinted with permission.

Those are among the findings of a rare look inside the Cuban government's secretive Border Guard, its judicial system and its prisons—all long off limits to outside observers.

For a week, Cuban authorities permitted a reporter to tour their aging naval fleet, accompany a Border Guard patrol in a speedboat confiscated from Florida smugglers and interview several of the more than 70 Cuban Americans who have been jailed here for illegally transporting humans.

For the government of President Fidel Castro, the unique access was meant to show Cuba's commitment to policing a trade that U.S. authorities privately concede they are powerless to deter.

A Castro Campaign During Elián Episode

Castro's campaign against the U.S. immigration policy reached new heights during the prolonged legal battle over custody of young Cuban castaway Elián González, who survived a smuggler's journey that killed his mother and 10 others in November 1999. The Cuban leader insists that the policy is a magnet that draws economic migrants to their deaths with little or no official deterrence from the U.S.

Cuban court records show that smugglers caught and prosecuted here routinely have been sentenced to 20 or 30 years in prison since tougher laws took effect in April 1999.

By contrast, thousands of pages of U.S. federal court records on file in South Florida show that smugglers convicted for similar offenses in Miami—even for those in which deaths occurred—received far lighter sentences from U.S. judges.

"The problem is that the U.S. side isn't doing its part to stop this terrible business," said Maj. Ernesto Hernández Gomez, a Border Guard commander. "The American government doesn't punish them. If they were doing what we're doing, the number of these journeys would diminish very quickly."

Hernández and half a dozen other Border Guard commanders interviewed along the island's northern coast, where they patrol a 12-mile territorial limit, echoed the frustration of many U.S. Border Patrol and Coast Guard officers, who are responsible for stopping the smugglers after they leave Cuban waters but before they reach the Florida coast.

Under the U.S. policy informally known as "wet foot/dry foot," Cubans intercepted by U.S. authorities at sea are sent home—an American commitment enshrined in bilateral immigration treaties signed in the mid-1990s. The Cubans in turn have agreed not to jail or prosecute those sent home.

But, in what Cuban officials have repeatedly asserted is a breach of those accords, their nationals who reach Florida's shore illegally are "paroled" into the U.S. and automatically get residency status in a year, although the smugglers who bring them are subject to federal prosecution.

Privately, several U.S. federal prosecutors say the seemingly contradictory policy makes smuggling cases difficult to try in South Florida, where many judges and juries view Cuban migrants as political refugees.

The net effect, Cuban and U.S. authorities agree, is that the numbers are on the rise.

Nationals who reach Florida's shore illegally are "paroled" into the U.S. and automatically get residency status in a year, although the smugglers who bring them are subject to federal prosecution.

Cuban Official Blames "Fast . . . Easy Money"

The Border Guard said that last year it recorded more than 150 human-smuggling missions launched from Florida, each picking up at least a dozen passengers from Cuba's northern coast. More than a third of those efforts were successful, according to the Border Guard. The agency, an Interior Ministry force with a mission similar to the U.S. Coast Guard, recorded fewer than 100 such journeys in 1999 and just 50 in 1998.

Coast Guard statistics show that, in the past year, as many as 1,000 Cubans were intercepted approaching the U.S. and sent back. But U.S. Border Patrol records indicate that at least double that number made land, and a spokesman said the Border Patrol arrested only a handful of smugglers in Florida waters last year.

Cuban Border Guard officials conceded that their own lack of resources, combined with the enormous profit potential in the smuggling trade, has added to the industry's growth.

"It's fast money, and it's easy money," said Lt. Col. Ramon Ramirez, the Border Guard's chief protocol officer.

Added senior State Security prosecutor Lt. Col. Orlando Soroa Clapera: "If we had the capacity to intercept every smuggling boat that came into our territory, there would be hundreds of U.S. citizens detained in our jails. Conservatively, I'd estimate we have been able to catch not even 5% of them."

Although small radar stations ring this nation's coastline, they use aging Russian and British equipment to monitor the shore and more than 4,000 islands and keys. There also are huge gaps in the radar net that Border Guard officials conceded are known to smugglers who were born and raised in Cuba.

But those officials added that they concentrate most of their radar assets on the coastal tourist resorts and industrial towns that are vital to the economy, rather than the more desolate coastline frequented by smugglers.

To beef up its patrols, the Border Guard recently intensified efforts to seize smugglers' speedboats, which are much faster than the agency's decades-old 74-foot vessels. The Cuban authorities have dozens of these speedboats and use them to catch more smugglers, though officials quickly added that the boats have only a limited value.

"The problem for us is that, even if we had 100 speedboats or 200, it won't help us much," said Ramirez, the protocol officer. "They guzzle very expensive gasoline—98 octane. We can't afford to use these boats anywhere near as much as we'd like.

"That's why our real effort is aimed at stopping the people on land, to frustrate their departure before they leave. Sometimes it's as simple as a boy telling his teacher he won't be in school tomorrow. We follow up on everything. Because once they're on board, the people think they're already in the United States. They become more aggressive, more defiant."

What is more, he stressed, the Border Guard has been under strict orders not to use force to stop smugglers at sea ever since a boat sank during a forcible interdiction in 1993 and a dozen people died. Instead, the Border Guard pursues speeding smugglers, appealing to them through megaphones to stop, until their boats either break down or reach U.S. waters.

In each case of a successful flight, Cuban authorities fax the U.S. Coast Guard in Miami details of the smuggler's boat registration, position and heading—a rare point of direct contact between the two nations' forces. But Ramirez complained that the faxes are rarely answered.

Replied Coast Guard spokesman Lt. Cmdr. Ron LaBrec in Miami: "We do get faxes in from the Cuban Border Guard pretty routinely. If we're able to act on it with vessels or aircraft in the area, we act on it. . . . Sometimes we do, sometimes we don't."

Just who ultimately is behind the trade and who profits most from it remain a mystery to the two governments. Investigators on both sides of the Straits of Florida say the speedboat pilots are mostly pawns in a game in which the major players, organizers and financiers are never caught.

Joel Dorta García and other smugglers imprisoned here appear to be living proof.

Dorta fled Cuba in a 19-foot wooden raft in 1994 and spent nearly five years fishing lobster and living well on Florida's Key West. He insisted in the interview that he ended up at the helm of the Scorpion only for the sake of his wife and children.

He denied assertions by Cuban prosecutors and witnesses that Miami-based organizers had paid him $45,000 for the July 3, 1999, journey, claiming instead that he did it to repay the boat owner for a successful run Dorta had made to Cuba the previous month to get his family out.

Dorta also said he was never given a chance to explain that during his one-day trial here, where he said he met his defense attorney only minutes before the opening gavel and was given only a few minutes to speak in his defense.

But the young smuggler, who said he didn't know of Cuba's harsh penalties before he was caught, insisted that he had no regrets; he is content knowing that his family is safe in Key West, where his wife works in a coffee shop.

When asked, though, whether repealing the wet foot/dry foot policy would eliminate much of the smuggling trade, as Cuba asserts, Dorta shook his head. As long as Cubans want to leave, he said, the business will thrive.

So what will it take to stop it?

"My answer," a hesitant Dorta replied with a wry smile, "may have a great cost to me. Maybe I'll get another life sentence."

Art and Politics in Miami[5]

BY JORDAN LEVIN
(AI) PERFORMANCE FOR THE PLANET, FALL 2000

The most contentious and consuming Cuban debate of the past year was over Elián González. But another dispute, over a Miami-Dade County Commission policy that kept presenters from bringing Cuban artists or art to Miami, also divided the city much of last year. Things came to a head when one of the city's leading non-profit presenters, the Miami Light Project, and four other small arts groups and independent music promoters joined an ACLU lawsuit that challenged the policy.

The depth of feeling and the questions raised by the fight over this Cuba policy said much about the power of culture and the way that Miami's art, politics and ideas—at least when it comes to Cuba—are connected. The policy's downfall, following a Supreme Court ruling in June, also did not get the attention given to Elián's return to Cuba. But the consequences could well be more significant, and longer lasting.

"It educates our community that there are democratic and constitutional values above our personal interests," said Alberto Sarrain after the Cuba policy was thrown out. Sarrain is the Cuban-born head of theater troupe Grupo La Ma Teodora, which was part of the ACLU lawsuit. "These are values that we have to learn."

In 1996, the County Commission unanimously passed a resolution stating that Dade County would not conduct business with companies or individuals who did any direct or indirect business with Cuba. It was passed amidst anger over the Cuban government's shooting down of two Brothers to the Rescue planes over the Florida straits.

But enforcement of the policy reached beyond business to control access to Cuban art and ideas. Arts groups receiving grants from Dade County—virtually all the non-profits in the city—had to sign a "Cuba affidavit" swearing that they would not present Cuban artists or works, or artists who had a broadly defined range of transactions with Cubans. Until 1999, arts groups signed without protest, not only afraid of losing important county grants but also of a backlash they believed could mean protests, boycotts, and loss of funding and support from Cuban-American donors and board members.

Given Miami's history of controversies over Cuban art—like the rock-throwing protests at a concert by Cuban dance band Los Van Van last fall, or the heated controversy over the Cuban Museum in the early 1990s, which resulted in bombings and the museum's closure—their fears seemed justified.

"The [Cuba] resolution has a 100% stranglehold on the cultural community," said Beth Boone, executive director of the Miami Light Project, in the fall of 1999. When Boone met with county officials to discuss what would happen if she presented Cuban music ensemble Grupo Vocal Desandan, she was told she could lose her county funding permanently. But it wasn't just the loss of money that made the policy seem threatening to her. "It's a politically sanctioned opinion," Boone said. "There's a palpable climate here that makes me self-censor."

Arts groups receiving grants from Dade County . . . had to sign a "Cuba affidavit" swearing that they would not present Cuban artists or works.

A series of events soon encouraged Boone and others to speak up. In January, organizers of the first Latin Grammy Awards, concerned that Cuban musicians would be barred from the Miami venue, announced that the internationally televised event would be held in Los Angeles instead. And in February the FIU-Miami Film Festival, one of the city's most popular cultural events, had almost $50,000 in county grants rescinded because it showed the acclaimed Cuban film *La Vida es Silbar* (*Life is to Whistle*). Meanwhile, corporations like AT&T and Carnival Cruise Lines that did lucrative business with the county were getting exemptions from the policy.

Such events made people begin to wonder whether the Cuba policy wasn't working against its intended purpose of encouraging democracy in Cuba, by closing Miami to artists questioning the system there. *La Vida es Silbar*, for instance, was widely interpreted as critical of the island's government.

"If there's been any group that has had a critical take on Cuba in the last 40 years, it has been artists and filmmakers," said Damian Fernandez, head of international studies at Florida International University. "If they don't have space there you'd think they could have an audience here. But they're damned by both sides."

Moreover, Federal law exempted cultural exchange from the Cuban embargo because it was believed to generate new ideas, understanding, and ultimately positive change in Cuba. Those critical of Miami's policy wondered how a local government could legally prevent exchange, and why they would want to. "To me art is the most important way to underscore democratic values," said

Boone. "Cultural exchange opens the door to democracy and the exchange of ideas. It's to the exile community's benefit if [this] happens."

Such statements challenged the feelings of a powerful portion of the exile community for whom any opening to the island—especially when they felt misunderstood over the Elián situation—meant accepting an unjust regime that had driven them from their homeland, often with great personal pain and loss. "If we had a sense that we had a shared ethic with other . . . groups, an understanding that [Cuba] was a dictatorship, cultural exchange could be allowed," said Ricardo Pau-Llosa, a poet and English professor. "But we feel threatened."

"Cultural exchange opens the door to democracy and the exchange of ideas. It's to the exile community's benefit if [this] happens."—Beth Boone, the Miami Light Project

---

Many local politicians agreed with or at least played to such sentiments. Mayor Alex Penelas spoke for many when he insisted that the Miami government was honoring the wishes of many exiles who didn't want to support Cuban artists. "This ordinance does not censor anybody—it just says that we will not get involved," he said. "It would be a slap in the face for this community if [Cuban] artists . . . appeared here." Even those who disagreed with the policy were not prepared to commit what was widely considered political suicide by challenging it.

And so it was that Miami Light, along with Grupo La Ma Teodora, the small theater company GableStage, and independent music promoters Debbie Ohanian, and Hugo Cancio, joined the ACLU lawsuit that challenged the policy. Ultimately, what drove them was not concern over Cuba, but over their rights in Miami. By effectively censoring their programming, they believed Miami's government was not only violating the U.S. Constitution and U.S. law on Cuba, but was behaving like the repressive government on the island.

"The issue is not right or wrong, it's the right to my own opinion," said Joseph Adler, artistic director of GableStage, who joined the suit although he had no plans to present Cuban artists. "We're being held hostage . . . by a very vocal minority. This community is afraid. It's like the Elián issue—it's not whether he should go or stay, but whether I could take a position on whether he should go without fear."

Although a local Federal judge did temporarily suspend the Cuba affidavit in May, whether the suit would have ultimately succeeded is unknown. This is because a Supreme Court ruling in June rendered the Cuba policy dead by July. The Court overturned a Massachusetts law that had prohibited companies from doing business with both that state and Burma. The ruling was based on the grounds that local governments could not make laws interfering with federal foreign policy—one of the central arguments made by Miami's ACLU attorneys.

But while the policy was dead, the attitudes that engendered it were not—something even the most ardent supporters of exchange acknowledged. "Because of the sentiment in the community it will take a long time to work on these issues," admitted Ohanian, the promoter who brought Los Van Van to Miami. "I don't think [the ruling] means it's easier to bring Cuban bands here. It's just that legally they can't stop us, which is half the battle."

Already, the change is being felt. Boone will include Grupo Vocal Desandan, the ensemble she wanted to bring to Miami last year, in her upcoming season. The director of the Rhythm Foundation, which presents worldbeat bands, hopes to soon present famed rumba group Los Muñequitos de Matanzas, which has always avoided Miami on its U.S. tours. In July Susan Caraballo, the Cuban-American head of Artemis Performance Network, a fledgling group in Little Havana, was hosting a workshop with noted Cuban film and theater director Enrique Pineda Barnet at her Little Havana space. And Ever Chávez, a recently defected theater director who works with her, was planning collaborations with Miami and Cuban artists.

"It opens the doors to so many things," said Caraballo. "I'm looking forward to [writing] on a grant application for an international exchange project: 'We'd like to send so and so to Cuba.' Before you couldn't even have the word in there."

For Sarrain, head of Grupo La Ma Teodora, the lawsuit was part of a larger process. He had twice suffered the consequences of intolerance—in Cuba he was jailed for trying to leave the island, and in Miami he had been ejected from his Little Havana space by a presenter fearful of the lawsuit's repercussions. "We have to learn to listen to each other," Sarrain said, speaking of Cubans on both sides of the water. "That is what I've learned by living in a democracy."

In Miami, art is playing a critical part in this learning process.

After Hurricane Elián[6]

By Max J. Castro
SALON, June 28, 2000

Now it is over. Elián González returned to Cuba Wednesday after the U.S. Supreme Court declined to hear the appeal presented by the boy's Miami relatives.

In the wake of "Hurricane Elián," Miami is a city asunder. The divisions, evident on the surface in the silent duel of flags waving from cars and homes—here Cuban, there American, yonder both—are deep, complex, contradictory and often intimate.

Flags are not the only symbol of the struggle. At the height of local tension, after the Immigration and Naturalization Service removed the boy from his Miami relatives' home in an April pre-dawn raid, critics of Miami's Cuban-American leadership threw bunches of bananas at City Hall.

Since that incident, the banana has become the symbol of opposition to the status quo, and "banana republic" is the favorite epithet used by those who are fed up with the hard-line exiles' clout in local government.

Is the Elián saga a turning point for the city, marking the beginning of the end of the exiles' control of Miami politics? And does it also herald a softening of the U.S. hard-line policy toward Cuba, a policy exiles have done so much to maintain? It seems no accident that this same week, Congress will approve measures to allow U.S. agricultural sales to Cuba for the first time in 38 years. It's the first significant break in the embargo and signals a major departure from the trend toward confrontation that characterized U.S.-Cuba relations five years ago.

It will be some time before we know the lasting impact of the Elián saga on Miami and the United States, but even now several things are clear. The Elián struggle has dramatically worsened ethnic tension in this multicultural city. The conflict pitted Cubans against Anglos, but also blacks against Cubans. African-American feeling grew so bitter that some blacks were willing to march with whites waving Confederate flags in the hastily organized "pro-American" demonstrations that drew several thousand protestors in the wake of the federal enforcement action to remove Elián from the Little Havana home.

---

6. Article by Max J. Castro from *Salon.com* June 28, 2000. Copyright © *Salon.com*. Reprinted with permission.

Black attitudes, in turn, have hardened many Cuban-Americans' feelings toward African-Americans, never very positive in the first place. Many Cubans see black involvement in the rallies—some of which had a xenophobic tinge—as meaning African-Americans have such rancor and envy toward Cubans they are willing even to consort with racists just to spite Miami's newly dominant ethnic group.

Virtually every racial and ethnic group in Miami is upset about the Elián drama, but many Cubans are feeling humiliated and besieged, and not just because of the repeated court defeats. The federal operation to retrieve Elián took place the very day the government in Cuba celebrated the 39th anniversary of the Bay of Pigs victory over exile invaders. For Cuban-Americans, the Bay of Pigs was a defining event, marking the end of hopes for an early return to the homeland, and giving rise to Cuban-American allegiance to the GOP in the wake of President Kennedy's perceived "betrayal."

When, 39 years later to the day, a Democratic administration seized Elián, the exile community exploded. Hundreds flew the Cuban flag, while others flew the American flag upside down and a few hotheads even burned the Stars and Stripes. And then the long pent-up anger of many non-Cubans, black and white, boiled over, prompting pro-American demonstrations and fueling ethnic strife.

Many Cubans see the local black and white backlash as anti-Cuban racism and xenophobia. That element was not entirely absent, but it was more than that. Liberal whites and blacks who would not dream of supporting English Only laws or other anti-immigrant initiatives were outraged by the exile community's hysteria. So they brought out the American flag and the bananas.

The "banana republic" label is laden with anti-Latin American connotations. It also doesn't fit. Family members of Jorge Mas Santos, head of the Cuban American National Foundation (CANF)—which bankrolled the fight to keep Elián in Miami—own controlling interests in telecommunications companies worth billions of dollars and listed on the New York Stock Exchange. CANF leaders are sophisticated about the workings of American capitalism and politics. That sophistication and clout, not bananas, is the secret of their success in plugging into the American political system and turning it to their own devices.

Miami's Cuban-American community is more like Taiwan circa 1960 than the stereotypical banana republic. It's a community of people displaced by a Marxist revolution. Here, economic success and professional expertise mixes with a fierce, anachronistic-sounding anticommunism and authoritarian tendencies.

Ultimately, the Elián case may signal a turning point in U.S.-Cuban relations. The decision to allow agricultural sales is a huge step toward change. U.S.-Cuba relations worsened four years ago, with the downing of the "Brothers to the Rescue" airplanes in 1996, and the resulting approval of the Helms-Burton Act. In the ensuing years, business and farm lobbies began to actively work against economic sanctions, and U.S. public opinion seemed to turn away from support for diplomatic isolation and the embargo.

But as late as 1999, the hard-line lobby and the three Cuban-American members of Congress and their allies were able to turn back an effort to exempt food and medicine from the embargo. Have these forces been fatally wounded by their actions in the Elián fiasco? The action by the U.S. Congress to ease the embargo is an important indicator that may be the case.

> *Virtually every racial and ethnic group in Miami is upset about the Elián drama, but many Cubans are feeling humiliated and besieged.*

One reason is that in the Elián saga, the iron triangle defined by the United States, Fidel Castro, and the exiles took on a new configuration. This time the governments of the United States and Cuba converged on a common position, leaving the exile community alone to fight a two-front battle. Even their Republican allies backed off when it became clear that there was no public support for citizenship for Elián González or for hearings into the INS raid.

But is the new geometry lasting? Or can Cuban-American conservatives make normalization as drawn out and excruciatingly difficult an affair as they made the resolution of the Elián saga?

In the Elián case, the hard-liners overreached so badly and looked so bad in the eyes of the U.S. public they gave their adversaries—the U.S. farm lobby, Cuban-American moderates and other embargo opponents—the enhanced political clout needed to finally make a breakthrough. Even Sen. Jesse Helms, fierce anti-Castro stalwart, friend to Cuban-Americans and sponsor of the Helms-Burton law toughening the embargo, voted to ease sanctions against the wishes of the Cuban-American lobby.

The story is different in Miami, where no changing of the guard can be expected, although there is a change in their tune. Some of the very people who helped fire tensions at the height of the controversy, including Miami-Dade mayor Alex Penelas, have been talking the language of dialogue and reconciliation ever since.

Yet the fruits of such efforts have been meager. For instance, top civic leaders met in the days following the INS raid to discuss scenarios in the event of Elián's return to Cuba. But they were not able even to agree that all communities would accept a final court ruling, and allow the boy to leave without protest. But a split in the Cuban-American leadership has become increasingly evident since the Elián affair. Some leaders—most notably business executive Carlos Saladrigas and Pedro Freyre, head of the advocacy organization Facts About Cuban Exiles—are pushing a new, more moderate approach for the Cuban-American community. They advocate focusing more on the post-Fidel future, and urge local leaders to draw a boundary between Miami governance and anti-Castro politics.

Calls for change have been rejected, however, by conservative Cuban-American icons like the nonagenarian retired banker Luis Botifoll and by CANF. Instead, CANF has gone on the offensive, lambasting critics and launching a campaign of ads in the U.S. media exposing the government of Fidel Castro for human rights violations, and claiming that the Elián affair was not a defeat.

In reality, hard-line forces have been dealt three tough blows in quick succession. First, the Supreme Court struck down the state of Massachusetts' sanctions against the government of Myanmar, invalidating Miami-Dade County's own ultra hard-line Cuba policy. Next the Miami relatives lost their last chance to keep Elián in the U.S. when their appeal to the Supreme Court was rejected. Finally, Congress agreed to ease the embargo, striking a blow against the hard liners' favorite policy, which they have fought tooth and nail to maintain and expand.

No community has been as touched by the Cuba debate as Miami. The Elián affair, like a seismic cataclysm, exposed deep social and cultural fault lines and brought to the surface long-suppressed resentments that, on many sides, seem to burn only hotter with time. Often, it is personal. In the wake of Elián, friendships were lost, affairs were ended and feuds flared: that is, wherever people did not opt for the more frequent recourse to a tense silence or to careful avoidance.

That toll was brought home to me with special force the day Elián was reunited with his father. On that night, I had a late dinner with my best friend and his girlfriend, both Cuban-Americans. I had just appeared on "Larry King Live," debating CANF chairman Jorge Mas Santos, and my friends had watched.

Inevitably, our conversation centered on Elián and the events of that morning. Although both my friends thought father and son should be reunited—a decidedly minority view among Cuban-Americans—it soon became clear they felt very differently about the case. Based on instinct and scuttlebutt, the woman, who comes from a family of 1960s exiles with an upper-middle-class background in Cuba, took a dim view of Elián's father, who she saw as a macho lowlife. But her boyfriend, my best friend—the child of dirt-poor Cuban immigrants who arrived in New York City in the 1940s—took personal offense, and countered with his own disparaging view of the Miami relatives. An argument ensued, turned bitter and ended in silence. The next day, my friend told me that his girlfriend had ended the relationship.

It's a tale that could be recounted by a depressing number of people in Miami these sad and searing seven months. Yet let's not write the city or the Cuban-Americans off just yet. My friends finally reasoned it out and decided to get back together. As Elián went home, there were no riots in the city, and the mood among militants was mostly quiet and resigned.

Maybe someday soon Miami will catch up with Taiwan, and Cuban-Americans will join the Koreans, North and South, who lately seem eager to settle their differences peacefully. I just hope I live to see and revel in that day.

IV. Life in Cuba: An Island Unto Itself?

A group of Havana school children holds a portrait of Che Guevera, the legendary leader of the Cuban revolution. Children in Cuba take the pledge, "Seremos como el Che (We will be like Che)."

Editor's Introduction

Cuban society is dynamic and complex, not defined exclusively by Castro and his revolution. Indeed, though many Cubans are critical of their government and frustrated by the socialist system, they also have a keen sense of pride in their country and its accomplishments. The international success of the documentary film *Buena Vista Social Club* shone a spotlight on Cuba's enduring traditions of music and celebration, sidewalk cafés and street life. Newer forms of art, including Cuban rap and film, provide evidence of the country's evolving cultural scene. The authors gathered in this final section attempt to look beyond the headlines, to explore Cuba's social, cultural, and intellectual life.

David Aquila Lawrence reports on the growing ranks of American academics who travel to Cuba, where they hope to learn more about the country before it changes. In Cuban universities, Americans find high standards and intellectual freedom, although—as in so many parts of Cuban society—they also discover that there are limits to free movement and expression.

Tom Miller reports on Cuba's national passion: baseball. From its earliest days, baseball has been intertwined with politics in Cuba. In the nineteenth century, baseball was seen as an anti-Spanish (and pro-American) sport, while in the twentieth century baseball games occasioned anti-Batista demonstrations. Interest in baseball flagged during the lean years of the mid-1990s, but enthusiasm for the game is again on the rise—as evidenced by the number of young children enrolled in Cuba's athletic training schools.

The 1994 Cuban film *Fresa y chocolate* (*Strawberry and Chocolate*), based on a groundbreaking Cuban novel and with a screenplay written by a committed revolutionary, launched a national discussion about the role of homosexuality in Cuban society. As John Casey learns, during the early days of the revolution, gays were made to work in labor camps and were persecuted as being too "*frágil*," or effeminate, for the revolution. (*Before Night Falls*, a recent film about the life of the gay Cuban writer Reinaldo Arenas, brought this shameful history to international attention.) Today, however, Castro is said to have "changed his mind" about homosexuality and, while homophobia is still pervasive, gays are becoming more visible and more accepted in Cuban society.

When Cubans are asked how they deal with deprivations and hardships, they often respond "*inventamos*," "we invent." Tracey Eaton's story about Cuban Harley-Davidson motorcycle fans provides evidence of the much-heralded spirit of Cuban ingenuity. Without access to spare parts and with little money, "Harlistas" have kept their motorcycles running through skill, determination, and sheer love for the machines.

Cuban society is less black-and-white than American society; intermarriage is far more common, and neighborhoods tend to be more racially diverse. And yet racism does exist in Cuba, in spite of José Martí—the 19th-century leader of Cuba's struggle for independence from Spain—having declared that race does not matter, that "we are all Cubans." Eugene Robinson reports that, in terms of educational and material standards, black Cubans are better off than they were four decades ago, a signal accomplishment of Castro's revolution. However, the economic crisis of the mid-1990s brought latent social tensions to the surface, and today many Cuban blacks feel shut out of the lucrative tourist economy. Recent art exhibits in Havana have explored black identity, and a new Afro-Cuban cultural center has opened downtown—both signs of the increasing awareness of race in Cuban society.

In the next article, Rosa Lowinger profiles Kcho, one of the most successful Cuban artists of the 1990s. Kcho builds sculptures out of wood, bottles, and debris washed up from the ocean. His sculpted boats, rafts, and docks evoke a Caribbean world defined by the sea, as well as a more recent Cuban history of refugees and migration. Lowinger describes the experience of viewing a particular sculpture as "witnessing a shipwreck from below."

The final article discusses "Castro's Children," the nearly two-thirds of all Cubans who were born since the revolution. After all the hand-wringing in the American press over what kind of life Elián González will lead in Cuba, Deirdra Funcheon decided to travel there herself to investigate the lives of Cuban youth. Funcheon meets university students who defend the revolution, and who are at the same time fascinated with American pop culture. Like American students, young Cubans hang out, listen to music, and drive around; unlike American youth, they often have to scrounge for food, wait in long lines for buses, or crowd into decaying buildings with their families. Like many Cubans, these young people seem eager—and impatient—for change.

American Academics Invade Cuba and Find a Vibrant Intellectual Scene[1]

BY DAVID AQUILA LAWRENCE
CHRONICLE OF HIGHER EDUCATION, SEPTEMBER 15, 2000

The heat from the sun is oppressive, clearing everybody off the broad sidewalk that winds along the harbor. Sea air, palm trees, and American cars dating to the 1950's pass by on the street. A student walks down the steps from the University of Havana's quadrangle. He's blond and wears a white baseball cap that says "Duke," with its visor expertly bent into a gentle curve.

He's not a Cuban poseur with a bootleg hat, but a genuine U. S. citizen. Hundreds of American students have visited Havana in the last two years for a month or two, joining a surge of thousands of other visitors. Charter flights from Miami to Havana have doubled during that time. This fall, the first full-semester program for American students in Cuba begins, to be run by Butler University, based in Indianapolis.

"Cuba is in," says Jorge Fornet, director of the Center for Literary Research, a government institute in Havana. At the *Casa de las Americas*, a government foundation in Havana that promotes cultural studies here, Mr. Fornet has served as a host to more than 100 students in the last two summers.

"It's been a real invasion—Berkeley, Duke, Tulane, Harvard," says Mr. Fornet. "At the moment we've got more offers than we can serve."

Fertile Ground for Research

After so many years of isolation from the United States, the island is fertile ground for research as it grapples with globalization, free-market pressures, and the wired world around it. Undergraduates are flocking to Cuba to learn Spanish in a more exotic place than Spain or Mexico.

---

1. Article by David Aquila Lawrence from the *Chronicle of Higher Education* September 15, 2000. Copyright © *The Chronicle of Higher Education*. Reprinted with permission.

Some groups in the United States that oppose Cuba's president, Fidel Castro, object, but the Cuban government is more than happy to welcome American visitors and to help show them around Havana's intellectual scene. Café conversation here can be a cornucopia of topics, including film, philosophy, and art.

But some of the Americans visiting Cuba also find that if they push, their academic freedom is limited. Visits to dissidents, for instance, may result in reprisals. And these so-called exchanges are often just one way, since Cubans have difficulty getting visas from the United States and an even harder time getting permission from their government to travel.

For 30 years, an economic embargo kept most American students and professors away from Cuba. But in the 1992 Cuban Democracy Act, the U. S. Congress encouraged academic exchanges, and American students now find it easier than ever to gain permission from the U.S. government to visit Cuba.

"The embargo is supposed to isolate Cuba. But we're the ones being isolated."— **Linda Howe, Wake Forest University**

Although the 1992 law's purpose was to tighten the economic blockade, another part of the legislation intended that academic travelers infiltrate Fidel Castro's Cuba with American ideas. Instead, the scholars who visit seem starved to learn about Cuban society, something they say they have been prevented from doing in the past.

"The embargo is supposed to isolate Cuba. But we're the ones being isolated," says Linda Howe, who directs the Wake Forest University summer program.

Ms. Howe's program includes classes in Cuban literature and culture at the University of Havana as well as community work, such as working with children in elementary schools. At the end of the six-week summer session, six other professors—four of them department chairs—joined Ms. Howe for a week in Havana. Many other summer programs have a similar approach.

"It's an opportunity to get beyond stereotypes and learn something about Cuban culture and society," says Professor Orin Starn, an associate professor of cultural anthropology and director of the Duke program in Cuba, also a six-week summer course.

"The students got a sense more than they could have from the U.S. of the vibrancy of Cuban culture and intellectual life," says Mr. Starn, speaking at the end of one of the study-abroad sessions. "And at the same time [they] saw how Fidel's government operates—the way that speech is restricted and the country controlled." Students also got to see, he says, the benefits of the revolution—universal health care, free education, a society largely free of crime.

A Firm Stance in Miami

Mr. Starn says that a group of Cuban-American students on the Duke campus opposed the establishment of the Cuban program, but the opposition never materialized as a formal protest.

Universities in Florida, a state where many residents have family members in Cuba, have adopted a variety of stances toward academic exchanges with the country. "The University of Miami's position has always been that we will have a relationship with the Cuban government when they allow us to pick and choose which academics we'd like to invite for exchanges and who we can send," says Andy Gomez, associate dean of the School of International Studies at the University of Miami, who was born in Cuba.

Many Latin American studies scholars, including some at the University of Miami itself, do not agree with the university's position. But Mr. Gomez doesn't see it changing anytime soon. "Academic freedom must be protected by higher education at all times, and we believe it doesn't exist in Cuba," he says.

Difficult Logistics

Florida International University, also in Miami, has a different approach. "You're not helping the academic freedom of people in Cuba by not having contact with them," says Lisandro Perez, who was also born in Cuba and is now the director of the Cuban Research Institute at the university. The research institute was founded in 1991, but the exchanges it has sponsored have been oriented toward scholarly research. Undergraduates from the university will be going to Cuba for the first time next summer. The university works with different Cuban institutions but tries to keep contact on an individual level between researchers, and has no formal agreements with the Cuban government.

At Duke, Mr. Starn says some parents were worried that Cuba might be a dangerous place, filled with anti-Americanism. Students say they have found hospitality, not hostility.

Travel logistics are the real obstacle—locating housing, finding a host organization on the Cuban side, and navigating U.S. law. One of the embargo's main provisions forbids U.S. citizens to spend money in Cuba. Most universities hire lawyers to make sure all of the students and professors are licensed to spend dollars and return to the United States with Cuban goods.

The most widely known anti-Castro group in the United States, the Cuban American National Foundation, is wary of the growing numbers of academics who visit the island. While the group supports the idea that students should go to see the Cuban system, its leaders aren't so keen on the dollars being spent.

"This type of situation lends itself to abuse," says Mariela Serretti, a spokeswoman. "If what they're doing is breaking the spirit of the law, that's wrong."

Any student who goes will doubtlessly see that Cuba is a totalitarian system, says Ms. Serretti, but she's afraid some may just be heading down to party. "We are against people traveling to Cuba for tourism—that doesn't benefit anyone except Castro's regime. He's the one who gets the dollars," she says.

Some of the students are just looking for a good time. When one was asked if he liked Cuba, he replied that a bottle of rum costs only $3. Many are more serious, and come looking for a sort of political forbidden fruit, says Mr. Fornet, one that may be disappearing soon.

"They want to see how Cuba is," says Mr. Fornet, "or maybe how Cuba was, before it changes."

Most American academics admit that their knowledge of Cuba has been seen through the narrow window of the American press and U.S. government policy.

The Cuba they encounter is not as many of them have suspected. Most American academics admit that their knowledge of Cuba has been seen through the narrow window of the American press and U.S. government policy.

"I thought everyone hated Castro here," says Tim Van Vorris, a 20-year-old junior in the Wake Forest program. "They do want change, but they don't hate him."

Many Cuban students take great delight in relieving visitors of their preconceived notions. "They leave thinking it's a different but a viable system," says Osmany Valdez, a 20-year-old Cuban student at the University of Havana. "And they're always impressed with our level of education."

The state of the Cuban economy results in visitors' encountering highly educated people mixing their drinks or carrying their bags. Orin Starn of the Duke program recalls that the first time he traveled to Cuba, the bellhop at his hotel noticed his name on the registration card. "He asked me if I was the same Orin Starn who had published a book on peasant organizations in Peru," Mr. Starn recalls, adding that even in Peru the book is obscure.

Common Misconceptions

Many Cuban students speak of jobs as bellhops or bartenders as a worthy goal. Who can blame them—after tips, hotel employees can make more money than Cuban brain surgeons. The darker side of the trend toward work in the tourist industry is that many young Cubans head into the sex trade. "We have some of the best educated prostitutes in the world here," says one Cuban professor.

Some American academics arrive with the common misconception that Cuba sits in stasis waiting for Mr. Castro's death. In fact the island faced drastic economic changes in 1991, when the country lost about $6-billion in annual subsidies from the crumbled Soviet Union. With their government food ration cut by two-thirds, most Cubans now scramble to make extra dollars outside their jobs, which have peso salaries fixed by the state. The new half-peso, half-dollar economic system is still in flux.

"It's not going to be an overnight change after the embargo ends and Castro dies," says Eric Popkin, a professor of sociology at Sarah Lawrence College. The government's allowing the use of dollars, he says, has already changed the country drastically.

Mr. Popkin is setting up a program that will make it possible for Sarah Lawrence students to spend a semester in Cuba beginning next fall. He says that despite what Cubans diplomatically call the "special economic period" over the last decade, Cuba still compares favorably to the abject poverty of some Central American countries. Most Cubans are living frugally, but they're getting by.

"You see some forms of poverty in Cuba," says Mr. Popkin, "but not people in misery. Not without shoes, or starving—people aren't begging."

Cuban academics are struggling to educate their students about a world that is capitalist and global when their country if still socialist and isolated. "Five years ago, we didn't have CNN or the Internet," says Juan Orlando Perez, a professor of journalism at the University of Havana. "Now my students can read Pulitzer Prize–winning stories online—I can't pretend not to know about them or that they're not excellent."

Mr. Perez, like his students, reads world news every day on the Internet—access is free at the university—and he's teaching his young students to be hard-hitting, thoughtful, even muckraking journalists. But when they graduate, they may be able to choose only which state-controlled, heavily censored news organizations they want to work for.

"But I tell my students: You'll still be journalists in the year 2050. I'm teaching. you for those years, not for you to work at *Granma*"—the official newspaper of the Cuban Communist Party.

"I'm a Good Revolutionary"

While the government continues to control the University of Havana, Mr. Perez, who has been teaching there since 1995, says he's never been told to change his teaching style. "The only limits placed on me are those of my conscience," says Mr. Perez. "My job is to teach them how to think. I think I'm a good revolutionary."

The last comment is distinctly Cuban, akin to someone saying he is a responsible citizen. References to the 1959 revolution—including the old tank sitting on the University of Havana campus—are common.

For professors, being a good revolutionary also means keeping Cuban students up to speed—though that mission may contradict the government's socialist ideals. An economics professor at the University of Havana prides himself on using the same textbooks as Columbia University in New York. Yet he knows that prevalent economic theory is not in line with the Cuban government's ideas. Still, he says, the department is free to teach.

"Complete Freedom"

"We talk with complete freedom in our department and are paid great respect," says the economist. "The government doesn't always agree, but they listen."

But the professor—and many other students and professors interviewed—requested their names be withheld, even when their responses were quite pro-Castro. The fact is that Cubans still defect in large numbers to the United States, and though most seek a better standard of living, some make a point of claiming political asylum.

The most prominent recent case is Emilio Ichikawa, a well-known sociology professor who fled Cuba in March. After attending the University of Havana and then teaching there since 1985, he says he couldn't wait any longer for change.

"It's not that I don't love Cuba, it's just the lack of opportunity," says Mr. Ichikawa, who now lives in Miami, where he has been doing research on the Cuban exile community since his defection.

"In recent years, they haven't been locking up writers and professors for having political opinions. But they can throw you out of work or keep you in a humiliating job," he says.

Many years ago, students at the university would report on professors who were deemed to be anti-revolutionary. Now the government still controls movement and contact with academics outside the country, including travel abroad.

Travel restrictions don't just mean the loss of intellectual stimulation: Professors can also lose out on income. During the economic hardship of the '90s, many professors found temporary teaching jobs in Mexico or other Latin American countries. While the academic standards may not measure up to Cuba's, the pay is enough to send money home.

Mr. Ichikawa's own problems began when he was denied permission to travel to New York for the Latin America Studies Association meeting in 1995. He says he isn't sure why the Cuban government denied him permission to leave, but his frustration at being unable to travel mounted. Last February, his request to make an academic trip to New York was granted just 24 hours before he was scheduled to depart.

Mr. Ichikawa decided to defect, and collected some of his prized possessions.

The Decision to Leave

"Castro could live 10 more years—that's a long time," he says. But exile isn't so easy either.

Being critical of Castro isn't very popular among academics in the United States, says Mr. Ichikawa, and they ask him just as often as Cubans did to justify why he left. "It used to be that exile was a triumph," he says, adding that the case of Elián González put the Cuban exile community in a bad light.

Mr. Ichikawa is only 37 and says he has every intention of returning to Cuba as soon as it is politically possible. While some dissidents do remain in Cuba, those who defect to the United States are not usually allowed back. And at least one college's academic-exchange program got a taste of Cuban government control. A program director who insisted on remaining anonymous says Cuban officials made it clear that the exchange might not continue if students made a visit to some well-known political dissidents on the island.

"A number of the students were interested in the meeting, and we were advised by our host institution that this would be a very bad idea and could lead to the cancellation of the program in the future," says the program director.

In the end, the students decided against meeting with the dissidents.

"It's about staying viable—the threat of not being able to return is an effective method—with academics as with journalists," says the director.

Those who continue teaching in Cuba are looking for the new limits in their rapidly changing society. While they know that the rest of the world views their system as a dinosaur, many Cubans want to preserve some of its merits when more change comes.

"Fear of Ending up Like Russia"

"We've been watching 10 years of change from Romania to Russia," says Juan Orlando Perez. "There's the fear of ending up like Russia—totally decimated by mafiosos and ex-communist functionaries. People in Cuba are aware that could happen, and that puts the brakes on other changes which we know are needed."

The intellectual landscape may be changing faster than the economic one. Only 10 years ago, subjects like homosexuality were still taboo for literature or research; then a Cuban film called *Strawberry and Chocolate* opened up a national dialogue. Likewise, in the last several years prostitution and drug addiction have become common topics of discourse. Now there is an open discussion of the new limits.

Writers and academics say they can criticize almost any aspect of Cuban society—the terrible public transportation, the food ration, the large number of educated young women driven to prostitution—as long as they don't directly blame the revolution or their president.

"It's not written down anywhere, but I imagine you still can't write a book about Fidel Castro," says Mr. Fornet, of the Center for Literary Research. "But it goes on changing. Just having dollars a few years ago was punishable."

Cuba's All-Stars[1]

By Tom Miller
NATURAL HISTORY, APRIL 1999

The score is 5 to 1 in the bottom of the seventh inning at Cuba's annual all-star game as the island's best baseball players show off for a Sunday afternoon crowd of fifteen thousand. Today's game, between the Orientales and the Occidentales, takes place in Ciego de Avila, a city of eighty thousand in Cuba's midsection that has been rewarded with this honor for having so greatly improved game attendance during the past year. José Ramón Cepero Stadium has been full since ten in the morning for the two o'clock game, and latecomers perch on the outfield wall. Attendance costs one peso (five cents); parking your bike in a lot adjoining the stadium costs the same.

An energetic man in his late fifties, with "Cuba" emblazoned on his red jersey, makes his way down through the stands and hops onto the home team's dugout roof. He has horn-rim glasses, smokes a Cohiba, and wears a silver whistle around his neck. This is Armando, from Havana, a man known universally as El Tintorero (the laundryman) for his day job: heading a crew that irons sheets for tourist hotels. Television cameras invariably focus on him at the Havana games—which he never misses—as he waves his cigar, shouts, toots his whistle, doffs his hat, jumps up and down, and rouses the crowd for the home team. El Tintorero has become such a part of Cuban baseball that the baseball commission pays his way to important out-of-town events, such as this all-star game.

"The only time I don't cheer is when Havana teams play each other," Armando tells me between whistle blasts. "And when I can't yell, I feel bad. At a regular game, people go crazy and everyone screams. They're happier when they participate—even the Palestinos" (Havana slang for people from the eastern part of the island who have taken up residence in the capital in recent years). Yet even this cheerleader acknowledges the turbulence that has tested his passion of late: "Many good players have either left for the States or only play overseas." In the latter case, some players "retired" to play in Latin America, Italy, or Japan, and the Cuban

---

1. Article by Tom Miller from *Natural History* April 1999. Copyright © *Natural History*. Reprinted with permission.

government collected 80 percent of their foreign pay. Cuba's baseball commission ended the practice last year but still allows coaches to work overseas under the same terms.

For the past few seasons, Cuban baseball has been battered by previously unheard-of losses in international competition, by players abandoning the country, by fans abandoning the stadiums, and by accusations of financial mismanagement. But heads have rolled at the government sports ministry, and a new crew has been brought in to straighten things out, bring back the luster to Cuban baseball, and get fans back into the stands. Cuba's once-invincible international primacy is now returning.

> *Cuba's reputation rests, above all, on its dominance of the Pan American games and, of course, the Olympics.*

At the end of each winter baseball season, Cuba's best players are selected for the national team that plays in tournaments throughout the Caribbean and the Americas as well as in Asia and Europe. Cuba's reputation rests, above all, on its dominance of the Pan American games and, of course, the Olympics. The national team is also scheduled to come to the United States to play the amateur standouts—essentially the college all-stars—but politics often dictates whether or not they will show up (they didn't last year).

Virtually all international competition is governed by the International Baseball Association (IBA), an organization that grew out of efforts in the 1930s—culminating only in 1992—to make baseball an official Olympic sport. Now headquartered in Switzerland, the IBA recognizes about one hundred national baseball federations. These send delegates to the IBA congress, which votes on measures related to world baseball. In 1996, in a significant move, the congress voted to allow professionals to represent their countries.

For Cuban baseball, the nationally televised eastwest all-star game is a climactic event, and the pregame festivities draw on the talent, youth, and emotions that the game thrives on. To show off for the fans, the allstars compete in batting, running, and throwing contests. Orestes Kindelán, whose home team is Santiago de Cuba, slugs four balls out of the park in rapid succession; hometown favorite Roger Poll sprints from home to first in 3.58 seconds; Oscar Machado of Villa Clara circles the diamond in 13.95 seconds. Catcher Eriel Sánchez of Sancti Spíritus is best at tossing out an imaginary base-stealer, and from the outfield, speedster Poll throws within eighteen inches of homeplate. There's also a three-inning youth championship game played by nine- and ten-year-olds (look for first basekid Joey L. Pérez Ramos to lead Cuba's national team in ten years). After they've played, the youngsters stand next to adult players along the base paths. Each all-star bends down and picks up a young athlete, hugs him, and affectionately carries him on his shoulders off the field. The kids get to watch the game from the dugouts as the Orientales beat the Occidentales 5 to 2.

No one can accurately pinpoint the day in the nineteenth century when the first Cuban hit a ball and ran toward first base. Sons of the well-to-do who went to college in the States (a tradition until the late 1950s) undoubtedly brought the game back with them. Havana-born Esteban Bellán, who played on Fordham University's baseball team in 1870–71 and then professionally for a few seasons, is generally credited with introducing the game to Cuba, although one account has a U.S.-schooled Cuban carrying it home in the 1860s.

> *Baseball, the United States' most benevolent and pacific export, hinted at Cuba's future free of Spain.*

It's also likely that Cuban workers in Florida cigar factories came back with the game. And merchant marines dropping off American goods and picking up Cuban sugar probably played ball in front of—and with—Cuban dockworkers and others. One theory has it that during the U.S. Civil War, ships unable to dock at Southern ports because of the Northern blockade continued south until they dropped anchor in Havana and that there, to entertain themselves, the crews played baseball. Whatever its passage to the island, the game was instantly popular wherever there was space for a field on the edge of town. The first written account shows Havana humiliating Matanzas 51 to 9 on December 27, 1874.

Cubans returning home from the States between 1868 and 1898, during the various wars of independence from Spain, saw baseball as a "paradigm of progress," suggests University of North Carolina history professor Louis A. Pérez, Jr., in *On Becoming Cuban: Identity, Nationality, and Culture*, to be published this coming fall. "Baseball," he writes, "promised the possibility of civilization: harmony among competing classes, orderly competition between conflicting interests. . . . Simply by not being Spanish, baseball embodied a critique of the colonial regime."

"Baseball was exotic and decadent," observes Roberto González Echevarría, "diametrically opposed to Spanish prissiness, hypocrisy, and (literally) bullish savagery." In his new book, *The Pride of Havana: A History of Cuban Baseball*, the Yale professor of Spanish maintains that the sport was "a powerful force in the democratization and secularization of Cuban culture." Bullfighting, Spain's most gory and traditional export, symbolized colonial rigidity and obtuseness; baseball, the United States' most benevolent and pacific export, hinted at Cuba's future free of Spain. Consider the affront suffered by the colonial powers as youthful Cubans gleefully swung for the outfield fences and conspired on double plays. In the eyes of the Spaniards, these were political acts, and for one year during Cuba's struggle for independence, Madrid banned baseball on the island.

Cuban literature and culture embraced the game as well. Nineteenth-century teams took on the names of Italian operas; Sunday afternoon competitions were followed by dinner dances; writers delighted in the game. Such was the early fervor for baseball that one sportswriter went on at length about Cuba's first bunt, in an 1890 game between Havana and Progreso. It was the bottom of the tenth inning, the score was tied 1 to 1, nobody out, and a man on first. The Havana manager "called his boys together, speaking to them in a low voice . . . and laughed with malicious satisfaction. [Juan] Antigas stepped up to bat, and while everyone expected him to swing for the fences, he just touched the ball lightly, hurriedly reaching first base, leaving the Progreso team in a stupor."

The manager who called for the bunt was Emilio Sabourín, a Havanan schooled for a while in Washington, D.C., and an enthusiast of both American baseball and Cuban independence. Arrested for insurgency and sentenced to twenty years' incarceration, he died in 1897 after two years in a North African Spanish prison. Now, more than a century later, a bust of Sabourín sits forlorn and uncared for in the backyard of Havana's maternity hospital. As a couple of friends and I pay our respects, a woman in her seventies walks by. "It's good that someone remembers him," she volunteers through a chain-link fence. "He was a great patriot and a great person."

Following three decades of intermittent struggle for independence, Cuba, with a last-minute assist from the United States, rid itself of Spain in 1898. But Spain turned over control of the island to the United States, not to the Cubans. During its three-year dominion, the United States outlawed bullfighting and its military played baseball, both among themselves and against Cuban teams. "It can only be imagined," writes historian Pérez, "what values and meanings were assigned to the outcome of games pitting the occupied against the occupiers."

After the turn of the century, professional leagues usually consisted of three or four teams that played in the winter months (accommodating the schedule of U.S. major league players), while amateur teams, profuse throughout the island, played year-round. U.S. players came to Cuba as part of barnstorming tours and to keep their skills up during the northern off-season. Among them were black athletes, who were not allowed into the major leagues but were accepted on Cuban professional teams. (Nevertheless, amateur teams on the island were all-white until the 1950s, since most Cuban blacks couldn't afford to play without being paid.)

Light-skinned Latin Americans, such as Cuban pitcher Adolfo Luque, played in the major leagues during this period. Luque, "the pride of Havana," began his big-league career with the Boston Braves in 1914 and wound it up twenty-one years later with the New York Giants. His best years were in the 1920s, with Cincinnati. Overall, he won almost two hundred major league games, with an earned run average of 3.24. What made Cubans particularly proud of Luque, however, was that while he starred and later coached in the States, he always came home for winter ball. In all, about eighty Cubans (more than the citizens of any other country) played in the major leagues between 1871 and 1959. But after Fidel Castro assumed power, the flow of players began to change dramatically.

U.S. players came to Cuba as part of barnstorming tours and to keep their skills up during the northern off-season.

Martín Dihigo, often referred to as the best player never to reach the major leagues, began his career in 1922. He played in his native Cuba but also in Mexico, Venezuela, the Dominican Republic, and the Negro league in the United States. Although he played all nine positions during his twenty-five-year career, it was his pitching and batting that earned him a reputation as one of the truly great players of this century. When Dihigo died, Cuba's poet laureate, Nicolás Guillén, wrote an elegy to him, concluding:

His face, ashen (death for black folks)
and his eyes closed, chasing
a white ball, this time the last one.

Between the two world wars, Cuban cigarette companies such as Billiken issued baseball cards. Today these rarities are sought not only by devotees of Cuban baseball but also by collectors looking for cards of Negro leaguers who played in Cuba. Many Negro league standouts, such as Hall of Famer John Henry "Pop" Lloyd, never appeared on cards issued in the States. As a result, a 1924 Billiken card of Lloyd recently fetched more than two thousand dollars at auction.

Between 1937 and 1959, Cuban fans got to see various major league teams conducting spring training on the island. Most notable were the 1947 Brooklyn Dodgers, a team that included three black prospects: Jackie Robinson, Roy Campanella, and Don Newcombe. The team selected Havana to avoid the racism of Florida towns, although the three black athletes were housed separately.

Before the Revolution, open betting was very much a part of Cuban baseball; it took place in parks, in private homes, and in the countryside, where a sack of beans or a pile of yuca might be the wager. At Havana's Gran Stadium, the stands behind the third-base dugout were the place to go, and one row became known as Wall Street. "I remember a game between Almendares and Cienfuegos in 1956 where the odds were 11 to 8," Ismael Sené, a rabid baseball fan in Havana, tells me. "One man waved eleven thousand pesos in the air, and another held up eight thousand. It got very intense at times." With the advent of the Castro years, betting was outlawed; still, in incidents in 1978 and 1982, a total of forty-two team members were suspended (and some of them jailed, along with some

---

Anti-Batista activists from the University of Havana . . . carried their noisy protests to the games, especially if the country's number one fan, Fulgencio Batista, was there too.

---

bookies) for betting on baseball. Havana's best team, people joked, was at the Combinado del Este, the prison just east of Havana.

If betting was integral to Cuban baseball, politics became so as well in the 1950s, just as it had sixty years earlier. Anti-Batista activists from the University of Havana on occasion carried their noisy protests to the games, especially if the country's number one fan, Fulgencio Batista, was there too. Once, in 1956, students took to the field shouting for freedom for their jailed comrades, and the police, instead of just clearing them off, clubbed them mercilessly. The whole country saw the incident on television, and this helped sway public opinion. The following year, Havana's mayor, a Batista sympathizer, was compelled to leave a game when fans booed him. "I was there that day," Sené recollects. "Everyone yelled, 'Long live Fidel! Down with Batista!' To me, those two events at the stadium were the two most important events of the Revolution."

Sené also recalls the time that the Sugar Kings, a Cuban minor league team, played a series in Havana against the Rochester Red Wings in the summer of 1959. Admission to the July 25 game was free for all the country folk and military filling the capital to commemorate the Revolution the following day. "There must have been thirty-five thousand people there," Sené says excitedly. "More than half of them carried arms. The game started at nine P.M. and went into extra innings. The game was still going on at midnight when it turned July 26, and everyone took out their weapons and fired them in the air to celebrate. Miraculously no one was hurt." But wasn't

Rochester coach Frank Verdi's plastic helmet grazed by a bullet? "No! That's not true!" The following year, by the way, the Sugar Kings of Havana, Cuba, moved to New Jersey, U.S.A., and became the Jersey City Jerseys. (A full account appears in the 1982 book *Baseball and the Cold War,* by Howard Senzel.)

While in high school, Castro himself played decent baseball and excellent basketball. But he was not, as popular mythology has it, offered a contract by the Washington Senators—or by any other team. So says Peter C. Bjarkman, author of numerous books on baseball, including two on Cuban baseball (forthcoming in 1999 and 2000). On occasion during his first decade in power, Castro would pitch a few innings, sometimes at public exhibition games

---

The propaganda value of beating America—literally at its own game—kept the sports ministry firmly entrenched and, until recently, almost untouchable.

---

and other times when playing within his inner circle. (The image of Castro pitching—especially against Americans—lends itself so well to literary metaphor that it has been the subject of some imaginative fiction, most notably Max Apple's short story "Understanding Alvarado." *Castro's Curveball*, a new novel by sportswriter Tim Wendel, uses the same conceit.)

Influenced by Eastern European models, Cuba did away with contractual professional sports within a few years of the 1959 Revolution and began its vigorous amateur system. "This is the first country in the Americas where sports went from being a commercial activity to one that is educational and cultural," Fidel Castro boasted. "It was the Revolution that made this possible." For years the national team would invariably be pictured receiving Castro's congratulations after yet another Olympic or Pan American Games victory. The propaganda value of beating America—literally at its own game—kept the sports ministry firmly entrenched and, until recently, almost untouchable.

Each Cuban province has a boarding school for young athletes. These "sports initiation" schools, as they are called, take in boys and girls as young as age eight and train them for just about every sport in international competition, from kayaking to women's volleyball. From ages eight to eleven, the students play all sports; after that, they specialize. In baseball they are required to practice every position, both left- and right-handed. With watchful coaching and steady progress, these athletes are ready to compete by the time they are fifteen or sixteen.

Surrounded by playing fields, the Havana school lies twelve miles east of the capital. Its one large building resembles rural schools throughout the country: two floors with dormitories, cafeterias, and classrooms, all wrapped around a maze of breezeways. On an unannounced inspection of one of the boys' dormitories, I find it clean, neat, and airy. Posters of Japanese baseball players and Che Guevara line one wall, while gymnastic bars take up a corner. A chess game between two twelve-year-olds on a bunk bed holds their teammates' attention. The boys in this dormitory, grouped by age and sport, spend half the day on the diamond and half in academic classes. On this particular day, out on the field, twelve- and thirteen-year-olds are learning bunting tactics.

In a physics class, the teacher lets me query her two dozen fourteen-year-olds. What, I ask, makes Cubans so passionate about baseball? "We cultivate it from birth," says one. "We have a gusto for the game," says another. One boy waves his hand and tells me, "It's part of ourselves, it's in our hearts. We have an emotional link to it." I ask them each to name the active baseball player they most admire. "Omar Linares," mumbles one kid, choosing the man who is perhaps Cuba's most outstanding all-around player. "Carlos Tabares," pipes up his neighbor, referring to another star. A fellow in the back then names Ken Griffey, Jr. At this, the room lights up. Soon it becomes practically unanimous: the baseball player most admired by Cuba's future all-stars is Ken Griffey, Jr., of the Seattle Mariners. (This was before the remarkable home run drives by Sammy Sosa and Mark McGwire.)

One enormous kitchen at the training center feeds three meals a day to 766 students. Birds fly into the kitchen, over the vats, then back out. The steam table has been sent out for repairs, and the staff does not seem to expect to see it back anytime soon. As a result, the cooks heat up food for Cuba's future international competitors using firewood foraged by students from the nearby woods.

The kids go home on weekends, and parents are encouraged to visit on Wednesdays. The province also provides for a psychologist to help young players who are trying to be adults too soon, who are having trouble adapting, or whose home problems are affecting their school performance.

The young baseball hopefuls get promoted—or weeded out—every two years until, at sixteen or seventeen, if they still qualify, they are sent to play on provincial development teams, the squads that feed Cuba's top teams. Beyond that, the opportunities become more restricted. "With only twenty spots on the national team, too many good young players are stuck on the island," says University of Texas political science teacher Milton Jamail, America's leading expert on contemporary Cuban baseball. "Rey Ordoñez of the New York Mets had been considered only the third best shortstop. The chance to play was one reason he defected."

Attending a game in the western city of Pinar del Río, at Capitán San Luis Stadium, I watch a perennial on the national team step up to bat. He is third baseman Omar "El Niño" Linares; the crowd stands and cheers his first appearance in three weeks, after an absence due to injury. Play stops while the batter, with a .373 lifetime average, reaches over to shake hands with the home plate umpire. Then the fifteen-year veteran shakes hands with the opposing team's catcher. These civilities and kindnesses are not showboating; they are characteristic of Cuban baseball and, for a foreigner, take some getting used to. Finally Linares faces the pitcher and grounds

---

"Rey Ordoñez of the New York Mets had been considered only the third best short-stop. The chance to play was one reason he defected."—**Milton Jamail, American expert on Cuban baseball**

---

out down the third-base line.

Pinar del Río is in a fight for the national title, a race it will eventually win. I have the misfortune this evening of sitting with the city's *peña*, the booster club that cheers on the local teams for every moment of every sport. I say "misfortune" because they have a piercing pump-action horn and an ear-splitting siren, both of which sound off at the slightest provocation. Rosendo Prieto, a retired truck driver and the *peña's* vice president, explains between horn blasts that it costs three pesos (about fifteen cents) to join. With all the ecstatic, rhythmic drumming and whistles, there are times late in a game when a ballpark feels more like a salsa nightclub than a stadium.

The *peña* siren goes off for twenty-five-year-old Pinar del Río pitcher Pedro Luis Lazo. Eight years ago, when I last saw him, he was a skinny rookie. At that time, he was pointed out to me as a future star; now, playing against the Metropolitanos of Havana, he shows how accurate that prediction was. Once Lazo reaches his sixth strikeout, the crowd begins to count them off, beginning the chant each time with "One!" By game's end, the count is up to sixteen.

The umpires pause after the third inning, and a master of ceremonies appears at home plate to introduce the 1978 national team and, one by one, the local Communist Party officials. Then play resumes. This Tuesday night game is significant not only because of the presence of Linares and Lazo but because the baseball season, begun amid fan disgust and hints of corruption, has once again excited the country with its verve, heroics, and red-hot rivalry.

Pinar del Río wins the game 4 to 1, and by the time fans throughout the nation sip their Wednesday morning coffee, word has spread of Linares's return and the unstoppable Pinar del Río nine.

Cuba Goes Gayer[2]

By John Casey
Spectator, August 15, 1998

Last Easter I attended the Saturday vigil service in Havana Cathedral. In front of me were four men, two older and two younger. They were fervently devout and liturgically rather bossy, eager to tell their neighbours (including me) when to blow out and when to relight their candles. But the main thing that caught my attention was that they were obviously and unashamedly homosexuals. With the first *Gloria*, when the bells as usual rang out and the electronic organ played with the accompaniment of a powerful samba beat, they hugged each other in demonstrative joy.

I was struck, not because it was a Catholic church in which they were so open in their sexuality, but because this was Cuba. The attitude of the Cuban state to gays has been harsh. How harsh it had been I discovered on that visit.

I had previously been in Cuba in 1993, and among the people I met then was a leading dissident writer. Miguel (as I shall call him) was a good friend of Castro's. He was also something extremely rare in the Cuba of the time, a more or less open homosexual. Castro had denounced homosexuality as "a bourgeois perversion."

So now I asked Miguel about the bourgeois perversion. "Fidel has changed his mind," he said. "Remember we are a military society, and Fidel thought that gays are *frágil* [i.e. feeble, unmanly]. But the real reason for his dislike was that two of his homosexual soldiers betrayed him in the Sierra Maestra." The Sierra Maestra is where Castro, with minuscule forces, began the guerrilla war that eventually took him to power in Havana. Any betrayal could easily have destroyed him, so his rage would have been justified.

Cuba certainly is a military society. Fidel Castro's preferred title is "Comandante" and he always wears military uniform. You have to doubt, however, how popular Fidel is in this military role. An English friend of mine had taken up with a black girl who was obviously working as a prostitute to support her family. We went to call on them at the top of a slum tenement. They were the poorest of poor blacks—unemployed, voodooists to a man and woman. Without the daughter's work they would be destitute. As we drank our rum, the father began to talk politics. The others turned the radio

---

up as he became loud with excitement: "We stand at the rallies listening to his speeches." He stood up theatrically: "I say, 'Yes, Comandante! You are right, Comandante! We are all behind you, Comandante!' And what do I really think? I think: You f—ing faggot!"

I did find evidence that Fidel had "changed his mind." I was staying in the flat of an actress/director and met quite a few theatre people, some of whom were explicitly homosexual or lesbian. One of them was my interpreter. Another was a film director, Cristobal—a flamboyant *grande dame*, who was keen that I should hear the story of his life and of the times before the Comandante's mind had changed. Cristobal entered dramatically, bearing a birthday cake with green icing which he had made himself for an English friend who was also staying in the flat, and for whom Cristobal professed hopeless love.

I called on him in his studio, where a friend of his, Esteban, an antiques dealer, was also waiting. An antiquated air-conditioner made so much noise that conversation was difficult. Once or twice I asked if it could be lowered, and Cristobal went through the motions of trying to adjust it, before saying it was impossible. Later I realised that he did not want the conversation overheard.

Cristobal remembered the revolution in 1959: "The beginning was beautiful. We both took part in the literacy campaigns, working in the countryside with the peasants. But what did we become? What did we give our youth for? The first sign of repression was that for a time we were forbidden even to listen to the Beatles."

The troubles of his friend Esteban began when he was called up for military service. The medical board examined him and excluded him from the call-up because he was severely asthmatic. A few months later he was ordered to report again. He found that the other men there were mostly gays: "I turned up with my toothbrush, when, to my amazement, I found that we were surrounded by men with machine-guns in the call-up office. We were taken to Camigue, at the other end of the island. It was a camp surrounded with barbed wire, with watch-towers manned by guards with machine-guns."

The camp included among its inmates homosexuals, Catholics and middle-class medical students. Half of it was reserved for common criminals. The prisoners began work at 3 a.m., walking to the sugarcane fields to cut the grass with scythes: "There was a gay schoolteacher in the camp. They began a roll-call, and when they came to him they said he was to be moved to the part of the camp reserved for the common criminals." Esteban explained: "I was on the same list; I too was to be made to sleep in the criminal part of the camp. The intention was clear—we were to be handed over to sexual assault by the criminals. The schoolteacher told me that if he was handed over he would take his own life. And he did kill himself. It was sad."

Cristobal is not *frágil*. Rather he is a brave and very determined theatrical queen. When he was caught up by the authorities he did his best to be punished for fighting and insubordination, because those were less shameful crimes than sexual deviancy: "I did military service. I volunteered for love. I was in love with someone who had gone for military service in 1967. We had been together for three years. I had been studying medical science, but I was put in the sappers, dealing with mines. My lover was to do the drawings of the mines we needed. It was a heavenly time."

> *Gays are no longer persecuted. Fidel has "changed his mind." Too late for some.*

The idyll did not last as Cristobal fell under suspicion for his sexual tastes. He was put to cutting sugar-cane from 5 a.m. each day. His *jefe* (military commander) began to persecute him: "He was a bit crazy. One day he put his gun in the refrigerator. It was a Russian gun, you see, and he said that it was used to a cold environment."

Cristobal was put on trial on charges of "passive or active pederasty." "They couldn't prove anything. But to make sure, I had a go at a stool-pigeon. I also tried to hit the *jefe*. So I got what I wanted. I was found guilty of insubordination and sentenced to six months. But, you see, that was infinitely better than being found guilty of being a faggot."

Sad stories, but also strange. Cuba is as far from sexual puritanism as any country can be. A favourite Cuban joke is to say that sex is the second most popular national activity. (The first? Getting money off foreigners.) Castro's revolution never went in for Maoist sexual austerity or Stalinist primness. Now the regime seems perfectly at ease with every sexual permutation and also with prostitution, the elimination of which had for years been one of Cuba's proud boasts.

So the supreme leader has spoken, and gays are no longer persecuted. Fidel has "changed his mind." Too late for some. At the end of our interview, Cristobal said, "If I came back to this world in a new life, I would not like to come back as a gay. You suffer too much." Esteban told me: "I would not like to come back at all. I have lost faith in human nature."

In Cuba a Vintage Harley Can Epitomize Life Itself

Keeping It Running a Difficult Labor of Love[3]

By Tracey Eaton
Times-Picayune, August 8, 1999

Legend has it that after the 1959 revolution, Cuban agents seized nearly 1,000 Harley-Davidson motorcycles, dug a huge hole in a secret spot and buried the fabled machines, dealing a blow to the American way.

Four decades later, Cubans argue furiously about whether the tale is true. But one thing is certain: The indomitable Harley lives on in the land of Fidel Castro, thanks to ordinary Cubans who go to extraordinary extremes to preserve their beloved "hogs."

"Our parents and our grandparents rode these machines. They're part of the family. And it's our duty to keep them alive," said Sergio Moráles, head of Cuba's only garage dedicated to restoring and repairing old Harleys.

Americans have heard this kind of story before: Man finds meaning in life while restoring or working on an old motorcycle. Now imagine Cuba, cut off from the United States, with no classified ads, virtually no spare parts from the United States, no junkyards, no Internet Web sites to help find that obscure 1955 crank pin.

"Maintaining a Harley is infinitely more difficult in Cuba than in the United States," Moráles said. "We go through hell."

Happy "Harlistas"

Yet it's a fate he seems to relish.

"It's all about sacrifice. You have to earn the right to ride these machines."

Moráles, a wiry man of 48, is the undisputed dean of Cuban Harley owners, who proudly call themselves "Harlistas." Besides running a tiny repair shop in Havana's gritty Luyano neighborhood, he is president of Cuba's Association of Classic Motorcycles.

"There have been times when we haven't been able to get tires for our motorcycles, so we have had to use Volkswagen tires," he said. "They're too big, of course, so we have to pad the rim. And we have to add spokes. All by hand."

As he spoke, it began to rain, soaking the vintage motorcycles parked in front of his modest home. All were knuckleheads, flatheads and panheads—Harley models produced in the 1940s and '50s.

Moráles puffed a soggy cigar while his wife, Miriam, served strong, sweet coffee. Their furry white pooch, named Harley, suddenly bounded outside and barked as the couple's son-in-law kick-started his battered old motorcycle, then roared down the street.

"We sometimes take the dog for motorcycle rides. He likes that, but he doesn't like the sound of the engine," said Moráles, taking a sip of coffee. "I guess it's too loud. Hurts his ears. But we like 'em loud."

His living room is decorated in the Harley motif: A color poster of a 1992 Harley Softtail graces one wall, a stuffed "hog" is perched atop the TV, and odd engine parts from 1940s-era Harleys are stacked neatly on the floor. A sign says: "God created the world in seven days and on the eighth, he created Harley-Davidson."

"Evangelists sometimes walk by, read that sign and get all upset," Moráles said. "They go into a long explanation about how God created the Earth in six days and rested on the seventh day. Then they stop and ask, 'By the way, what's Harley-Davidson?'"

Cuban Hybrids

He stepped outside and walked across the street to his repair shop, crammed with cycle parts.

"We take parts from Alfa Romeos and other cars and from other motorcycles and adapt them to fit our Harleys," he said. "Or we make our own parts. Our motorcycles have so many Cuban-made parts, we consider them 'Made in Cuba.' It fills us with pride."

He estimates that there are at least 100 working Harleys in Havana. American motorcycle experts say the Cuban Harleys would likely have value in the United States even if they are "hybrids."

"You could make a ton of money if you could get those Harleys out of Cuba," said Dick Winger of the Antique Motorcycle Club of America, with 8,000 members worldwide. "They're very collectible."

The price of vintage Harleys in the United States has dipped slightly after peaking three or four years ago, but "everyone still wants" an old Harley, said Steve LeMay, 40, a California man who restores old motorcycles.

"Basketcase Harleys," with their parts literally piled in baskets and cardboard boxes, start at about $4,000, he said. Restored models average $18,000. And some of the rarest and most coveted Harleys, such as the 1936 knucklehead, "can run $35,000 to $50,000."

It is extremely difficult, under Cuban law, to export old Harleys. But some foreigners who have moved to Cuba have bought some of the old motorcycles and had them restored, a trend that saddens Harlistas.

"We're the ones who have made the sacrifices to keep these motorcycles running. I'd hate to see foreigners come in and buy them all," Moráles said. "They wouldn't appreciate them. You have to work on them yourself to appreciate the beauty of a Harley."

Classic motorcycle experts who have journeyed to Cuba have been amazed by the Harlistas' dedication and know-how. Consider what happened when Toronto mechanic Donny Petersen did a workshop for Harlistas in Havana in 1997.

Diehard Harlistas refused to abandon their motorcycles, but say it takes lots of sweat and ingenuity to keep them going.

The Harlistas "wanted to get right to their favorite subjects, which involved the redirection of internal oil passages inside the engine," Petersen wrote. "There wasn't anything they didn't know about their machines. They can take a motor apart blindfolded and put her back together again."

Moráles, his hands blackened by motorcycle oil and grit, said he once cut in half a perfectly good Harley exhaust system just to see how it worked. Harlistas have to be fanatical about the care of their machines, he said.

Poor Man's Cadillac

"We use these motorcycles for work, for transportation. We can't survive without them. This isn't like the United States, where you have to have money to buy a Harley. In Cuba, it's the poor who have Harleys."

Hogs fell out of favor in Cuba in the 1970s and '80s as motorcycles from the Soviet bloc flooded the island.

"People didn't want Harleys anymore," Moráles said. "They were too much work to keep up, and the price of them dropped. You could get an old Harley for $500. They became the motorcycle of Cuba's poor."

Diehard Harlistas refused to abandon their motorcycles, but say it takes lots of sweat and ingenuity to keep them going.

"It was especially difficult in the 1970s," Moráles said. "We couldn't get even simple equipment, like air pumps to inflate the tires. We stuffed grass into the tires so we could still ride. That actually worked."

Moráles learned to repair Harleys under the late Jose Lorenzo Cortez, nicknamed Pepe Milesima." His friends called him Milesima, meaning a thousandth, because of his never-ending quest for mechanical precision.

Harlistas honor "Milesima every Father's Day, the day of his death. They climb onto their machines, ride to Havana's Colon Cemetery and gather around a tomb marked "Pepe Milesima, Harley-Davidson mechanic."

"Pepe learned to fix Harleys before the revolution," Moráles said. "He was a true master."

In those days, Harley-Davidson had a bustling dealership in Havana.

"Harleys sold like hot bread. They sold like crazy," said Lourdes Bretos, daughter of the late Luis Bretos, who ran the dealership.

She did stunts on Harleys, even riding one along the top of the narrow seawall on the edge of Havana.

"Those were the best days of my life," said Bretos, a Miami resident who left Cuba in 1961. "We toured the entire island by motorcycle, going where there were no roads."

Hundreds of regular Cubans, along with dictator Fulgencio Batista's police and soldiers, rode Harleys. Castro loyalists despised the soldiers, which might have fueled the tale about the mass burial of hogs.

Harley-Davidson Motor Co. executives hope to again do business in Cuba and visited the island in 1995 to explore the possibilities.

The company, founded in a backyard shed in Milwaukee 96 years ago, sees Latin America as a potentially lucrative market. Already, demand for Harleys in Europe, Japan, Australia and other countries is soaring.

But back in Havana, Harlistas say money and profit is hardly what matters to them. Sounding like the characters out of the 1974 book *Zen and the Art of Motorcycle Maintenance*, they say owning a Harley in Cuba is more about life and truth. Friends and family. And don't forget hardship.

"Take the way we start our motorcycles," Moráles said. "It's by kick-start. There's no electronic ignition. No button to flick. You have to give it a kick. You have to use some muscle. It's a ritual. And it's not always easy.

"Like I said, it's about sacrifice."

Cuba Begins to Answer Its Race Question[4]

By Eugene Robinson
Washington Post, November 12, 2000

Maria del Carmen Cano, a scholar at the Cuban Institute of the Book, studies race in Cuba. For years that was an obscure and lonely task, but now people are beginning to pay attention. To illustrate why, she tells a story about her husband.

He is tall and very dark-skinned. Not long ago, on a day off from work, he was making his way through a downtown Havana neighborhood in shorts, tennis shoes and T-shirt, a bulging knapsack slung over his shoulder—he was taking the family's computer to be repaired. Approaching from the opposite direction was a white man, also in sneakers and T-shirt and shorts, also toting a full knapsack. They crossed paths right in front of one of the policemen who stand, sphinxlike, on Havana's busy street corners.

The officer stopped Cano's husband and demanded to see his identity papers, letting the white man pass without a second look.

When the policeman learned that he had just detained a lieutenant colonel in the Cuban military, he was effusively apologetic. "But from then on," Cano says, "my husband had a greater appreciation for my work."

Breaking a long-standing taboo on discussing Cuban society in racial terms, scholars and even officials here are delving into issues of race, racism, racial stereotypes and stubborn patterns of discrimination. They have found, as Cano says, that "it's unrealistic to assume that a good communist or a good revolutionary can't also be a racist."

Black Cubans, by any material or educational measure, have made great advances in the past four decades, their progress often cited by officials as one of the signal accomplishments of President Fidel Castro's revolution. As one example, officials report that in this country of 11 million people, there are more than 13,000 black physicians; by comparison, in the United States, with a black population four times as large, the 1990 census counted just over 20,000 black doctors, according to the leading U.S. association of black physicians.

Intermarriage between whites and blacks is commonplace in Cuba. Race relations, especially among individuals, are much more relaxed and amicable than in U.S. neighborhoods—and unlike in the United States, virtually all Cuban neighborhoods are racially integrated.

But many young Afro-Cubans—those too young to remember what things were like before the revolution—contend that a form of structural racism exists in Cuba, and that it is getting worse.

The Cuban version of the "New Economy" is based not on computers or the Internet but rather on tourism, which is growing by leaps and bounds while the rest of the Cuban economy languishes. Young blacks say they are underrepresented on the staffs of the big new five-star hotels and the ancillary service businesses springing up around Havana, the Varadero beach resort and other major cities. In today's Cuba, with the economy substantially "dollarized," those with access to tourists—and the dollars they spend—form a kind of new elite, and this elite of waitresses, doormen, tour guides and cab drivers appears much whiter than Cuba as a whole.

> *Unlike in the United States, virtually all Cuban neighborhoods are racially integrated.*

The government's position, famously expressed by Cuba's independence hero Jose Martí, is that race does not matter, that "we are all Cubans." But to scholars, including those who remain fully committed to the revolution, some worrisome racial issues have become self-evident.

Academics say that black Cubans are failing to earn university degrees in proportion to their numbers—a situation to which Castro has alluded publicly. The upper echelons of the government remain disproportionately white, despite the emergence of several rising black stars. And while perceptions are difficult to quantify, much less prove true or false, many black Cubans are convinced that they are much less likely than whites to land good jobs—and much more likely to be hassled by police on the street, like Cano's husband, in a Cuban version of "racial profiling."

Even the most outspoken critics of the way the government has handled, or ignored, the issue of race in Cuba do not believe the racial problems here are as acute or widespread as in the United States. They share the worry of Cuban officials that foreign observers will oversimplify the situation, seeing it in stark terms of black and white when the more appropriate image is a spectrum of beiges and browns.

Several black Cubans interviewed for this article were especially anxious that reports of Cuba's racial problems not be seized on by the Cuban-American community in Miami, which is overwhelmingly white—and which was founded by a core of people who made up much of Cuba's pre-revolution white elite. Many here question whether there would have been such hubbub in Miami over Elián González had the boy been black instead of white.

"There is a feeling that to talk about this issue is to divide the unity that is necessary to face American imperialism," said Tomas Fernandez Robaina, senior researcher at the Jose Martí National Library and a preeminent scholar on race. But he added, "In many places, blacks have more problems getting a job than white people. I'm not telling you a secret."

Recently Castro has acknowledged lingering traces of racial discrimination, using a speech last year to pin the blame on racist attitudes introduced during the U.S. occupation of Cuba following the Spanish-American War.

Many here question whether there would have been such hubbub in Miami over Elián González had the boy been black instead of white.

His brother, Vice President Raúl Castro, the second most powerful man in Cuba, tackled the subject in March, in a speech that black Cubans still remember and parts of which they cite verbatim. He used a more down-to-earth example that people could relate to their everyday lives: If a hotel denies entry to a person because he is black, he said, then the hotel should be shut.

When black Cubans gather, the topic of racism readily emerges. But the government does not permit clubs, associations or movements based on race; there is no NAACP in Cuba, nor would one be allowed.

Cuban race relations are thus conducted on the individual level, and because of cultural factors they lack the element of confrontation. This is a nation where a man can refer to his dark-skinned girlfriend as *"mi negra,"* or "my black woman," without giving it a thought or raising any hackles. It is a society where friends can tease each other about how dark their skin is and no one takes offense; where a tan-skinned woman can casually say of a party she attended, "Oh, there were a lot of negros there, so I left," and no one seems uncomfortable or embarrassed. Cubans love to laugh, love to employ their well-developed sense of irony.

"There is an important difference between our two countries," said Alexis Esquivel, an artist who has helped organize groundbreaking exhibitions here on the theme of race. "In the United States, you can't joke about race, not at all, but you can talk about it seriously. Here in Cuba, you can joke about race all you want. But you can't talk about it seriously."

Cuba's Racial History

Cuba has a familiar history of slavery and emancipation, but also a history of widespread intermarriage. The result is that racial lines are not nearly so clearly drawn, or so immutably fixed, as in the United States. There has not been a census since 1980–81, and at that time a majority of Cubans identified themselves as white. Most Cuban scholars discount that result, estimating that the Cuban population is between 60 percent and 70 percent black or mulatto (mixed-race). They also question the usefulness of official government statistics on race that are based on that census.

Cubans reserve the term "black" for people with very dark skin and kinky hair. Many African Americans who consider themselves black would be called mulatto in Cuba, and some—with light skin and straight hair—would be called white. The pre-revolution racial hierarchy put whites on the top, blacks on the bottom and mulattos

---

The pre-revolution racial hierarchy put whites on the top, blacks on the bottom and mulattos somewhere in between.

---

somewhere in between; the revolution ended all official discrimination, but as in virtually every country with a history of slavery, traces remain.

"The economic crisis has taken the lid off," said researcher Cano. "Now there is new space for racist attitudes to exist."

She referred to the implosion of the Cuban economy following the dissolution of the Soviet Union and the Eastern Bloc, which ended a lifeline of subsidies and eliminated the only viable markets for Cuban goods. The early 1990s were desperate years in Cuba, a time when people accustomed to a reasonable standard of living were suddenly hungry, when gasoline was in short supply and power outages were a daily occurrence. The government calls it the "Special Period"—and although the situation has greatly improved, Castro has not yet declared it at an end.

The crisis exacerbated tensions, and many black Cubans began to feel that in this egalitarian society, they were getting the short end of the stick. After Castro made it legal to possess and spend dollars, remittances from overseas relatives eased the pain for some Cubans. But since so many of the Cubans in Miami and elsewhere who could afford to send money home were white, the relatives on the receiving end in Cuba also tended to be white.

During the leanest years there were episodes of unrest. The worst came in the summer of 1994 along the seafront in Central Havana, a neighborhood that happens to have a high percentage of black residents. Crowds took to the streets and police officers came under attack. It did not qualify as a race riot, but arguably was the closest thing post-revolution Cuba had seen.

The turmoil prompted Castro to allow a limited safety-valve exodus of rafters to set out for Florida—the first mass departure in which there were substantial numbers of blacks as well as whites.

The conventional wisdom to that point had been that blacks were among Castro's most faithful and avid supporters—beneficiaries of both concrete benefits and memorable gestures, from Castro's legendary choice to stay in Harlem during his first New York visit to his decision to send thousands of Cuban troops to faraway wars in Africa. Shortly after the 1994 disturbances, the government accelerated a move to promote young, activist black officials to key posts, even inviting them into the inner circle.

The Communist Party leader in Havana city, Esteban Lazo, is black, as is the party leader for Havana province, Pedro Saez.

Blacks also hold the top party posts in Santiago, Cuba's second-largest city, and Camaguey, as well as leading positions in several other party organs.

It is unclear, though, the extent to which these brash, can-do officials have convinced black Cubans that the government is addressing their concerns about race.

In Santiago, a young black man named Lazaro—he did not want his last name used—spoke of how he admired black leaders in the United States, like Jesse L. Jackson.

Asked who were the black leaders in Cuba, he gave a sardonic smile.

"Look, man," he said. "In Cuba, there's only one leader."

Carving Cultural Space

"The first thing you're accused of when you do work like this," said artist Alexis Esquivel, fingering his long dreadlocks, "is that you're doing something to damage the image of Cuba."

"Work like this" means the exhibitions that Esquivel, 31, and a group of Cuban artists, black and white, organized on the theme of race in Cuba. The first was called "Keloids," a reference to the raised scars that form when African skin is wounded.

One artist, Manuel Arenas, showed two paintings that dealt with black Cubans' experience in the streets—one titled "Look Out, There's a Black Man," and the other titled "ID Card" and showing a black man, set against the national emblem, opening his identity card as if to show it to a policeman. Another artist, Rene Pena, played against the stereotype of the Cuban black man as sexually voracious with a photograph of a black man's nude torso in which the penis is replaced by a knife blade.

Esquivel's work in this show, mounted at the Center for Development of the Visual Arts, centered on the soga—a rope that was used long ago at dances and other functions to separate blacks from whites. The soga is a theme he returns to again and again, sometimes installing a rope high in a gallery so that only the observant notice it, sometimes using the rope as a barrier, sometimes tying rope tightly around his face like a horse's bridle—or an instrument of bondage.

To Esquivel's surprise, the exhibition was reviewed in the official Communist Party newspaper *Granma*. The review was generally positive, if somewhat cool, but the significant thing was that the show was acknowledged at all. Esquivel went on to help mount a second "Keloids" exhibition.

Esquivel's own history is instructive. A mulatto by Cuban standards, he grew up in a small town in the interior. His artistic talent was recognized and he was sent to another province, Pinar del Río, to attend a special school. Almost all of his classmates were white, and to hear him talk of the experience is like listening to a young black man talk about how he felt going to St. Albans or Sidwell Friends.

"I had to suppress my musical tastes," he said. "I liked traditional music, music you could dance to, but my friends were all into rock. I was conflicted."

"People would say something like, 'Those blacks, they're horrible.' Then they'd turn to me and say, 'Oh no, Alexis, we're not talking about you, you're fine.' Imagine what that does to a person."

He recalls the moment of his radicalization: For an assignment in school, he read *The Autobiography of Malcolm X*. From that point, he identified himself as black.

"I remember going home on a visit," he said, "and telling my mother not to use hair straightener anymore."

Esquivel's partner in putting on the exhibitions was a Cuban art historian, Ariel Ribeaux, who wrote the manifesto for this gathering movement of black-themed art. Ribeaux's award-winning essay was entitled "Neither Musicians Nor Athletes."

That title was a comment on the space that blacks traditionally occupied in Cuban society, praised for their athletic prowess—Fidel Castro himself went out to the airport to greet Cuba's returning Olympic athletes, most of whom were black or brown—and their contributions to broadly defined Cuban "culture," especially religion and music.

Black Cubans have begun to use that cultural space to express racial pride and to comment on their position in the society.

The Afro-Cuban religion that most Americans know as *santería*, but that most believers in Havana call "the Yoruba religion," recently was allowed to open a cultural center in an airy downtown building near the pre-revolution capitol. Rafael Robaina, a researcher at the Center of Anthropology who specializes in the religion, calls it "the only black organization that we have in Cuba."

Antonio Castaneda, president of the Yoruba Cultural Center, says the building, with its museum devoted to the Afro-Cuban saints, is "a bastion in defense of black people, a source of pride." Castro helped fund the $2 million project by instructing banks to lend the necessary money for construction.

> ### *The Afro-Cuban religion that most Americans know as* santería . . . *recently was allowed to open a cultural center in an airy downtown building near the pre-revolution capitol.*

In music, meanwhile, young Cuban songwriters slip in sly lyrics about skin color, about unemployment, about racism. At a recent performance by the popular group NG La Banda, for example, the singer added a line about a black man being stopped by police on the street.

In a bit of commentary that would do Richard Pryor or Chris Rock proud, the singer, who is black, used the Cuban slang word that most closely approximates "nigger."

Walking While Black

That is the one concrete, on-the-ground issue that almost all black Cuban men, especially young men, can relate to: being halted by police and made to produce their documents. To foreigners, the officers are unfailingly polite—even if, for example, the foreigner happens to be barreling the wrong way down a one-way street. But when they are not just standing and watching, generally they are stopping young men and asking to see their papers. Anecdotally, but also in the universal opinion of black Cubans, the men being stopped are more likely to be black than white.

Recall the case of Maria del Carmen Cano's husband, who was stopped in Havana while an identically dressed white man was allowed to breeze by? According to Cano, her husband was so indignant that he demanded to know why he had been singled out. "We were looking for someone with physical characteristics like yours," the policeman replied.

A few days later, Cano says, she and her husband went to a party where there were a number of black couples, and he told the story. Everyone laughed. "Four or five black men there had had the same thing happen to them. And they had been told the same thing—'We are looking for someone with physical characteristics like yours.'"

She goes on, "My husband was even more angry. He said, 'If you're going to lie to me, at least be original.'"

Making Waves[5]

By Rosa Lowinger
Art News Online, June 2000

In Ghent earlier this year, the Cuban artist Kcho leaned over the side of a small motorboat to lay strips of wood on the Lys River. He had been commissioned by the city of Ghent and its Stedelijk Museum voor Actuele Kunst to create new work for the group exhibition "Over the Edge." It had been raining for three days, and his Belgian assistants wondered why Kcho, wet and covered with mud, chose to plot the dimensions of his on-site installation in the freezing weather rather than sketch his idea on paper and contract an engineer to build it. Kcho explained that he first needed to "make the drawing in the river" himself by using the cast-off wood he found in the city's harbor. The completed piece, on view through the third of this month, is a 66-foot-long dock that spirals out into the water from a medieval castle on the riverbank.

Water—its presence usually just implied—is a powerful point of reference for Kcho (pronounced KAH-cho). Docks, boats, oars, rafts, inner tubes, and debris washed up from the ocean are among the objects he has included in his installations. For the 30-year-old artist, creating work that points to the sea is a natural result of having been born and raised on a small island off the southern coast of Cuba. "Where I grew up, all the limits were liquid," says the artist, who is now based in Havana. To reach the main island required a four-hour boat ride.

Travel and migration in the context of his country's recent history also figure prominently in Kcho's work. In 1994, just months before a massive wave of emigrants embarked for Florida from all over Cuba's northern coast, he created *La regata (The Regatta)*, a flotilla of toy boats and beach debris—rocks, driftwood, twigs, pieces of rubber—that was installed in one of the fortresses that line the Havana harbor, as part of the Fifth Havana Bienal. *Lo mejor del verano (The Best of Summer)* was created that same year for "*Cocido y crudo*" (Cooked and Raw), an exhibition at the Museo Nacional Centro de Arte Reina Sofía in Madrid, organized by Dan Cameron, now senior curator of Manhattan's New Museum. That installation included rowboats, kayaks, bits of wood, oars, baskets,

---

5. Article by Rosa Lowinger from *Art News Online* June 2000. Copyright © *Art News.* Reprinted with permission.

and fishing nets suspended from the ceiling and reflected in the black polished floor. One had the impression of being submerged in water, witnessing a shipwreck from below.

"People went into that gallery and cried," says Manuel E. González, a Cuban exile and current director of the art program for Chase Manhattan Bank in New York, describing how the installation evoked the tragic fate of so many Cubans who have taken to the seas over the years. And while his choice of imagery draws directly from the collective psyche of his nation, Kcho's penchant for discarded objects mirrors the contemporary Cuban practice of salvaging and recycling materials because of the scarcity of basic items. "Kcho is the quintessential Cuban artist of the 'Special Period,'" says González, referring to the era of economic crisis in Cuba that began after the breakup of the Soviet Union in 1991.

> *The installation evoked the tragic fate of so many Cubans who have taken to the seas over the years.*

Today, Kcho is celebrated as the island's most internationally established artist since Wifredo Lam (1902–82). In the last decade, his poetic and sometimes nostalgic works have been featured in more than 50 group shows and biennials around the world and in 15 solo exhibitions, at such venues as the Museum of Contemporary Art (MoCA) in Los Angeles (1997), the Jeu de Paume in Paris (1998), and the Palacio de Cristal at the Reina Sofía (2000). *Para olvidar* (*To Forget*), an installation consisting of a rowboat set atop a pile of empty and half-empty beer bottles, won the $50,000 grand prize at the 1995 Kwangju Biennale in South Korea. The artist's first show in the United States took place in 1996 at New York's Barbara Gladstone gallery, which continues to represent him. His work sells for between $4,000 for a drawing and $75,000 for larger sculptures. Many of his pieces are in the collection of major museums, including New York's Museum of Modern Art and the Museo de Bellas Artes in Havana.

In all of his installations, Kcho tends to use the same basic vocabulary of images and objects associated with the sea. "He works with few symbols, but every time you see a new drawing or a boat, it's like seeing it for the first time," says Alma Ruiz, assistant curator at MoCA in Los Angeles, who organized Kcho's 1997 exhibition "*Todo cambia*" (Everything Changes). The artist created two installations for the show. One was a series of totemic sculptures of unbaked clay and wire fashioned in the forms of a raft, sailboat, kayak, oar, and inner tube. The other consisted of a large boat constructed of wooden racks of the sort used by Havana booksellers and filled with Spanish, English, and French texts representing a wide range of literature available in Cuba. Visitors were encouraged to board the boat and spend time reading the books. "These works have tremendous physicality," remarks Ruiz. "Just like him."

Kcho's presence is palpable even before he enters a room. At Casa de las Americas, a Havana cultural institution where he recently showed, he could be heard thundering down the hall, calling out to friends he had not seen since his residency at Alexander Calder's studio outside Paris. Not especially tall but as thick and solid as a football linebacker, Kcho was in constant motion, dominating the offices of Casa de las Americas with his voice, enormous smile, and seemingly boundless energy. It was a hot day, and he pulled off his shirt, cinched his pants with a rope belt, put the shirt back on, then shouted to fellow artist Tania Bruguera, literally lifting her off her feet as he hugged her. One gallery assistant offered him water and another brought out highball glasses with ice and Chivas Regal. This was star treatment, Cuban-style.

"I'm so happy that this place would invite me to do this show in Cuba, where my friends are and the people I love," he said that day, talking at breakneck speed. "The last time I exhibited in Cuba was in '97 at the Bienal. I wanted to do the MoCA show here but no one wanted it."

Kcho's lament is familiar among young Cuban artists, and it is due, in part, to the political subtext that exists in much of their work. In the 1980s, many artists were making art that overtly critiqued the government. This led to censorship and, finally, mass emigration of many of the island's most prominent figures, such as José Bedia, who now lives in Miami. Now, a decade later, the artists of Kcho's generation tend to cloak their messages in poetry and symbolism.

The Casa de las Americas show, which ended in March, was modest in size, but Kcho nevertheless managed to use the awkwardly divided gallery and low ceiling to their best advantage to convey his themes of migration and impermanence. The most effective piece was a simple boat made of chain-link fencing that filled almost an entire room. The boat's prow protruded through a narrow doorway between rooms, and one got inside the boat by walking through an opening in the prow. "Upon entering the gallery, we were obligated to board the boat," says Cuban curator Cristina Vives, recalling her visit to the exhibition with a group of curators from Minneapolis. "Those who went inside became temporary travelers, emigrants, and those of us who chose to stay outside—on land, as it were—watched this mass of humanity crowded together like immigrants on any latitude of the planet." The title of the installation, *No me agradezcan el silencio* (*Do Not Thank Me for Silence*) is typically poetic and ambiguous.

"Kcho's titles are essential to understanding his work," says Ruiz. "He is purposely enigmatic so he can say things indirectly. '*Todo cambia*,' the title of his show at MoCA, was his way of saying that in the island everything changes, but everything stays the same." Kcho explains that his titles play a role in his art-making process. "I was in a bar last night, having a beer with one of my assistants. A small thing suddenly became something: don't hammer two nails in one line. I was explaining it to him and, at the same time, I knew the expression would be the starting point for a new work. I have notebooks full of phrases like that," says Kcho. "Sometimes it takes me a year or more to do something with them, but my process always begins with the title."

Kcho was born in 1970 on the Isla de la Juventud. His father, a carpenter, had always wanted to name a son Cacho, which means "chunk" or "piece." His mother, the person in charge of the decorations for the island's annual carnival, protested, and he was named Alexis Leyva Machado. Still, the nickname stuck throughout his youth. In high school, the artist changed the spelling. "Crooks had aliases, I wanted one, too," he wrote in the catalogue for "*La columna infinita*."

Kcho learned to use hand tools and to make wooden toys from his father. "If I had not gone to art school," he says, "I would have ended up a carpenter like him." But he began early academic training in art, after a local teacher was impressed by his talent. He attended school on his island until he was 14, when he was accepted into the prestigious Escuela Nacional de Artes Plásticas in Havana, Cuba's national fine-arts school. He began as a painter but soon switched to sculpture because, he says, "painting seemed too methodical, too much about process, and there's an element of deceit in it." Now he eschews most applied color in his work, but he credits his painting background for enabling him "to see that trash also has color."

Unlike many Cuban artists of his generation, Kcho was not accepted at the Instituto Superior de Arte, the university level of the fine-arts school. Consequently, he began his professional career much earlier than most. At the age of 21, he was in group shows in Havana and Caracas and was given a solo exhibition at the Havana gallery Centro de Arte 23 y 12. Titled "*Paisaje popular cubano*" (Cuban Folk Landscape), the show featured Kcho's 1990 *La peor de las trampas* (*The Worst of Traps*), a ladder made of branches that culminate in fake palm fronds and whose rungs are machete blades, and the elegantly spare *Como el garabato se parece a Cuba* (*How the Hook Resembles Cuba*), a 1991 piece consisting of a farmer's grass-cutting tool that looks remarkably like the profile of the island.

In 1992 Kcho traveled outside of Cuba for the first time to participate in shows in Mexico, Holland, Belgium, and Spain. While abroad, he encountered works by artists who had been influencing him for years. "Picasso and Duchamp are gods," says Kcho. More direct influences come from the work of Constantin Brancusi and the Russian Constructivist Vladimir Tatlin. *A los ojos de la historia* (*To the Eyes of History*), Kcho's 1992 spiral tower made of twigs, sticks, and twine, was modeled after Tatlin's never-realized *Model for the Monument to the Third International* (1919–20). Kcho's tower, however, is topped with a used conical fabric coffee filter, recycling a failed monument into a quasi-functional item.

Kcho makes frequent reference to Brancusi in his "La columna infinita" series. Since 1995, he has been constructing columns composed

> *"Cuba is not Fidel alone.
> . . . Cuba is also its
> artists."*—Cuban artist Kcho.

of everything from bent wood to stacked boats to rubber inner tubes to bottles. The recent show at the Palacio de Cristal brought together eleven of these pieces from collections around the world.

Sly political references are tucked here and there throughout Kcho's work. Included in the Madrid show was a series of drawings of docks—each dock in the shape of a letter that spells out, among other things, Elián, the first name of the six-year-old Cuban boy who survived a boat wreck and whose contested custody put a spotlight on Cuban-American relations.

Like most Cuban artists, Kcho rejects a purely political understanding of his work. Still, sometimes he cannot help having the political discussion imposed on him. His 1996 show at Barbara Gladstone was picketed by angry Cuban exiles who claimed that any support for a Cuban artist directly assists the Castro regime. The following year he was denied an entry visa by the U.S., making it impossible for him to create the wall drawing that was to be part of the MoCA show. Once it became clear that no amount of lobbying by MoCA would overturn the U.S. decision, the artist had Ruiz include their correspondence and the rejection notice from the State Department as part of the installation that contained the book racks.

Meanwhile, Kcho has been able to travel to different parts of the world for numerous exhibitions. And when he's home in Havana—where the money he makes from sales abroad affords him a degree of wealth—Kcho enjoys an international cachet. Wherever he is, when discussing his work he continues to stress its universal themes—travel, nostalgia, loss, and impermanence—rather than letting it be pigeonholed as purely political. After all, he says, "Cuba is not Fidel alone. . . . Cuba is also its artists."

Castro's Children

Cuba's Youth Study, Party and Scrounge[6]

By Dierdra Funcheon
NEW YORK PRESS, NOVEMBER 22, 2000

It's 50 years since Fidel Castro received his law degree from the University of Havana, and everyone at his alma mater is playing hooky. Instead of studying, students from different academic departments are competing in water polo, soccer and racquetball, running races, holding swim contests and karate chopping each other. The annual Caribe Games, a three-week-long university-wide athletic event, are in progress. Although class is not officially canceled, one of the truants assures me that no one attends.

I've wandered onto the campus just hours after disembarking from my flight from Montreal, motivated by a post-Elián curiosity about how young people live on Castro's island. Sitting in the crowded blue-cement bleachers by the outdoor pool, I'm approached by a copper-skinned 23-year-old with soft, light eyes who introduces himself as Alejandro. He's looking for sneakers to borrow so that he can compete in the next race. Many students run barefoot.

Alejandro studies English and German, despite having little hope of ever visiting England or Germany. He lives with his father, his mother, his uncle and his four brothers in the nearby suburb of La Lisa. They lived in Russia for a few years when his father, a military officer, was stationed there. The father is now retired, and Alejandro's mother tutors students for extra cash, a practice that is illegal but common.

Students are paid 30 pesos a month, the equivalent of $1.50, to attend university in Cuba, Ale tells me. He shows me the ration card that entitles him to five cafeteria meals each week. His family gets a separate ration card for groceries. He is handsome, but his body—even his face—is bony, angular, gaunt.

"I agree with the government ration card," he says. "They are trying to give everyone the same, but everyone does not have the same. It is impossible, but it is good that they are trying to solve problems."

---

6. Article by Deirdra Funcheon from *New York Press* November 22, 2000. Copyright © *New York Press*. Reprinted with permission.

Ale empties his backpack, showing me his student identification card, a Metallica tape, a notebook. He asks if I like Cher. Did I know that her full name is Cherilyn LaPierre, and that she was born on May 20, 1945? He got this information, he tells me, from *The Encyclopedia of New Groups*. I don't argue with him.

"I don't know if you know about this child, Elián González," he continues, as though I might have missed the dozens of city billboards depicting the child's face behind bars. "But we don't need to fight to win. We always win, with our ideas."

So you like Cuba, then? I ask him. You're not itching to innertube your way across the Florida Straits?

> *"A lot of people go to America because they see all the things that you can have there. They think if they go there, life will be better. But it will not necessarily be better."*—Alejandro, a student

"Well," he answers thoughtfully, "a lot of people go to America because they see all the things that you can have there. They think if they go there, life will be better. But it will not necessarily be better." Still, he understands why they leave. "You have to make it on your own. If I had a good opportunity in another country, I would take advantage. It doesn't have anything to do with politics."

"But if I lived in another place," he continues, "I could not hold my desire to be near the beach. When I lived in Russia, I lived near the river. I was eager to take a swim, but when I saw that the water was not like our beaches, and there were Russians sunbathing and swimming in their underwear, I wanted to come back to Cuba."

He pauses. "Is that how you say it? Beaches?" He is concerned about his accent. "Because I don't want to say 'bitches.'"

Making a friend in Cuba is like being adopted. When Alejandro leaves for his race, I am transferred to the care of his *amigos*. David, a gangly kid with a deep voice, is the school's star athlete; Omar, a shaggy-haired Bob Dylan fan, "used to play" the guitar but cannot get replacements for the strings he broke; Dayron is a graduate student who has studied in Belize. All of them speak English and hope to be assigned jobs—jobs are assigned here, not applied for—as translators once they graduate.

I am also introduced to "a VIP," the president of the Young Communist League. He is a handsome black man with a huge smile and the poise of a leader. He wears a tucked-in t-shirt bearing the word "Beijing" and a picture of a panda bear. The boys say that most of the university students belong to the Young Communist League. Students who criticize the government are not punished, they say, but "people look at them differently." Patriotic members of the League "try to show them that our government is the right way."

But enough of politics; there is a celebration at one of the university's student hangouts.

"We are referred to as 'party animals,'" Dayron says.

"Oh yeah?" I grin. "So what makes a party in Cuba? Alcohol?"

"Yes, alcohol and dancing."

"Drugs?"

"No! We don't have that problem here."

"Food?"

"No. Just rum. And dancing."

"Does the university provide the rum?"

"Of course. You sound surprised."

"Well, in the U.S., we aren't exactly encouraged to get drunk at school."

"Well, my friend," he laughs, "this is a free country."

We walk a few blocks to the Federación de Estudiantes Universitarios headquarters, which, it turns out, is quite an exclusive establishment. It takes some finagling to get past the ID-checkers at the gate, but the boys herald me as an ambassador of peace, which I am happy to fancy myself. A sweeping staircase leads up to the door of a three-story house, and brightly colored, Warholesque posters of Fidel Castro and Che Guevara adorn the outdoor walls.

The party, though, is on the open-air patio, where a DJ booth looms above a cement dancefloor surrounded by iron tables and chairs. Rum is dispensed from two giant vats and sold for centavos to students who have brought their own empty pint bottles. Dayron was right—there is no food. By now it is 7 p.m., the sun has set, and people haven't eaten since noon, but no one finds this unusual.

The place is packed with young women and men on their way to becoming biologists, psychologists and lawyers. People randomly shout, "I love English!" and invite me to stay at their homes. I dance with several guys, betraying the comparative rigidity of my American hips, and venture up to the DJ booth. The two DJs are happy to let me inspect their collection, which consists not of records, not of CDs, but of cassette tapes. Not just tapes, but copies of tapes. Second- or third-generation mix tapes. The DJs' headphones are broken in half.

The next night, I am summoned to a party in a Havana suburb called Alamar. As I move farther from the city center, the crumbling, vintage architecture of the capital is replaced with towering, boxy apartment complexes that look like they'd be condemned in the

United States. Cinderblocks are exposed; telephone poles and electric wires are bundled and strung up in haphazard ways. The streets lie empty and dark.

The interiors, though, are different. The apartment I'm visiting has a tiled floor, wicker furniture and 8-by-10 framed Picasso prints on the wall. David plays borrowed CDs on a stereo he has smuggled in for the occasion. We pass around crackers with garlic butter, pork rinds, homemade wine and bottles of rum. I play dominoes for the first time in my life, and my partner, a thin guy who could pass for Jerry Seinfeld, is incredibly congenial about our losing 100-0. He keeps yelling the few English words he knows: "We are the winner!"

Short on mind-altering substances but long on imagination, we play some games reminiscent of those played at middle-school slumber parties. In one, every person writes a compliment or question to another partygoer, anonymously. For example, "Why do you seem quiet tonight?" Or "You are a great volleyball player." The recipient reads the note, writes a reply, scratches off his or her own name and then places the note in a pile to be read aloud. I write to Alejandro, "You are very intelligent." When one of the girls reads through all the notes, I learn his reply: "Obviously, you underestimate me." I tell him, "In America, we call you a smartass."

Sex is one of the few forms of affordable entertainment here, but it's difficult to find a secluded place in which to have it.

We play another game in which the boys, as a group, choose a question to ask the girls. While they are conferring, the girls decide which of us will answer truthfully; the rest of us will lie. The boys ask, "Where do you most like to make love?" and "On what part of your body do you most like to be kissed?" Then we each answer, in turn, and the boys guess whose answer was honest.

Sex is one of the few forms of affordable entertainment here, but it's difficult to find a secluded place in which to have it. You can rent rooms in Cuba by the hour, and there's a popular Spanish term that translates as "vertical love." Someone tells me that condoms are the preferred method of birth control, but doesn't mention that Cuba's abortion rate is the highest in the hemisphere. Abortions have been legal since the 1940s and are performed for free at state hospitals. As in the United States, people postpone getting married until they're in their late 20s, and the divorce rate is high. "Ninety-nine percent," someone joked to me. (The actual rate is 3.7 divorces per 1000 people, close to the U.S. rate of 4.3, according to United Nations statistics.)

When a Backstreet Boys song comes on, five of the guys suddenly line up and bust moves that would make the American boy-band weep. Around 4 a.m., I try to call a taxi from the outdoor pay phone. I have no currency smaller than a dollar, which, if it could be inserted into the phone, would buy a hundred calls. But it can't, so Alejandro pays. We have no success with the phone system; it looks like I will be staying until morning.

Twelve of us retire to David's apartment. We move into his bedroom, where we won't disturb the assortment of sleeping relatives. The room is sparse, cold and lit by fluorescent bulbs; pictures of Alicia Silverstone and NBA stars are taped to his wall. Seven people pile on the twin bed; Alejandro and I take the floor. We joke around until a rooster in the yard starts to crow.

At sunrise, there is already a long line for the bus. An official passes out tickets to people in the order that they arrive, because only a limited number of bodies can board at once. We manage to catch the next bus, Dayron paying my fare, even though, with the dollar I'm holding, I could buy a hundred fares. Chivalry lives in Cuba.

The city of Santa Clara, where one of the defining battles of the revolution took place, is quite famous for its giant statue of Che Guevara. Batista fled as soon as the rebels took Santa Clara, and a spirit of energy and optimism lingers in its streets. On every block, people are playing: baseball, hopscotch, dominoes. Couples on motorcycles putter by, carrying loaves of bread; a man pushes a tv in a wheelbarrow. People light fires and cook stew in the middle of the street, and 26-year-old Ernesto (named after Ernesto "Che" Guevara) hands me flowers when I walk by. I am adopted again.

Ernesto would like to run a restaurant. And no wonder. He and his friend Tony lead me to a *paladar*, an incognito restaurant run in someone's home. We sneak up a narrow spiral staircase to a tiny room with covered windows and two small tables. I order food, but the guys insist they want nothing. I order them beers anyway, and tell the owner to bring extra plates. Once the spread arrives—chicken, shrimp, rice, beans, salad and bananas—the two relax, but only a little. The bill comes to almost $30; I have just spent on our dinner a sum it would take a Cuban three months to earn.

Tony is a music technician for bands that play in Santa Clara. "Do you like Metallica?" he asks me. "Guns 'N Roses? Whitesnake? Nirvana? Santa Clara is the capital of rock." When we move on to a bar, he does me what he thinks is a favor, and keeps requesting these bands at the DJ booth.

On the way back to my room that night, I am stopped by a car-load of kids hanging around a purple Cadillac preserved from the 1950s. Such old cars are common in Cuba, but it's still weird to see a young person driving one. Ten girls are crammed in the back; the owner and his two friends are obviously proud.

The girls, I find, study pharmacology at the university in Santa Clara, and two of the boys go to school. The one with the car did not finish college, and when I ask if he plans to go back, they all giggle. It's as if I've asked Bill Gates why he doesn't go back to pick up those last credits at Harvard. He has a car! He's already loaded! One of the boys says he knows a guy who went to Miami and managed to buy two cars in six months. This elicits "oohs" from the girls, who look at me to confirm that this could be possible. Such is the stuff of legend.

I'm asked whether I own a car back in the U.S., and I answer yes. Twelve pairs of critical, curious eyes fixate on me, and I feel a little guilty. Trying to deflect the attention, I ask the kids what they do besides go to school.

"We drive around," says the most talkative girl, the leader.

Just drive around?

"And look for food."

Not all young people in Havana are fortunate enough to be university students. To get into U of H, students must pass a series of rigorous admissions tests. Once in, students must pass more tests to be admitted to the program of their choice. What about those who don't make it? I ask Dayron. He shrugs. "They do something else."

For some, something else means being a *jinetero*. The term literally means "jockey," and refers primarily to prostitutes, but is also used to describe young capitalists who hustle tourists for dollars. *Jineteros* come in both male and female versions, and in Havana they hang out near the Coppelia, which is the place to see and be seen.

One night at the Coppelia I am approached by a smooth 25-year-old girl named Alicia and her young friend, who, it seems, is in training. Eager to please, Alicia asks if I want to go to a party, or to a movie, or to a club. She guides me to a bar called La Red. She says that both she and her friend are salsa teachers, which I later learn is a popular, and vaguely defined, occupation in Cuba.

In this particular club, which is close to many hotels, a tv channel broadcasts American videos with a Latin feel—Christina Aguilera, Jennifer Lopez, Elvis Crespo. The "salsa teachers" give me an impromptu lesson while everyone else at the bar eyes them jealously. They are all learning, together, how to work this economy.

Alicia orders a round of sodas. How generous, I think. It is only later, when we are ready to move on, that I get passed the bill for the four drinks, and am charged eight dollars for entering. Alicia consults with the doorman. I think she just earned her week's pay. I tell her that I am tired, and ready for bed. Am I sure? she asks. Is there anything she can get for me? Alcohol? Drugs? Marijuana?

In Cuba, it is frowned upon *not* to pick up hitchhikers. If you have a car, and even a little bit of free space in it, you're expected to take on passengers. In fact, government workers in yellow jumpsuits, stationed along the roadside, flag down drivers and organize the process.

> *In Cuba, it is frowned upon not to pick up hitchhikers. . . . In fact, government workers in yellow jump-suits . . . flag down drivers and orga-nize the process.*

About 15 miles outside the city of Trinidad, I stop my rented teal Peugeot to pick up Ivan, a 26-year-old swimming teacher. He works two mornings a week at an elementary school several towns away. Because of the haphazard transportation system, he leaves his house at 5 a.m. to make his 8:30 class. But what about the other five days?

He laughs. "The girls think I am *loco* because all I do is fish." Around 8 a.m., he tells me, he ties a net to his ankle, grabs his harpoon gun and swims five kilometers into the ocean. Alone, he treads water until he has either speared 70 fish or it gets dark. It is illegal to catch lobsters; they are reserved only for export. He sells the fish for five pesos apiece to *casas particulares*—homes that are run as bed-and-breakfasts for tourists, at a rate of about $15 a night.

Ivan calls himself an "Indio" because of his reddish-brown skin—not that skin color is much of an issue here. Fifty-one percent of the population is mulatto, people of all races work and socialize together and discrimination is barely detectable to the American visitor. Racism, I am told, is a minor problem and most noticeable in the provinces.

Ivan lives with his grandmother, mother and stepfather. He would like to move out, but says it isn't possible. Housing is in such short supply that many married couples cannot get a place of their own; slim chance that a young, single man would be granted his own apartment. He would like to live in the U.S., but only temporarily. "I could open a Cuban restaurant for a few months and make enough money to come back and live like a king."

Later, we walk around the town. The bars are full of Canadians, Italians, French. I ask Ivan if we can visit a bar where the locals hang out, but there really isn't one. A giant cave on the mountainside has been turned into a nightclub. Ivan has only been in it a few times, when he has sold a lot of fish and can afford the seven-dollar cover charge. The town, it seems, does not belong to natives. It belongs to tourists.

At one club, a compact young guy in black pants, a skintight camouflage t-shirt and sunglasses dances flamboyantly. Ivan points to him and says: "Gay." He makes a face of disgust and says that there are many homosexuals in Cuba. "They are a problem!"

Two mornings later, I wake up to a loud banging on the door. It's not quite 7 a.m. An immigration officer in green army fatigues orders me to come to his office and meet with his boss. Still bleary-eyed, I follow him to a complex of boxy concrete buildings on a dirt road, where I am ushered into a small office and interrogated by two soldiers.

They're stern but sympathetic. They are just doing their jobs, making sure that all news gets dispensed by the only national daily newspaper, the government-backed tabloid *Granma*. I am asked to confirm what they have heard about the U.S., and my responses stun them. Yes, college costs $24,000 a year. Yes, kids shoot other kids at school. And yes, we must pay to see the doctor. "*¡Dios mío!*" they mumble.

I get a talking-to about the difference between a journalist visa and a tourist visa from the higher-ranking of the two men. "Many people do not understand Cuba," he says. "They come here for a few days, and go to their country and write negative things.

"With this visa," he continues, holding it up, "you can go the waterfalls, go to the beach, and take pretty pictures. Stop asking questions."

There is a Cuban saying that goes, "*Si tu tienes amigos, tienes un central*"—if you have friends, you have a factory. Anything can be produced.

I need a place to stay on my last two days in Havana, and through word of mouth find room at the home of a family anchored by Elisa, a woman pushing the upper limit of the Gen-X range. Four generations' worth of Elisa's clan live on the premises; they scurry to rearrange their quarters to make room for me and feed me, and they give me a rare three-peso coin engraved with Che Guevara's image. They shield me from the television every time someone on it raves about the evil Miami Cuban mafia (which is often), and tell me I am "*familia*."

The hospitality is amazing, but the house is crumbling. The walls and ceilings are pocked with holes, a roach runs through the living room and the bathroom is filthy. Grayish underwear hangs on hooks beside the shower. The toilet flushes only occasionally, and the wiping materials (which aren't necessarily toilet paper) must be put in a trash can because the septic system cannot handle them. To shower, one must stand in a colorful plastic tub inside the bathtub, or else the hundreds of miniature flies that live in and around the drain will come swarming out in a black cloud.

Trying to lighten my load for the return trip home, I filter through my backpack. Elisa accepts all that I offer, including a shirt, shampoo, soap, zit cream and a half-used deodorant. She is especially pleased with film and batteries, and when she admires my shoes, I give those to her as well. Her mom goes nuts over a bottle of nail polish.

Elisa has the air of a powerful woman, so I am not surprised to learn that she used to work in high-level government offices, and at one point with Fidel Castro's brother, Raúl. Many Cuba-watchers have speculated that Raúl will take Fidel's place when he goes, but Elisa gives me a sidelong glance when I bring that up, and wags her finger.

"No, no, no," she says. Raúl has no personality, no leadership skills, the people don't like him. "But don't think for a second that Fidel hasn't thought about this," she says. She taps her forefinger on her temple and says, "He knows. He has been training people. . . . I can't tell you the names, but they are good people." She nods and winks. "Don't worry, good people."

Will Cuba become a democracy then, I ask? Will there be capitalism? She squints and thinks about it. "Small chance," she says pinching her thumb and forefinger. "Very, very small chance."

The next day we cruise around with Elisa's friend Lili. I still don't quite understand the Cuban work ethic. Anyone who's not selling something roams slowly through the streets, or waits for a ride somewhere. A garbage truck passes at midday; three men on the back take turns loading trash while three in the cab sip a bottle of rum. Folks hang lazily out the windows of the cigar factories, watching passersby. We stop to see a group of Elisa's friends who are relaxing in their living room.

Elisa says she's between jobs. Lili, a jai-alai teacher, says she works Monday through Saturday, but it is Friday, at noon, and she's cruising around Havana in my rental car (*"Fidel's* rental car," they correct me), blasting Elvis Crespo tapes and going to drink beers at Ernest Hemingway's house. "It's okay," she says, laughing.

That night, I meet the university students back at the pool to celebrate the end of the Caribe Games. About 1500 people, including the DJs with their mix tapes, surround the makeshift stage beside the pool, below the banana-tree-covered hill. A guy named Miguel ("Like Michael Jordan!" he declares. "I like Mike!"), who, in an Hawaiian print shirt and khakis, looks like LL Cool J modeling for the J. Crew catalog, offers me some rum.

"I love English," says the 27-year-old, over the music. "But I could never live in America. America is too fast. Here it is paradise." He beams, sweeping one arm through the air, gesturing at the night sky. "I love my country, I love my government and I very much love my family."

Everyone shakes, the two DJs stand on a chair and pump their fists, and some people fall into the pool. I am trying to salsa with the soccer coach when the music cuts off, people start shrieking and 1500 bodies spit away from the dancefloor. A fight has broken out.

Joel, an acquaintance of mine, grabs me and leads me through the hysterical crowd as people file out of the gate. The party has ended. Sadness looms.

"This really pisses me off," says Joel, in English. One guy walks by, shirtless, blood dripping down the side of his face. Our friends huddle, disappointed.

"This never happens," they say urgently, like they must convince me of this.

"It's okay," I say. "Fights happen everywhere."

"They don't usually happen in Cuba, and never at the university," says Joel.

Military police have come to investigate, and we leave. As we move across the dark soccer field, a hefty woman in a long white nightgown, with flocculent gray hair and spectacles, comes across the field, yelling, "Miguel!" My friend Michael Jordan runs up to her, kisses her head and walks off with his arm around her—his mom.

Just when I thought I might leave Cuba without meeting someone who wants to defect, Joel tells me he wants to go to Miami. Seriously. Within the next year.

"Here there are so many problems. It is difficult to get soap. They give you a house, but the house is falling apart. They give you food, but the food that is supposed to be for a month is really only for seven days. I have little brothers, and my parents, and I want to go the U.S. and send them money."

Doesn't the government block you from leaving?

"No! If you want to go, fine. Bye. Leave."

The problem is getting a U.S. visa—"For every visa given, 20 people apply," Joel tells me—and then finding a way to get to the States. Joel knows a girl who won one of the U.S. visas in the Cuban lottery; she's agreed to marry him so that he might leave as well.

"I have a friend who went to Miami on a boat," he tells me. "He said that he had so much fear, to be at sea for a few days, in the black night. He said if he had known what it was going to be like, he would never have gone. But I must go now. I am young, and I am like a ram. Always fighting."

To finance his trip, Joel has brokered a black-market deal on a laptop computer. With the $50 he made, he bought a rewritable CD-ROM drive that he can use on a friend's computer. He plans to download music from the Internet, record CDs and sell them for profit. In light of the fact that few Cubans have ever sent an e-mail, much less downloaded something, Joel's entrepreneurial skills are striking.

His naïveté about the States soon becomes evident, though. "I think the U.S. government gives every Cuban who arrives the money to live for a year," he says.

I tell him to think of a backup plan. His dream job, he says, would be to manage a computer store. He adds that he can fix computer hardware, and that he knows Microsoft Access and Microsoft Excel. It occurs to me that, with these skills, and given that he's bilingual, Joel is possibly more employable than I am.

The next night, my last in Cuba, I invite all the people I have met in Havana to a picnic at a park overlooking the bay, just under the statue of El Cristo, Jesus Christ. I shop at a modern grocery store that only rich Cubans and tourists can afford. Hair dye and toothpaste are displayed in a locked glass case, and a security guard patrols the aisles. At the closely guarded deli counter, I buy 45 slices of ham for 20 American dollars. Rum costs three dollars a bottle.

Seven friends make it to the picnic, where I introduce the concept of the footlong sub and try to describe McDonald's.

"You mean you don't even have to get out of the car?" Alejandro asks.

They teach me some Spanish slang. *"Nadar a la pelota,"* they explain, means to go skinny dipping, which none of them have ever done, and they give me a *"Salvemos a Elián"* t-shirt that they got at one of the rallies. We sing "Hotel California" and some Bon Jovi songs.

I tell them that I want to send a package when I return to the U.S., and they warn me that it may be pilfered if I send it through the mail. I promise to write them at their university e-mail addresses, but we know that could be unreliable. They tell me I should hurry back, and I am flattered; but when I suggest that they come visit me, I can tell from their faces that it is as though I have made a cruel joke.

Bibliography

Books

Alvarez, José, and Lázaro Peña Castellanos. *Cuba's Sugar Industry*. Gainesville: University Press of Florida, 2001.

Azicri, Max. *Cuba Today and Tomorrow: Reinventing Socialism*. Gainesville: University Press of Florida, 2000.

Block, Holly, and Gerardo Mosquera, eds. *Art Cuba: The New Generation*. New York: Harry N. Abrams, 2001.

Canizares, Raul. *Cuban Santería*. Rochester, VT: Inner Traditions International, 1999.

Castro, Fidel. *Capitalism in Crisis: Globalization and World Politics Today*. Hoboken, NJ: Ocean Press, 2000

Chomsky, Noam. *Latin America: From Colonization to Globalization*. Hoboken, NJ: Ocean Press, 2000.

Daniel, Yvonne. *Rumba: Dance and Social Change in Contemporary Cuba*. Bloomington: Indiana University Press, 1995.

Díaz-Briquets, Sergio, and Jorge Pérez-López. *Conquering Nature: The Environmental Legacy of Socialism in Cuba*. Pittsburgh: University of Pittsburgh Press, 2000.

Erisman, H. Michael. *Cuba's Foreign Relations in a Post-Soviet World*. Gainesville: University Press of Florida, 2000.

Espin, Vilma, and Deborah Shnookal, eds. *Cuban Women Confront the Future: Three Decades after the Revolution*. Hoboken, NJ: Ocean Press, 1992.

Evenson, Debra. *Law and Society in Contemporary Cuba*. Hoboken, NJ: Ocean Press, 2000.

Fernández, Damián J. *Cuba and the Politics of Passion*. Austin: University of Texas Press, 2000.

Foss, Clive. *Fidel Castro*. Gloucestershire: Sutton Publishing, 2000.

Hatchwell, Emily, and Simon Calder. *Cuba: A Guide to the People, Politics and Culture*. Northampton, MA: Interlink Publishing Group, 1999.

Hunt, Christopher. *Waiting for Fidel*. New York: Houghton Mifflin, 1998.

Jatar-Hausmann, Ana Julia. *The Cuban Way: Communism, Capitalism and Confrontation*. West Hartford, CT: Kumarian Press, 1999.

Kirk, John M., and Leonardo Padura Fuentes. *Culture and the Cuban Revolution: Conversations in Havana*. Gainesville: University Press of Florida, 2001.

Lobo Montalvo, Maria Luisa, Zoila Lapique Becali, and Alicia gar Santana. *Havana: History and Architecture of a Romantic City*. New York: Monacelli Press, 2000.

Lumsden, Ian. *Machos, Maricones, and Gays: Cuba and Homosexuality*. Philadelphia: Temple University Press, 1995.

Mendoza, Tony. *Cuba: Going Back*. Austin: University of Texas Press, 1999.

Mesa-Lago, Carmelo, ed. *Cuba after the Cold War*. Pittsburgh: Pittsburgh University Press, 1993.

Moses, Catherine. *Real Life in Castro's Cuba*. Wilmington, DE: Scholarly Resources, 1999.

Pérez, Louis A. *On Becoming Cuban: Identity, Nationality, and Culture*. Chapel Hill: University of North Carolina Press, 1999.

Pérez-Lopez, Jorge, ed. *Cuba at a Crossroads: Politics and Economics after the Fourth Party Congress*. Gainesville: University Press of Florida, 1994.

Pérez Sarduy, Pedro, ed. *Afro-Cuban Voices: On Race and Identity in Contemporary Cuba*. Gainesville: University Press of Florida, 2000.

Pérez-Stable, Marifeli. *The Cuban Revolution: Origins, Course, and Legacy*. New York: Oxford University Press, 1998.

Price, S. L. *Pitching Around Fidel: A Journey into the Heart of Cuban Sports*. New York: Ecco Press, 2000.

Ripley, C. Peter, and Bob Shacochis. *Conversations with Cuba*. Athens, GA: University of Georgia Press, 1999.

Rodó, José Enrique, and Margaret Sayers Peden, trans. *Ariel*. Austin: University of Texas Press, 1988.

Roy, Joaquín. *Cuba, the United States, and the Helms-Burton Doctrine: International Reactions*. Gainesville: University Press of Florida, 2000.

Suchlicki, Jaime. *Cuba: From Columbus to Castro and Beyond*. London: Brasseys, 1997.

Szulc, Tad. *Fidel: A Critical Portrait*. New York: Avon Books, 2000.

Web Sites on Cuba

For those who wish to find more information online about Cuba, this section lists various Web sites that may be of interest. These sites are only a small fraction of the many sites on the subject, but we hope they will serve as a starting point. Due to the nature of the Internet, the continued existence of a site is never guaranteed, but at the time of this book's publication, all of these Internet addresses were in operation. Many of these sites are published both in English and Spanish.

AfroCubaWeb

www.afrocubaweb.com
In addition to posting articles about Afro-Cuban art and culture, this site functions as a clearing-house for news, discussions, organizations, and events surrounding Afro-Cuban identity.

Castro Speech Database

lanic.utexas.edu / la / cb / cuba / castro.html
Maintained by the University of Texas Latin American Network Information Center, this is a searchable database of Castro's speeches, in English and Spanish, from the 1950s to the present.

CubaNet

www.cubanet.org / cubanews.html
Founded in 1994 by Cuban-Americans in Miami, CubaNet works to promote free press in Cuba. The site publishes uncensored news about Cuban politics and daily life, provided by independent press agencies and freelance writers based in Cuba.

Center for Cuban Studies

www.cubaupdate.org
In existence since 1972, the Center for Cuban Studies dedicates itself to providing information about contemporary Cuba and lobbying to normalize relations between Cuba and the United States.

Cuba Web

www.cubaweb.cu
Cuba's official government site details business, technology, arts, and politics in Cuba.

Cuban American Alliance

www.cubamer.org
The Cuban American Alliance is a lobbying group that "educates on issues related to hardships caused by current United States–Cuba relations."

Cuban American National Foundation

www.canf.org

Founded in 1981 by Cuban exile Jorge Mas Canosa, this organization exists to "promote freedom, democracy and human rights for Cuba and an end to Fidel Castro's dictatorship."

Cuban Research Institute

lacc.fiu.edu / cri / #Mission

Established in 1991 under the auspices of Florida International University, the Cuban Research Institute administers one of the most extensive Cuban and Cuban-American studies programs.

Granma International

www.granma.cu

This is a multilingual version of *Granma*, Cuba's official newspaper.

Additional Periodical Articles with Abstracts

More information on Cuba can be found in the following articles. Readers who require a more comprehensive selection are advised to consult *Reader's Guide Abstracts* and other H.W. Wilson indexes.

Cuba: Is American Business Missing Out? Sí: A Bright Future. Ana Julia Jatar-Hausmann. *Across the Board* v. 37 no. 7 pp20–5 July/Aug. 2000.

With the passing of time, the embargo of Cuba becomes more costly to the United States. The embargo was imposed on Cuba in an effort to destroy the country's trade and investment. However, the embargo is unilateral and as such, trade opportunities are merely diverted away from the United States to other countries, without overly damaging the Cuban economy. As time passes, the Cuban economy is likely to continue to grow, thus creating more lost opportunities for U.S. business. Given the fact that Cuba's trade levels would be higher without an embargo, the trade opportunities foregone by U.S. businesses are, in reality, a fraction of a much larger trade that would have existed but for the embargo. If the United States just waits for the dust to settle with regard to the Cuban situation, other countries will have seized most of the trade. A response from Marc A. Olshan to this viewpoint is presented.

Elián's Fevered Island. David S. Toolan. *America* v. 182 no.17 pp6-11 May 13, 2000.

There is a certain irrationality to the U.S. embargo of Cuba. The idea behind the Helms-Burton Act, which penalizes foreign companies that trade with Cuba, was that turning the screws of economic pressure would drive Cubans to rebel and force Castro to hold free elections. In reality, the law has solidified Castro's position and intensified repression inside Cuba because it gives substance to Castro's charge that the island is under siege by Goliath-like America. Given that the embargo does not stop Cuba from obtaining American or any other nation's products, it is ineffective. It has struck Canadians, Mexicans, and many Europeans as an infringement on their own trading rights and led such nations to go out of their way to increase diplomatic contacts, trade, and investment in Cuba. During his 1998 visit, Pope John Paul II repeatedly called for an end to the embargo, and U.S. bishops have continued that call in the wake of his visit.

Strangling Cuba: Effects of U.S. Embargo. Brian Brown. *Commonweal* v. 126 no.14 pp16-17 Aug. 13 1999.

America's trade embargo is directly responsible for Cuba's critical shortage of medical equipment. Until the late 1980s, Cuba's imports from communist bloc countries and Western Europe offset the 38-year-old blockade that prevents Cuba importing from America such essentials as medicine and food. The collapse of the Soviet Union in 1991 together with the introduction of the 1992 Cuban Democracy Act and the 1996 Cuba Liberty and Democratic Solidarity Act, which prevent numerous transactions between Cuba and foreign corporations, have made the embargo extremely effective, however. As a result,

Cuban doctors have access to less than half of the new medicines available on the world market and are in short supply of vital equipment, including defibrillators, kidney dialysis machines, and incubators. On April 29, bills were introduced in both houses of Congress to end the blockade of food and medicine to Cuba.

Not Here: Cuba Still Has State-Run Medical System. *The Economist* v. 351 no. 8118 pp28-9 May 8, 1999.

In Cuba, health care is still free to all of its citizens, despite the ongoing trend to privatize in many nations. Cuba has many doctors, and it has earned money abroad for its medical research, but parts of the free system are in trouble, with poor equipment and few supplies. Cuba blames the American embargo for the lack of supplies and equipment, and this is partly true. However, it is also the case that Cuba can afford to buy very little. Nevertheless, the problems facing the Cuban health care system are not reflected in its infant mortality rate or life expectancy, with first-world figures suggesting that the system is still performing well.

Dissent, and Diplomacy: Ibero-American Summit in Cuba. *The Economist* v. 353 no. 8146 pp38-9 Nov. 20 1999.

With the cold war long over, the treatment of dissidents by Fidel Castro's regime in Cuba looks nastier than ever. Castro's neighbors took the opportunity of the Ibero-American summit, held in Cuba at the end of 1999, to criticize his regime. The summit's official topic was the challenges of globalization, but the real theme was human rights. Problems have been brewing since March 1999, when Cuba tried and jailed four prominent activists. Tension grew on the eve of the summit, and dozens of dissidents were arrested to prevent them from disrupting the occasion. Castro took advantage of the situation by holding a press conference to condemn counterrevolutionaries. Nevertheless, opponents such as Elizardo Sánchez of the Cuban Commission for Human Rights received almost as much attention as Castro from the visiting summit members.

Big Trouble in Havana. Bob Drury. *Gentlemen's Quarterly* v. 69 pp204-11+ May 1999.

The four decades of American subterfuge that Fidel Castro's revolution outlasted pales in comparison to the next wave of imperialist aggression. The Sicilian Mafia, the world's most ruthless capitalist organization, is back to take control of Cuba. With Castro's demise in sight, it is hardly surprising that the Mob would target a place so central to its history. The Sicilian Mafia will take over the Americans' capitalist role and, as a by-product of their business plan, bankrupt the nations of the Caribbean whose economies depend on the U.S. tourism dollar.

A Jewish Renaissance in Castro's Cuba. Dana Evan Kaplan. *Judaism* v. 49 no. 2 pp218-36 Spring 2000.

The writer describes the Jewish community of Cuba today and places contemporary events in the context of the historical background of the past four decades. Most Jewish immigrants came to Cuba in the early years of the 20th century, and the Havana Jewish community became quite prosperous. Following the Cuban Revolution in 1959, the majority of Cuba's Jews emigrated. The Castro government, however, went to considerable efforts to avoid any action that could have been construed as anti-Semitic. The Jewish community in Cuba is currently undergoing a revival, with substantial levels of Jewish activity in both Havana and Santiago de Cuba.

La Vida Loca: The Life of the Artist in Cuba. Edward Rubin. *New Art Examiner* v. 27 no. 3 pp24-7+ Nov. 1999.

Part of a special section on politically engaged art. Art in Cuba since the Revolution is closely linked to the political history of the island. In the early 1960s, artists received state support. In the 1970s, when Cuba was controlled completely by the Soviet Union, the heavy hand of authority was brought down, and all kinds of artists were marginalized for ideological reasons. At the end of the 1970s, the Instituto Superior de Arte (ISA) in Havana was created, giving life to what became known as the "New Art of Cuba." This work emerged in the 1980s and focused on the social and the political. The 1980s also saw the establishment of the Havana Bienal, the most formidable agency of Third World and Cuban art promotion. Cuban art in the 1990s is still referred to as the "New Art of Cuba," but younger artists seem more concerned with identity than a decade ago. The ISA today is full of students, and more and more Cuban artists are receiving international grants, participating in foreign residency programs, and appearing in international exhibitions.

Sexual Revolution: Communism versus Prostitution. Silvana Paternostro. *The New Republic* v. 223 no. 2/3 pp18-22 July 10/17 2000.

Cuba's campaign against prostitution is not primarily about higher moral standards but is a response to the flourishing industry's threat to communism. In the early 1990s, Fidel Castro and the Cuban government successfully used the women to promote tourism. The so-called *jineteras* are often highly educated professionals who earn meager state salaries. They acquire gifts and hard currency from foreigners through prostitution, which they use to support themselves and their families. Their ethic of consumption, entrepreneurship, and independence is having social and ideological effects that Castro's government feels unable to control, however. Special Brigades of the Revolutionary National Police have begun stopping the girls and checking their identity cards, expelling those not from Havana back to their native regions.

Best of Friends, Worlds Apart. Mirta Ojito. *New York Times* ppA1-A20 June 5, 2000.

Ojito examines how the interracial friendship between Cuban-born Joel Ruiz and Achmed Valdés has changed since coming to Miami. In Cuba, skin color came second to nationality, while in Florida, race has defined the outlines of their lives.

Rap Takes Root Where Free Expression Is Risky. Brett Sokol. *New York Times* ppC28 Sept. 3, 2000.

El Rap has become very popular among young Cubans, to whom the traditional music of the Grammy-winning *Buena Vista Social Club*—classic bolero and son—is literally the music of their grandparents. Brett Sokol reports on the Sixth Annual Rap Festival in Cuba, where the rappers and their fans remind him of the early rap scene in 1980s New York City. Although the Cuban government initially sought to shut down rap concerts, they have now switched gears and support rap festivals. Cuban Minister of Culture Abel Prieto says that Cuban rappers are "the next generation of Cubans and they are saying powerful things with this art."

The Old Man and the Boy. Jon Lee Anderson. *New Yorker* v. 76 pp224-31, 233-7 Feb. 21/28, 2000.

The Elián González saga has been a successful public relations exercise for Fidel Castro's dwindling socialist regime in Cuba. To counteract the economic emergency that followed the demise of the Soviet Union in the early 1990s, Castro legalized the use of the dollar and permitted a limited market economy. The increasing number of outsiders who are gaining a foothold in Cuba provides evidence of an emerging capitalist society. In addition, economic necessity has created more relaxed attitudes toward nonconformist ideas and lifestyles. Despite economic and cultural improvements, a huge percentage of Cubans wish to leave the island. Nonetheless, the dispute over whether young illegal immigrant González should stay in the United States or be returned to his Cuban father has galvanized popular opinion in Cuba, providing a sense of national identity.

A Tale of Two Teens: **R. Peña of Havana and H. Hernandez of Miami**. Rachel Louise Snyder. *Seventeen* v. 59 no. 5 pp194-8 May 2000.

The writer compares the standard of living available to 16-year-old Raul Peña in Havana, Cuba, with that available to 16-year-old Jenny Hernandez, the daughter of Cuban exiles living in Miami, Florida.

Cuba: Background to a Revolution. Alejandro de la Fuente. *Social Education*. v. 64 pp88-92 March 2000.

Despite 40 years of Soviet-style socialism, the fate of Cuba—both in its future promise and the formidable obstacles facing it—remains linked with that of the surrounding island nations. Cuba shares with other Caribbean nations a common past of conquest, colonization, ecological disaster, and foreign domination; in shifting its dependency from the U.S. to the U.S.S.R., Cuba did not outgrow its dependence on sugar industry and tourism. The country's course in the future remains to be seen.

Clash of Faiths. Johanna McGeary. *Time* v. 151 pp26-32+ Jan. 26, 1998.

Two titans of the 20th century, Pope John Paul II and Fidel Castro, will collide in January on the small island of Cuba. Communism, a 100-year-old ideology that proposed a collective utopia of social justice and economic equality on Earth, will face Catholicism, a 2,000-year-old belief in the enduring power of devotion to the divine and reverence for human dignity. The pope's aim is nothing less than the worldwide establishment of a wholly Christian alternative to the once attractive Marxist philosophies of this era. Meanwhile, even after communism collapsed in practically every other corner of the planet, Castro still believes history will absolve him in his belief in a god that failed. The two men and their agendas are compared.

The Dictator's Dilemma? The Internet and U.S. Policy Toward Cuba. Taylor C. Boas. *Washington Quarterly* v. 23 pp57-67 Summer 2000.

Authoritarian leaders in the information age are faced with an irrefutable dilemma. The Internet and associated information and communication technologies provide enormous economic potential for developing countries, and the increasingly interconnected global economy thrives on openness of information, but the information revolution presents new challenges for regimes that rely on centralized political control. So far, however, Cuba has managed to stave off such political dangers of the Internet. Cuba's cautious response to the Internet has been shaped by the economic and political incentives that the regime has faced, in addition to the dynamics of its antagonistic relationship with the U.S.

The Other Tempest. Bob Shacochis. *Wilson Quarterly* v. 24 no. 3 pp14-24 Summer 2000.

Shacochis asks an elusive question: What will happen to Cuban national identity in the future? He speaks to writers and artists, some of whom express fears that Cuban culture, including its vital literature, performing arts, and film communities, will be threatened by capitalist culture. After watching a Cuban adaptation of Shakespeare's *The Tempest*, *La Otra Tempestá* (*The Other Tempest*), a parable about Cuba's history as a tropical island inhabited by *santería* gods, Shacochis meditates on the future role of Cuba in an increasingly homogenized world.

Index

ACLU lawsuit 124
Adler, Joseph 124
African-Americans' attitudes towards
    Cuban-Americans 127
AG 38
agricultural reform
    exports increase 24
    farmer's markets allowed 2, 60, 61, 75
    loss of oil and fertilizer imports 85
    pest management innovations 86
    Soviet collapse impact on 83
    urban agriculture encouragement 84–
        85
AIDS 70
Alarcón, Ricardo 21, 46, 55, 57
Albright, Madeleine K. 112
Alexander, Noble 42
Allan, David 80, 81
American academics in Cuba
    benefits of exchange to U.S. students
        135–136
    CANF opposition 137–138
    educational freedom in Cuba 139–140
    government oversight of Cuban aca-
        demics 140–141
    knowledge obtained by visits 138
    opposition of some U.S. schools 137
    travel logistics 137
American farmers anti-embargo senti-
    ments 111
anti-Cuban art resolution in Miami
    ACLU lawsuit 124
    background 3, 122–123
    counterproductive aspects of 123–124
    impact on cultural community 123
    Supreme Court rulings and 3, 125
art in Cuba
    Kcho's works. See Kcho
    Miami anti-Cuban resolution. See
        anti-Cuban art resolution in
        Miami
    race depictions in 163
Ashby, Timothy 76
Ashcroft, John 111
atheism 37

Bacardi rum company 62
"banana republic" 126

baseball in Cuba
    betting on 148
    fan enthusiasm 151
    game with U.S. team 3
    pre-revolution league activities 146–
        147
    reputation of teams 144
    resurgence of popularity 143–144
    start of 145
    symbolism of playing 145–146, 148–
        149
    U.S. players involvement 147–148
    young athletes school 149–150
Baxter, Kevin 23
Bay of Pigs 1
Bellán, Esteban 145
Bible imports 34
bicycle use in Cuba 12, 14, 87
Biltmore Yacht and Country Club 69
biotechnology
    advances in 79
    dedication of scientists 80–81
    foreign licensing agreements 79–80
    foreign partnerships 81–82
    government support of 80
    research facilities 81
    See also health care
Blyth, Peter 72
Boone, Beth 123
Botifoll, Luis 129
Bourget, Elizabeth 76
Bradley, Tom 113
Brittan, Leon 55
Brothers to the Rescue 2, 36–37, 128
Brugeras, Miguel 70, 71, 72
Bush, George W. 113–114
Butler University 135

Cabrera Delgado, Vicente 15, 16
Calvo, Vicente 35
Calzon, Frank 107
Campus Crusade for Christ 40
Cancio, Hugo 124
CANF. See Cuban American National
    Foundation
Cano, Maria del Carmen 159, 162
capitalism
    Cuban youth's interest in 177–178,
        180

foreign capital benefits to workers 74
juxtaposition with socialism 13, 24–25, 28–29, 58–59, 60–61
Cardenas, Jose R. 114
Caritas Cubana 35
Carnival 18
Casanova, Alfonso 74
Casey, John 152
Castro, Ángel 19
Castro, Fidel
  attitude towards religions 33
  Cuba's transition from 48
  dislike of homosexuality 152
  dislike of U.S. 101, 118
  family farm 19
  longevity of rule 44–45
  love of statistics 18–19
  succession possibilities 21, 45, 180
  timeline of rule 1–3
Castro, Lina 19
Castro, Max J. 126
Castro, Raúl
  liberalist leanings 45–46
  succession possibilities 21, 42, 45, 180
Castro's Final Hour (Oppenheimer) 53
Catholic Church
  growing tolerance for 15–16
  role in Cuban political changes 47, 97
  See also religion
CDA (Cuban Democracy Act of 1992) 103
CDR (Committee for the Defense of the Revolution) 11
Center for a Free Cuba 107
Centre for Genetic Engineering and Biotechnology (CIGB) 13, 81
Centres for the Reproduction of Entomophages and Entomopathogens (CREES) 86
Céspedes, Rafael 36, 37
China
  argument against PNTR 95–97
  move towards market democracy 93–94
Christianity. *See* religion
cigar industry 13
CIGB (Centre for Genetic Engineering and Biotechnology) 13, 81
Clinton, Bill
  contradictions in statements on relations 103, 104
  "people-to-party" policy 114
Cobián, Rolando Suárez 35
Collazo Valdés, Odilia 20

Committee for the Defense of the Revolution (CDR) 11
Cortez, Jose Lorenzo "Pepe Milesima" 158
Council for Mutual Economic Assistance (COMECON) 54
CREES (Centres for the Reproduction of Entomophages and Entomopathogens) 86
Cruz, Humberto 41
Cuban American Alliance Education Fund 112
Cuban-American Military Council 42
Cuban American National Foundation (CANF)
  Elián González situation and 127, 129
  opposition to academics' Cuba visits 137–138
  strength of lobby 62, 110
Cuban-Americans
  anti-Cuban art resolution in Miami 122–123
  civil war with Cuba 62, 63
  dollars sent to Cuba 25
  strength of lobby 62, 100, 110
  See also Cuban American National Foundation
Cuban Committee for Democracy 109
Cuban Council of Churches 33, 34
Cuban Democracy Act of 1992 (CDA) 2, 103, 136
Cuban Federation of Sport Fishing 16
Cuban Liberty and Democratic Solidarity (LIBERTAD) Act. *See* Helms-Burton Act
Cuban Missile Crisis 1
currency. *See* dollar economy
Custin, Charles M. 109

daily life
  baseball popularity. *See* baseball in Cuba
  food markets 11
  growing use of dollars 12, 25
  municipal services status 28
  remembrances of prosperity 15, 16
  residence occupation rules 11–12
  social life of youth 176–177, 178–179
  student's views of future 21
  visitor restrictions 15–16
DeLay, Tom 93
Díaz-Balart, Lincoln 37, 42, 114
Dihigo, Martín 147
dollar economy

currency crisis impetus 56–57
foreign exchange increase 58–59
growing importance 12, 23, 24
impact on daily life 12, 25
legalization in 1993 2, 25, 58
Donohue, Thomas J. 114
Dorta García, Joel 117, 121

Eaton, Tracey 155
Echevarría, Roberto González 145
economy
    agricultural reforms. See agricultural
        reform
    currency crisis 56–57
    dual monetary system. See dollar
        economy
    fiscal deficit reduction 59–60, 61
    fiscal policy 63
    food markets 11, 60, 61, 75
    foreign capital benefits to workers 74
    foreign direct investment 59, 60
    GDP growth 61
    government wages 11
    hard currency shortage (1990-93) 56
    information technology sector growth
        76–78
    market reform strategy 24, 25, 46, 57,
        58
    self-employment allowed 60
    Soviet Union collapse and 23–24, 53,
        54–55
    tax system establishment 59
    tourism importance. See tourism
    transformation policy basis 76
    U.S. embargo impact 61, 63
Economy and Planning Ministry 74
education
    freedom in Cuba 13, 139–140
    government oversight of 140–141
    stipends for university attendance
        172
    young athletes school 149–150
embargo, U.S.. See trade embargo
energy policies in Cuba 85, 87
Erickson, Audrae 111
Esquivel, Alexis 161, 163, 164
European Unions Trade Commissioner 55
exchange rate 63

Facts About Cuban Exiles 129
farmer's markets 2, 60, 61, 75
Feinberg, Richard 110
Fernandez, Damian 123

Fernandez Levy, Delvis 112
Fernandez Lopez, Daniel 78
Fernandez Robaina, Tomas 161
fertilizer imports loss impact 83, 85
Fidelismo 25
Fineman, Mark 117
Finlay, Carlos 80
fiscal deficit reduction 61
Florida International University 137
Fontaine, Roger 44
foreign direct investment 59, 60
Fornet, Jorge 135, 138, 142
Free Cuba PAC 110
Freyre, Pedro 129
Fuller, Craig L. 111
Funcheon, Dierdra 172

GableStage 124
GDP growth 61
Giga 77
God's Love in Action 41
Gomez, Andy 137
Gómez, Graciano 19
González, Angel Tomás 24
González, Elián, situation
    anti-sanctioning interests in U.S. and
        100
    Cuban-American response 127
    cultural divisions exposed by 126
    immigration policy and 118
    legal and legislative defeats during
        129
    split in Cuban-American leadership
        128–129
    timeline of 3
González, Lourdes 11
Gore, Al 112–113
government of Cuba. See socialism
Griffey, Ken, Jr. 150
Grupo La Ma Teodora 124
Grupo Vocal Desandan 125

Habanos, S.A. 13
Harley-Davidson. See motorcycle popular-
        ity in Cuba
Harlistas. See motorcycle popularity in
        Cuba
Hastert, J. Dennis 111
Havana
    dual character of 10
    tourism heritage 67
health care
    alternative medicine encouragement

88
block doctors system 10–11
de-emphasis on foreign drugs 88
facilities condition 28
government wages 11
lack of medicines 28, 102
research advantages 13
See also biotechnology
Helms, Jesse 100, 101
Helms-Burton Act
    CANF's role in 62
    content of 47–48, 104
    impact of 36–37, 61, 62
    impetus for passing 2
    international criticism of 55, 99
    on funding of independent groups
        105–107, 108
    restrictions on agriculture imports 84
    restrictions on medicines 82
Hernández Gomez, Ernesto 118
hitchhiking 178
HIV infection rate 70
homosexuality
    Castro's dislike of 152
    increasing tolerance for 142, 153, 154
    persecution during revolution 153–
        154
Howe, Linda 136
human rights
    dissident intolerance 20
    persecution of homosexuals 153–154
    religious practices intolerance 30, 33–
        34
    violations in Cuba 97
human smuggling
    Border Guard and 117, 119, 120
    increasing rate of 117
    motivation of participants 121
    numbers intercepted 119
    smuggler's sentences 118
    U.S. "wet foot/dry foot" policy 118–119
Hunter, Héctor A. 32, 33, 34

IBA (International Baseball Association)
    144
Ichikawa, Emilio 140, 141
immigration
    Castro's 1994 allowance for 2
    restrictions in U.S. 20
    U.S. policy towards refugees 103,
        118–119
information technology
    bypassing of U.S. embargo 77–78

electronics manufacturing industry
    77
government support of 76
public access to 77
Institute for Democracy in Cuba 62, 106
International Baseball Association (IBA)
    144

Jamail, Milton 150
Jatar-Hausmann, Ana Julia 53
John Paul II visit 3, 15, 31

Kcho
    background 170–171
    boat and water themes 167–168
    commercial success 168
    migration and impermanence themes
        169
    political references in work 171
Kennedy, John W. 30

Lage, Agustin 81
Lage, Carlos 46, 57
La Plata 9
La Vida es Silbar 123
Lawrence, David Aquila 135
Lazo, Pedro Luis 151
leadership in Cuba
    new generation of officials 46
    succession possibilities 21, 45, 46
    transition from Castro 48
    U.S. role in transition 47–48
Levin, Jordan 122
LIBERTAD (Cuban Liberty and Demo-
    cratic Solidarity) Act. *See* Helms-Bur-
    ton Act
Limonta, Manuel 13, 81
Linares, Omar "El Niño" 151
Lloyd, John Henry "Pop" 147
Lowinger, Rosa 167
Luis Brito, Henry 10, 11
Luna 38–39
Luque, Adolfo 147

market reform
    decision in 1993 57
    GDP growth 24
    new commercial buildings 28
    new leadership possibilities 46
    strategy 24, 25, 46, 57, 58
Mas Canosa, Jorge 62, 110
Mas Santos, Jorge 127
Maximum Leader. *See* Castro, Fidel

McGovern, James P. 95
medicine. *See* biotechnology; health care
Mendez, Hector 34
meningitis vaccine 79
Metcalf, Edward 87
Methodist churches 33
Miami Light Project 122, 124
microenterprises 60, 73–74
Miller, Tom 143
Ministry of Information Technology
    (MINIT) 76
Monreal, Pedro 57
motorcycle popularity in Cuba
    background to use 157–158
    pride in repair work 155–156
    value of motorcycles 156–157

National Association of Sugar Mill Own-
    ers of Cuba 62
National Centre for Scientific Investiga-
    tion 80
nickel production 24
Ñico López school 14
Nuccio, Richard A. 100, 101, 102, 112, 115

Odén Marichal, Pablo 39, 107
Ohanian, Debbie 124, 125
Oliva, Erneido A. 42
Open Doors with Brother Andrew 38, 40
Oppenheimer, Andres 53
Ortega, Jaime 31, 32
Overseas Council 41
Owensby, Barry 41

Partagás 13
Pastors for Peace 36
Pau-Llosa, Ricardo 124
Penelas, Alex 124
"Pepe Milesima" 158
Perez, Juan Orlando 139, 140, 142
Perez, Lisandro 137
Pérez, Louis A., Jr. 145, 146
permanent normal trade relations
    (PNTR) with China 93–94, 95–97
pest management innovations 86
Peters, Philip 73
Pons Palaez, Alexander 37, 41
Popkin, Eric 139
Portal, Marcos 59
Pro Human Rights Party of Cuba 20
prostitution
    government reaction to 27
    tourism related increase 26–27, 70

Protestant house churches 33–34
Putman, John 9

racism in Cuba
    black leaders in government 163
    government policy of no discrimina-
        tion 161
    increasing references to race 165
    race in art 163
    race relations in general 160, 161,
        164, 178
    racial profiling prevalence 159, 160,
        165–166
    racial tensions 162–163
Ramirez, Ramon 119
Ramos, Marcos Antonio 31, 32
religion
    American missionary activity 40–42
    cases of cooperation with government
        34–35
    Catholic Church. *See* Catholic Church
    expansion of church's relief role 35
    extent of government tolerance 15–
        16, 31–32
    lack of strength in Cuba 32–33
    loss of leaders during revolution 40
    membership growth 33–34
    pastor shortage 39–40
    predictions for Cuba 42–43
    restrictions on churches 33, 37, 38–39
    restrictions on foreign missionaries 40
    role in Cuban political changes 97
    santería practice 18, 39, 165
    significance of pope's visit 15, 31
    torture of activists 30, 33–34
    U.S. embargo impact on ministry 36
revolution history
    baseball leagues 146–147
    Carnival celebration 18
    Castro's La Plata camp 9–10
    persecution of homosexuals 153–154
    personal assets confiscated 16
    timeline of events 1–3
    tourism prior to 66–68
Rice, Condoleezza 113
Robaina, Robert 57
Robinson, Eugene 159
Robinson, Linda 66
Rodriguez, José Luis 57
Roman Catholic Church. *See* Catholic
    Church
Ros-Lehtinen, Ileana 109
Rosshirt, Tom 113

Ruiz, Roy 33
Russia 54

Sabourín, Emilio 146
Saladrigas, Carlos 129
Sánchez, Celia 9
Sanchez, Elizardo 108
santería religion 18, 39, 165
Santiago de Cuba 17
Sarrain, Alberto 122, 125
Section 109, Helms-Burton Act 105–107,
    108
self-employment restrictions lifted 2, 60,
    73–74
Sené, Ismael 148
Serretti, Mariela 138
Shapiro, Charles 112
Shea, Nina 31, 38
Simendinger, Alexis 109
small businesses 60, 73–74
Smith, Wayne S. 103, 110
SmithKline Beecham (SB) 79
socialism
    dissident intolerance 20
    foreign capital benefits to workers 74
    government salaries 74
    ideology maintenance 13, 60, 172,
        173–174
    juxtaposition with capitalism 13, 24–
        25, 28–29, 58–59, 60–61
    medical facilities decline 28
    military's role in economy 65
    new economic strategy 64
    organized crime avoidance 64–65
    political prisoners 20
    political watch groups 11
    rules governing public dissent 20
    stipends for education 172
    universal health care system 10–11
    visitor restrictions 15–16
Soroa Clapera, Orlando 119
Soviet Union
    impact of collapse 2, 23–24, 83
    predicted impact of collapse 53
    timeline of Cuba relationship 1
standard of living in Cuba. *See* daily life
Starn, Orin 136, 138
Strawberry and Chocolate 142
Suárez, Raúl 34–35, 38
sugar industry 12, 87

Tackett, Steve 41
tax system establishment 59

Taylor, Stuart, Jr. 99
Tejeda, Vicente 18
telephone system 77
Thiessen, Marc 106
timeline of the Cuban Revolution 1–3
Tippitt, Sammy 41
tobacco industry 13, 24
Torres, Rubén Araujo 9
Torricelli, Robert 103–104
tourism
    beach resort growth 71–72
    economic importance of 12, 14, 56, 69
    embargo ignored by 70
    expected growth in 72
    Havana's heritage 67
    impact on daily life 25
    late 1990s revival 66, 69
    market reform strategy and 24
    pre-revolution 66–68
    prostitution increase due to 26–27, 70
trade embargo
    anti-sanctioning interests in U.S.
        110–112
    arguments for lifting 98, 101–102
    bypassing by technology sector 77–78
    Cuban energy policies due to 87
    inadvertent support of Castro 109
    lack of international support 2, 99
    medical care impacted by 1, 88, 102
    political pressures to maintain 100–
        101
    relaxation of some restrictions 3, 111
    religious leaders opposition to 36–37
    tourism's ignoring of 70
    U.S. tightening of. *See* Helms-Burton
        Act
Trinidad 17
TV Martí 107

U.S.–Cuba relations
    contradictions in Clinton's statements
        103, 104
    Cuban revolution timeline 1–3
    policy towards refugees 2, 103, 118–
        119
    presidential candidates' platforms
        112–114
    shift in U.S. public opinion 115, 128
    Supreme Court rulings on state's
        interpretations 125
    time element in Cuba transition 114–
        115
    U.S. funding of independent groups

105–107
United States
  academic exchange programs. *See* American academics in Cuba
  argument against PNTR for China 95–97
  argument against trade with Cuba 94–95
  Cuban public's dislike of 27
  embargo against Cuba. *See* trade embargo
  illegal immigrants policies 103, 118–119
  international criticism of Helms-Burton 55
  PNTR with China 93–94
  revival of pre-revolution regattas 69
  role in future transition 47–48
University of Havana 21
University of Miami 137
Urban Agriculture Department 85
US Agency for International Development (USAID) 105–107

Valdés Vivó, Raúl 14
Varadero 71–72
Veguilla, Eliezar 30, 43
Veguilla, Leoncilo 33, 43
Vera, José M. 37
Vesco, Robert 82
Vila, Naomi 38

Vila, Orson 33, 38
Viñales 15, 16
Voice of the Martyrs (VOM) 40

Wake Forest University 136
Walker, Lucius 36
Wallace, Gregory C. 41
Warwick, Hugh 83
Western Baptist Convention of Cuba 33
"wet foot/dry foot" policy of U.S. 118–119
Whitaker, Daniel 79
White, Tom 40
Williams, Sam 38
Wolfson, Micky 71
World Street Evangelism 41

York Medical 79
Yoruba religion. *See santería*
Young Communist League 174
youth in Cuba
  athletes school 149–150
  daily life 176–177, 178–179
  hospitality 179–180
  interest in capitalism 177–178, 180
  interest in U.S. 173, 174, 180
  on immigration to U.S. 181–182
  socialism support from 172, 173–174
  social life 174–176, 181
  stipends for university attendance 172
Youth With a Mission (YWAM) 40